Developing Critical Awareness at the Middle Level

Using Texts as Tools for Critique and Pleasure

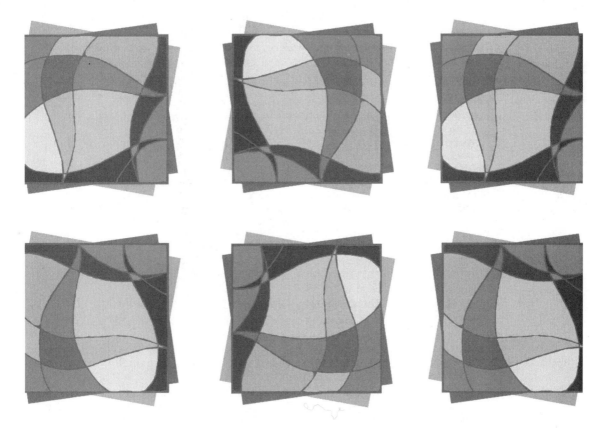

H O L L Y   J O H N S O N
University of Cincinnati
Cincinnati, Ohio, USA

L A U R E N   F R E E D M A N
Western Michigan University
Kalamazoo, Michigan, USA

INTERNATIONAL
Reading Association
800 BARKSDALE ROAD, PO BOX 8139
NEWARK, DE 19714-8139, USA
www.reading.org

The International Reading Association attempts, through its publications, to provide a forum for a wide spectrum of opinions on reading. This policy permits divergent viewpoints without implying the endorsement of the Association.

Director of Publications Dan Mangan
Editorial Director, Books and Special Projects Teresa Curto
Managing Editor, Books Shannon T. Fortner
Acquisitions and Developmental Editor Corinne M. Mooney
Associate Editor Charlene M. Nichols
Production Editor Amy Messick
Assistant Editor Elizabeth C. Hunt
Books and Inventory Assistant Rebecca A. Zell
Permissions Editor Janet S. Parrack
Assistant Permissions Editor Tyanna L. Collins
Production Department Manager Iona Muscella
Supervisor, Electronic Publishing Anette Schütz
Senior Electronic Publishing Specialist R. Lynn Harrison
Electronic Publishing Specialist Lisa M. Kochel
Proofreader Stacey Lynn Sharp

Project Editor Charlene M. Nichols

Cover Design, Linda Steere

Web addresses in this book were correct as of the publication date but may have become inactive or otherwise modified since that time. If you notice a deactivated or changed Web address, please e-mail books@reading.org with the words "Website Update" in the subject line. In your message, specify the Web link, the book title, and the page number on which the link appears.

Library of Congress Cataloging-in-Publication Data
Johnson, Holly, 1956-
  Developing critical awareness at the middle level : using texts as tools for critique and pleasure / Holly Johnson, Lauren Freedman.
      p. cm.
  Includes bibliographical references and index.
  ISBN 0-87207-571-0
 1. Critical pedagogy. 2. Children's literature Study and teaching (Middle school) 3. Language arts (Middle school) I. Freedman, Lauren, 1946- II. Title.
  LC196.J64 2005
  370.11'5--dc22

2005006222

Contents

"We're all fighting a war whether we know it or not—a war for our minds and souls and what we believe in...."

From *Stand Tall* (Bauer, 2002, p. 177)

Preface

Middle-level students are active participants in this war for their minds, souls, and what they believe in. They also are just developing ideas about who they are and what they believe in. Given the slightest encouragement about their ideas and beliefs, they will respond with a multitude of questions, questions seemingly off topic and personal, and often beginning with How come? or Why? Students in grades 6 through 8 are eager to know all they can about how the world works and their places in it. Too often, though, young adolescents are characterized by the adults who fear or are annoyed by them as beings whose focus is everywhere but on academic learning. Yet when viewed through the eyes of adults who understand, appreciate, and encourage their openness, candor, and naiveté, adolescents' questions usually are seen as uniquely connected to the subjects under study because these questions are, more often than not, ones only 11- to 14-year-olds—"tweens" as they are sometimes called—would ask. Their questions come from the deep connections only someone that age might make with a text, an experience, or a comment by a teacher or peer. For example, during silent reading time in their language arts class, two students had the following brief exchange initiated by one student's reading of *The Giver* (Lowry, 1993).

> Anthony: How come we have to line up single file to go to lunch? And can only walk on the right side of the hallway? I wouldn't want to live in Jonas's world, but sometimes our world looks just like it.

> Rebecca: Yeah, I thought of that when I was reading that book, too. Like they just want us to be a bunch of robots.

In response to a piece of literature, these students are attempting to confront adults' rules. Many adults might respond by explaining their own need for rules or by simply ignoring the questions. Too often, the opportunity for rich discussion precipitated by students' questions is lost because adults underestimate young adolescents' ability to engage in substantive discussion. As a consequence, adults control students' questions by keeping them silent.

It is through discussion, and the critique and pleasure that accompany real conversations, that teachers can invite their students to become critically conscious, or aware, of how the world around them beckons for their attention, their beliefs, their allegiances, and sometimes even for their acquiescence to injustice. Students often become animated during discussion, and by using literature to target students' concerns, teachers can empower them to work with text and issues that they will encounter outside the classroom.

This text is born out of our desire to provide middle-level students with opportunities to voice their thinking and explore the complex answers to their unique questions about their own life experiences and the wider world. Through our experiences as middle-level language arts, reading, and social studies teachers, we know how important it is to encourage students to ask difficult and complex questions and to say with little hesitation or self-censorship what they think and feel about the things we are reading, writing, discussing, and studying. Having worked with young adolescents as they struggle to become competent, capable, and strategic literacy learners so they might unlock the mysteries of texts and the worlds those texts represent, we know that they need and want more than the traditional literacy curriculum of worksheets and rote skills that asks them to think very little and talk even less. By addressing some of their desires within a curriculum that provokes discussion, passion, and connection, we find that young adolescents have much to share with us and with the world. By adjusting curriculum and instruction to include literature circles that allow them time to discuss their ideas, teachers can provide middle-level students the opportunity to develop the skills necessary to confront and connect their ideas with those of the texts they are reading. Presenting and exploring ways to engage students' emotions, criticism, and pleasure in being part of what Frank Smith has dubbed the "literacy club" (1988) is the challenge we attempt to meet in this book.

We and many of the teachers with whom we have worked as school colleagues and as school and university partners find middle-level students inspiring and profound, especially when engaged in pondering and discussing the issues that provoke, disturb, anger, or delight them. We also have found issues of social justice, such as racism, sexism, and ageism, especially engaging to young adolescents. Given an issue or an action that raises their sense of justice, fairness, or freedom, middle-level students rise to the challenge with passion, compassion, and personal understanding. Many of these students have not assimilated the myth that levelheadedness always accompanies reason. Often our students are not levelheaded; they respond from the gut, the same place from which many of us first find ourselves responding when confronted with inequity, unfairness, and injustice. When confronted with issues of unfairness as in *Nothing but the Truth* (Avi, 1991), injustice as in *Leon's Story* (Tillage, 1997), persecution as in *Torn Thread* (Isaacs, 2000), discrimination as in *The Moonbridge* (Savin, 1992), prejudice as in *Witness* (Hesse, 2001), or corruption of power as in *Rag and Bone Shop* (Cormier, 2001), these students often champion the underdog who is seeking equity with those who hold the power. They relate well to the injustice of power imbalances mostly because they are working hard to establish themselves as equal partners in running their lives as they mature toward adulthood and independence from their parents and other significant adults in their lives.

Middle-level students' criticisms of the world can be cutting, profound, and provocative. Their thinking can also be uplifting, heartening, and exciting. Providing them with the opportunity to respond with passion engages young adolescents in the thinking required by members of a democratic society, whether in the workplace or as citizens responsible for governing their country. The promises for the future inspire us to create classrooms where middle-level students can find pleasure in the critical processes that will help them develop as thinkers and learners.

In our work as teachers, we have found few middle-level students who are not concerned with social justice. They are concerned about their world and, with the help of their teachers, can discuss such matters in rigorous and thoughtful ways. We also know, however, that when we have discussed such matters with middle-level students we have wished we had a guide that would have helped us in addressing the issues of power, oppression, identity, and critical consciousness. This text begins that work.

The Purpose of This Book

Our intent with this book, as in our teaching, is to ask students to think about what literature has to say about them, other people they know, and the world at large. With this text, we hope to put young adolescents and their literacy needs squarely at the forefront. As Alvermann (2002) suggests,

> [Our concern is that] despite the work of conscientious teachers, reading supervisors, curriculum coordinators, and principals in middle schools and high schools across the country, young people's literacy skills are not keeping pace with societal demands of living in an information age that changes rapidly and shows no sign of slowing. (p. 189)

Helping students gain the critical literacy skills and strategies they need to enter the world beyond high school is part of the pleasure of being a middle-level teacher.

Providing opportunities for young adolescents to develop critique and pleasure in the context of a language arts classroom means weaving together threads of questioning and analysis with threads of emotional and intellectual enjoyment and interest. Through this weaving students deepen their relationships with texts by responding to and discussing why they might feel or think the way they do, what in the text they are connecting with and in what ways, what they find invigorating and intriguing, and what they find troubling. With the help of their language arts teachers, middle-level students are able to intertwine critique and pleasure in ways that will enrich them academically while also encouraging them to become active in the conversations that connect their experiences with the wider world. Through dialogue they also come to realize the diverse world they live in and the multiple ways in which people view similar phenomena. We find that by asking students to work with us as we "read the word and the world" (Macedo & Freire, 1987), students not only enter the conversations, but also they add substantially to them.

At first glance, blending critique and pleasure seems a contradictory idea. Luke (1997) and Alvermann (2002) assert that to ask students to critique the texts they find pleasurable would be tantamount to asking them to lie. Luke (1997) further suggests that young people "are quick to talk a good anti-sexist, anti-racist, pro-equity game," yet what they tell their teachers may not reflect "what goes on in their heads" (p. 43).

Yet, middle-level language arts classrooms are the very places where critical thinking and the pleasure of emotional engagement find a natural home. It is in the literature students read, their responses to the literature, and in subsequent discussions that the potential for middle-level learners to investigate themselves and their connections to the world is created. It is in these connections that we find the most inspiring evidence that middle-level students have minds that matter, and want to be engaged in the matters of the world. To embrace certain texts, certain content, is a right we wish our students to hold. Yet, we wish for them to take ownership of the "why" behind the embrace and come to realize what it might be about particular texts or specific subjects that holds their interest and passion. At the same time, while discussing certain pieces of literature with others, their interest and curiosity may be piqued by another student's connections, which can then broaden their desire to read beyond their initial selection.

With this book, we wish to be clear that we are not asking middle-level students to forfeit their pleasure of certain texts, but rather to broaden this pleasure through an awareness of what it is they love and perhaps through interrogating why they enjoy one genre, topic, or author more than others. By reflecting on their passion and becoming aware of these connections, young adolescents become better equipped to discuss particular ideas or content or texts with deeper insight. And by asking students to create spaces in their lives where they can both critique texts and take pleasure in them, we are suggesting that their teachers can negotiate these spaces in the classroom and that literature read in the classroom is a place where critique and pleasure often intertwine.

We, as readers, also realize how much easier it is to critique texts that we initially may not appreciate. Yet, through engaging in dialogues with others about what makes a text interesting, racist, sexist, inclusive, discriminatory, or engaging, we find that it becomes much more difficult to dismiss a text without consideration. Often, we even develop an interest or pleasure in reading texts we previously thought uninteresting or uninspiring. We found that the process of reading and discussing literature widens middle-level students' interests by introducing them to literature they did not know was available. For this reason it is essential that middle-level students participate in critique to become more astute at evaluating the information they read and the messages they receive.

The Audience of This Book

Because we find middle-level students fascinating, the reading of quality young adult literature a worthy endeavor, and the ability to engage in critical conversations a privilege, we wanted to share our thinking with other middle-level educators. Assisting middle-level students as they learn to think critically—both independently and with others— about the information they encounter in the media as well as in their lives is one of the most important goals of a middle-level educator. We want to facilitate the ways in which middle-level teachers can engage their students in the reading of young adolescent literature with a focus on critical consciousness and social justice.

Although this text is geared toward middle-level language arts teachers, we also want to suggest that using literature in social studies, science, and math classes and engaging students in critique as well as pleasure in these subject areas can deepen the students' connections with and subsequent interest in the concepts being studied. Especially in social studies, students' innate sense of fair play often comes to the fore with little coaxing and can turn what they had perceived as boring into a burning interest. For example, the reading and discussion of a novel such as *Out of the Dust* (Hesse, 1997) can initiate students' questions about the U.S. Depression, a period with which they may have initially thought they had little connection. The same holds true for a novel such as *Catherine, Called Birdy* (Cushman, 1994) and students' engagement with the topic of the Middle Ages.

This text also can be used within university classrooms with inservice or preservice teachers. Understanding how texts can be used as tools for both critique and pleasure is one way those interested in becoming middle-level teachers can learn how to engage their language arts students. This book can be used with preservice teachers as a guide to initiating the discussions of critical consciousness that might be difficult to broach with young adolescents.

How to Use This Book

In this book, we discuss the concepts of critical pedagogy and the "pedagogy of possibility" (Simon, 1992), which allow teachers to create conditions for the pleasurable reading of young adolescent literature in ways that will have young adolescents at any reading level asking to "do that again." We also share strategies addressing critical awareness for empowerment and social justice. These strategies create a "discourse of potential" (Powell, 1997, p. 4) to engage students across cultural boundaries and traditional patterns of participation.

Within each chapter, we highlight particular young adolescent texts by selecting excerpts from them that seem to us to be especially salient passages to use with middle-level students as a way of addressing the focal concept under discussion.

Many of the young adolescent novels highlighted in this book may be unfamiliar to teachers or may not be used by many teachers within their classrooms. However, we selected these texts for two reasons. First, we have found that few texts are considered "classics" at the middle level. By this we mean that few school districts or states in the United States have required reading lists (Johnson & Chen, 2004), and many language arts teachers are looking for thoughtful pieces of literature to share with their students. Second, this book allows us to introduce a number of amazing pieces of literature that directly relate to the issues we discuss within it. The novels we highlight only suggest what is available across the world for adolescents and their teachers to use in their exploration of power, privilege, oppression, and the ways these concepts are enacted between and among people, groups, and perhaps even societies.

Throughout this book we provide Questions for Students to Consider, or general prompts, for teachers to use within their language arts or social studies classrooms. These questions are general because they are what many educators might consider common, traditional, or even beginning reader response questions. We agree. We created these prompts with the intent that they would be used as a way of initiating discussions with students. Because we know that middle-level students have unique voices and make connections that we would not anticipate, we did not want to create prompts that seemed too rigid or controlling. Our hope is that students will drive the dialogue about the concepts within these books. We know, however, that often their teachers have to get them started. We believe these general prompts will help teachers to do just that.

Another aspect of this text is the examples of literature circles and class discussions that have occurred between middle-level students and their teachers. Teachers from Texas and Michigan kindly worked with us on the development of this text by allowing us to visit their classrooms and initiate discussions with their students or by engaging their students in the texts we selected for this book. We also draw from our own interactions with middle-level students to exemplify how discussions about power and oppression, language and privilege are possible between young adolescents and the adults with whom they work.

In this book we also highlight picture books that can introduce topics related to critical consciousness, critical literacy, and social justice. Through the use of picture books, just as in novels, young adolescents can make that leap from the world of the text to the world of which they are a part. Picture book illustrations allow middle-level students to "see" how social justice may or may not be manifested in the world. Picture books, because they are short, streamline the issue of social justice and how it cannot be just a concept but also must be a lived experience.

Through addressing student voice, concepts of injustice, and the use of young adult literature and picture books, this book weaves together a fabric of potential for a better understanding of social justice as well as classroom critique and pleasure—for middle-level teachers and students.

The Organization of This Book

We begin by defining critical terms in chapter 1. We discuss critical thinking, critical consciousness, and critical literacy and the similarities and differences between them. We also discuss the element of critical pedagogy and a "pedagogy of possibility," which has the potential for expanding middle-level language arts classrooms and the discussions of literature to include aspects of critique and pleasure.

Chapter 2 addresses the transition from theory to practice. In this chapter, we explain the concept of literature circles and how they can be used to discuss the literary theories we highlight throughout the rest of the text. We discuss pragmatic issues in connection with literature circles, particularly peripheral participation, materials and access, and student resistance.

In chapter 3, we discuss literary theory and its potential use in middle-level classrooms. We outline the five major theories we have used with middle-level students and why these theories might be introduced with sixth- through eighth-grade students. We address literary theories early because we focus on one particular theory as well as one particular genre of adolescent literature in chapters 4 through 8.

Chapter 4 is an exploration of the concepts of identity and representation, which we find are crucial elements for understanding power, oppression, diversity, and social justice. We address the issue of privileging and how assumptions about individuals and groups should be problematized. In this chapter, we focus on reader response theory because we find this to be a foundational literary theory that middle-level readers can most easily accommodate, and it is a theory upon which teachers can build the subsequent theories discussed in this text.

In chapter 5, we address the issue of power and how to discuss it with middle-level students. We begin with a definition of power, and then we share how realistic fiction can be used to examine power in individual relationships and between groups. In this chapter we highlight rhetorical criticism because this literary theory addresses the particular use of language by an author to bring about an intended response in the reader. We end this chapter with a discussion of how power is also used in literature circles or discussions.

Chapter 6 focuses on the issue of oppression. To understand power, students must also understand that oppression often is its result. We highlight how oppression must be named, recognized, and discussed by middle-level students and their teachers. Oppression often is as tricky to name as power, and it is also an aspect of human behavior that needs to be disrupted. We explore feminist criticism and the genre of science fiction in this chapter, bringing together elements of oppression and domination that often go unrecognized in the world at large and in this genre in particular. We end the chapter with a discussion of assessing oppressive behaviors in our interactions as teachers about literature.

Addressing multiple perspectives is the highlight of chapter 7. We focus especially on the issues of race and class in young adolescent literature. Using culturally situated response as the focal literary theory, we examine one piece of multicultural literature that brings into relief how people and situations are viewed differently by various individuals or cultural groups. We then conclude with a discussion of diversity issues and adolescents.

In chapter 8, we share the importance of contextualizing critical consciousness by examining historical fiction and the literary theory of New Historicism. We discuss the element of context and how it can change, and thus, explore how our responses might change or not depending on the context.

We conclude this book with a discussion of where we as educators might go from here. The critical issues for us involve not only the reading of texts but also the real issues of when to address such issues with middle-level students and how that in turn might affect their thinking and living.

It is our hope that you will use this book to plan opportunities for your students to read young adult literature and become critical consumers of that fiction. By providing the time and the structures for them to strengthen their pleasure and critical skills, you guide students toward connections that give them "the kind of present experiences that live fruitfully and creatively in subsequent experiences" (Dewey, 1938, p. 28). Thus, you enable your students' learning to grow and their educational opportunities to develop exponentially.

Acknowledgments

No work can be completed without the help of essential people who help see the project to fruition. For us, those people include Mrs. Mueller and Mrs. Saunders, middle school teachers who are concerned about educating the young people with whom they work to become more critical consumers of texts and to use this knowledge for a more just and humane world. We also acknowledge the help of our editors, Matt Baker and Charlene Nichols. Your guidance and care of this work humbles us. Finally, we would like to thank our colleagues and teachers from around the United States and world. No work stands alone. It is built on the ideas and struggles of others. This work is no different.

"The world is a strange place, she thought...full of contradictions and conflicting ideas."

From *Kezzie* (Breslin, 1993, p. 241)

CHAPTER 1

Becoming Critically Conscious: Theoretical Understandings

As teachers, we have learned that middle-level students have many talents, including the ability to wonder and to ask questions. Because these talents extend in many directions, we often do not realize the importance of middle-level students' wondering and question posing. We forget that they want to know all kinds of things and to ask all types of questions that cover a wide variety of interests and topics, conflicts and contradictions. However, given the conflicting ideas and contradictions of the world, it is no wonder young adolescents have so many questions.

We assert that questioning is an aspect of becoming critically conscious and an aspect of schooling that engages many young adolescents. Questioning encourages students to think beyond the standard curriculum. *Critical consciousness*, a term used by Brazilian educator Paulo Freire (1994), means to become aware of the historical, social, and cultural mores or ideologies that create what is acceptable or not within a particular society. Critical consciousness, or awareness, is also a feature of a "pedagogy of possibility" (Simon, 1992), which can transform middle-level language arts classrooms, reading instruction, and students' lives by allowing students to envision the possibilities of a better world.

Defining Critical Terms

When discussing issues of schooling, terminology should be defined to ensure that there are similar understandings of these terms among participants in the discussion. The terms we wish to outline include *critical thinking*, *critical consciousness*, and *critical literacy*. We also discuss the concepts of social justice, pedagogy of possibility, and critical pedagogy, ending our discussion with how teachers can pull all these concepts together to transform their middle-level language arts classrooms into places of engagement for themselves and their students.

When discussing the concept of "critical" in the field of education, a number of definitions might come to mind. For some, it is the idea of critical thinking. For others, it is about critical theory and critical pedagogy. For still others, it is about critical consciousness and critical literacy. By assimilating the skills of summarization, analysis, and evaluation, which are typically the skills associated with critical thinking, middle-level students become more proficient readers and learners (Harvey & Goudvis, 2000). Becoming critically conscious and accommodating the questioning stance linked with critical literacy, middle-level students become better readers of the word, the world, and the types of representation within the texts they read (Macedo & Freire, 1987). Knowing what differences exist between these terms, however, does not mean that we necessarily see a hierarchy of knowing and learning. Often, these skills and strategies work together, relying on each other for more comprehensive understanding.

Table 1 differentiates the three concepts of critical thinking, critical consciousness, and critical literacy. It is the elements of critical consciousness and critical literacy from which the discussion of pedagogies of engagement extend.

Critical Thinking

Because the definition of critical thinking is fluid and the term is used by educators in multiple ways—as a cognitive ability that is content or context specific or as a generalized skill that can transcend contexts—when we read about critical thinking, we often do not know what the writer means by the term without him or her explaining it. Researchers suggest that knowing how those in the discipline think about its content is

TABLE 1

Definitions of the Critical Concepts		
Critical Thinking	**Critical Consciousness**	**Critical Literacy**
The ability to use logical thinking, analysis, comparison and contrast, questioning, evaluation, and summarization.	The ability to recognize the conditions that result in the privileging of one idea over another within a particular culture or society.	The discussion of how power is used in texts by individuals and groups to privilege one group over another.

a way of learning the content (Rathes, Jonas, Rothstein, & Wasserman, 1967), suggesting a more content-specific way of thinking about particular topics and concepts. For instance, we would think about concepts in science using hypothesis testing, while in history we would use cause and effect and context as ways to think about content. More recently, researchers have asserted that inquiry, and the more general idea of thinking through wondering and questioning, can be used across the curriculum and that it involves the more commonly believed skills of critical thinking such as evaluation, synthesis, application, and inference (Freedman & Johnson, 2004; Short, Harste, & Burke, 1996). Other critical thinking curricula "favor the view that critical thinking skills must be taught in the context of specific subject matter" (Kuhn, 1999, p. 17). Kuhn further asserts that critical thinking is developmental, cognitive, and metacognitive.

By combining these definitions, we can define critical thinking as an attitude or "habit of mind" (Meier, 1996) encompassing a skepticism that allows for divergent ways of knowing about the world and about the knowledge emphasized in any content area or discipline. Meier (1996) suggests that habits of mind allow students to develop problem-solving and thinking skills through questions that address the following aspects of any situation, problem, or issue:

- Cause and Effect/Connections: How did this happen? How is this connected to other things?

- Point of View/Perspective: Who is telling/writing this? What other perspectives are there?

- Evidence: What are the facts? Where did these facts come from?

- Suppose/Wondering: Asking "what if" questions such as "What if the community agrees to an airport?" and "What if the school goes to school uniforms?"

- Debate: Asking questions such as "So what?" "Who cares?" and "What difference does it make?"

By asking middle-level students to become critical thinkers through the use of a habits-of-mind curriculum, teachers can ensure that students learn specific content and gain the knowledge necessary for engaging the world in a critical manner. (See Table 2 for an example of how to use habits of mind in your curriculum.)

Kuhn (1999) suggests that critical thinking addresses specific intellectual skills that include

- Metacognition: The process of thinking about your thinking and the awareness of when you are having difficulty comprehending.

TABLE 2

Using Habits of Mind

Directions: Set a scenario that is relevant to and presents an issue for middle-level students, for example, moving lockers from the hallways to inside homeroom classrooms. Then, investigate the issue through the five habits of mind.

Cause and Effect/Connections: Why would the school decide to place lockers in homerooms instead of in the hallways? How is this change connected to other changes or issues in the building?

Point of View/Perspective: Who wants this change? Who would this change affect and in what ways? Who doesn't want this change and why?

Evidence: What facts are connected to this change? How much time do students spend at their lockers? What is the purpose of lockers?

Suppose/Wondering: What if lockers were removed entirely? What if students could store books in classrooms rather than their lockers? What would happen if the lockers were placed in the cafeteria or gym rather than a classroom?

Debate: How would the change improve or worsen conditions for students and teachers? What other alternatives exist and how would they improve or worsen conditions? Why is this change necessary?

- Metaknowing: The realization that knowledge is constructed by human beings, rather than existing external to humans and awaiting discovery.

- Metastrategic knowing: The realization of the repertoire of strategies an individual has available and the ability to select the proper strategy for the task at hand.

These skills are frequently part of inquiry strategies that are not content specific, but rather have "wide applicability" (Brown, 1997, p. 399) and are useful across the curriculum or in different contexts within the same content area. For instance, the use of metacognition in language arts or reading classes is a skill beneficial for reading, writing, and literary analysis. Students also can have metacognitive awareness of decisions they make after school and whether these decisions might lead to complications they are not prepared to handle. Strategies used for a particular process in one content area also can be used for other processes in other content classrooms or experiences to arrive at similar understandings or products.

In terms of language arts classrooms and the literary analysis necessary for exploring literature in a critical manner, we find that when students are able to ask questions, evaluate the text from various literary perspectives, and make connections to their lives and to the world, they are using critical thinking to comprehend the text. We also find that this type of thinking enhances their critical consciousness and that the elements of higher-order comprehension—such as metacognitive reading strategies and understandings of reader response theories— become essential elements of the language arts classroom (Luke, 2000).

Ultimately, critical thinking leads to a way of looking at the world that involves a question-posing stance. Such a stance allows readers to ponder what is revealed and what is not within the literature they read and the lives they live. This critical awareness also addresses the limitations and potentials of the lives lived within the literature—lives that may touch ours because the characters cause us to vicariously experience their lives or because their situations address our own or help us see the world through new lenses.

Critical Consciousness

Critical consciousness stands at the juncture between critical literacy and critical thinking. As we previously mentioned, to become critically conscious is to become aware of the historical, social, and cultural mores or ideologies that create what is acceptable or not within a particular society (Freire, 1994). We all live with ideas of what is acceptable, what is right, or what is "natural." Yet, there are multiple ways to be in the world, and not all of these ways are compatible with one another. We often make decisions about what is the best way to be, what is the most acceptable, or what is more correct. Typically, those decisions result in our way of thinking or being in the world, and we do not often question our own ideas, but rather wonder about others' ideas. We also rarely question where our ideas or beliefs came from, assuming that they are the right ones, the most evolved, or the most sensible.

For example, middle-level students are not often asked to think about living in another culture where school is not mandatory. They would have difficulty understanding how some countries do not have the financial support necessary for educating all its citizens, thus families must pay for their children to go to school. In such places, families are forced to make decisions about their children's future. Questions such as who should go to school and for how long become challenges for each family that cannot afford the books, the uniforms, and the other costs associated with going to school. Middle-level students in countries such as the United States, Australia, the United Kingdom, and Germany would find these decisions foreign to their way of thinking. Thus, part of understanding cultures other than their own means that students must examine their ideas of the world and how a person may not always understand the decisions another person makes.

There are times when we must question our own ideologies, simply because they do conflict with others' in critical ways. For instance, as teachers, we realize that we have ideas about what teaching is, what teachers should be like, and what students should be like. We also have ideas about the kinds of things that should happen at home with our students, what their parents should do or be like, and what values they should place on education. We live with these assumptions about ourselves and the world. In becoming critically conscious, however, we must begin to situate these ideas in the times we live in, the ways we were raised and educated, and the ways that the media and the laws of our societies have decided are right, good, or important.

By using literature as a venue for addressing assumptions, students are better able to articulate a critical consciousness in reference to their own lives. For instance, the following excerpt from *Stone-Cutter: A Novel by Leander Watts* (Watts, 2002) challenges some of the assumptions that litter our world and our ideas of it. Albion Straight is a young stonecutter who has just been commissioned to work for a stranger named John Augustus Good. He is supposed to help with Mr. Good's estate but must be gone from his home village for three months.

September 20

Another long day of travel, but today Mr. Williams spoke more and this lifted the forest gloom a bit.

At times his talk was as strange and disordered as Little Watty's midnight rambling. I recognized in his discourse the name Swedenborg, who I believe is a renowned philosopher. He made references to spirits, but whether he meant liquors or angels I couldn't determine. And what he says about Mr. John Augustus Good does not put my heart at ease.

"He is a great man, but not as others are great. Wealth does not guarantee greatness. Nor does walking in the halls of power like a judge or senator. Having a thousand followers means nothing if the words you lead them with are mere beautiful puffs of air." He slapped his horse, not to goad her on, but to capture my attention completely. "Mr. Straight, it is of utmost importance that you understand the gravity of our mission. You have contracted a three-month period of service to Mr. Good, but you may find that it will last a lifetime."

I asked what he meant, and he repeated himself. When I asked for an explanation, he was mum.

QUESTIONS FOR STUDENTS TO CONSIDER

1. What assumptions is Mr. Williams disputing?
2. What makes a person great in this society? Why?
3. What could Albion assume about his service to Mr. Good lasting a lifetime?

For instance, when discussing question one, students might ponder the idea of greatness and how Mr. Williams might think about it in reference to Mr. Good. Students also could discuss their concepts of greatness and how greatness is defined differently by different groups in their school, community, or nation. From the "why" in question two, teachers could ask students to become more questioning or critical about how societies may use the same word, but that meaning could be quite different in particular contexts or cultures. For question three, we can envision students wrestling with the idea of chronological time or psychological time. Could Albion's contract last a lifetime? In what ways? Could he find himself connected psychologically to Mr. Good and the work he will do for Mr. Good far longer than his three-month service? How might Albion be contracted to Mr. Good after his first three months? Do humans do things longer than they planned and why? Do we always like that our contracts have lasted longer than we first wished?

With these types of questions to consider, students can begin to understand the subtleties of language and how it is used to mean more than its literal interpretation.

Once we begin to understand how assumptions and values work, we must question who gets to decide the parameters of acceptability or impropriety. We must also look at how these ideas disadvantage others who may not hold the same ideas of the world. For instance, Gomez (1993) asserts that "presently an undisputed mismatch in the race, social-class, and language backgrounds of teachers and students [exists] in the United States" (p. 460). As part of this mismatch, students and teachers often do not understand each other's value systems, which can be reflected in their classroom relationships. The difference in values between home and school can produce a wide gap for students to cross, but if teachers can work toward understanding students' home cultures and their "funds of knowledge" (Moll, Vélez-Ibáñez, & Greenberg, 1988) these gaps can be decreased.

As the number of children of color increases within the United States, teachers will need to question their assumptions about children, families, and learning. Thus, to become critically conscious, teachers and students will need to negotiate what they read about the world as well as the texts that represent the world. They will need to learn how to share across cultural borders so that all students will have opportunities for social, economic, and political power.

Becoming critically conscious, then, means having an understanding about the diversity of cultures and people within particular communities and societies, as well as the world. Becoming critically conscious also means coming to realize the conditions under which people live—some privileged, some disadvantaged, depending on how they measure up to a society's idea about the world. Teachers' work, then, may include discussions about privilege and oppression, about identifying this privilege and oppression in students' own lives or the lives of others. Middle-level readers also need to become conscious of "how all texts (print, visual, and oral) position them as readers and viewers within different social, cultural, and historical contexts" (Alvermann, 2002, p. 198).

Through the use of children's and young adult literature that presents protagonists struggling in situations that students may face in their own lives, students can become more conscious of how the world works for or against certain groups of people. And by reading literature that shows a dynamic protagonist and an evolving plot or situation, students will come to realize that we are different kinds of people in different contexts. For instance, in *Trino's Time* (Bertrand, 2001), Trino is the oldest son to a single mother, a brother to two younger siblings, a friend to his buddies, a boy interested in a studious girl, a student who does not especially like school, a helper to an older man at the local grocery, an outsider who is trying to make new friends, and a teenager with decisions to make about street activities that killed two of his friends. In each of these contexts, Trino is a slightly different person. Students heading into adolescence will understand this as they attempt to discover who they truly are.

"Lisana, what are you doing here with the gorilla guys?"

This question came from Janie, Lisana's friend, who sat down across from Lisana with her food tray. Today, Janie was dressed completely in orange.

"Hey, Janie, doing your shopping at the Halloween Bargain Basement again? You look like a pumpkin," Hector said before taking a bite from a hamburger.

Janie just rolled her eyes and said to Lisana, "Don't you want to sit some place else?"

"No, I like it here by the windows," Lisana said. "Besides, Trino and I were talking about looking for books for Coach Treviño's report."

"I sure lucked out," Janie said. "Mr. Chaffee doesn't make us do extra stuff in his history class."

But Lisana didn't seem to be listening. "It would be so interesting to read more books written by *latinos*." She smiled at Trino.

"There she goes again with the books stuff," Hector said to Trino, shooting the words out of the side of his mouth. "Next, it'll be poetry junk."

Trino gave Hector a nudge with his elbow to quiet him. "There's got to be some place besides Maggie's store that has the books we need."

"Hmmm." Lisana cocked her head to one side. Suddenly, her face brightened. "I know! We can go to the university. My sister told me that a college library has a lot of books for research. I bet Coach would give us extra credit if we used college books."

"Are you crazy? You think they're going to let a bunch of seventh-graders into a college library?" Hector said. He spoke with a mouthful of hamburger. Bread and meat pieces smashed together as he talked. "Besides, Trino and I don't have a library card for a college library. Do we, Trino?"

Trino wanted to say that he didn't have any kind of library card, but kept silent. He looked from the gross sight in Hector's mouth back to Lisana's annoyed expression.

"You don't need a college library card, Hector. You must stay and read the books there. You take notes from your reading. My sister used to do it all the time."

Trino thought Lisana's idea was crazy, too, but he wanted to look nicer than Hector; so Lisana would like Trino better. "I've never gone to the college library, Lisana. But I'll go with you if you think we can find books by *latinos* there."

She rewarded him with a glowing smile. "That'll be great, Trino. Thanks. I'll talk to Amanda and see if she can come with us." She looked around Trino to give Hector a questioning look. "Well? Hector, are you coming with us? You're Trino's partner, right?"

"I have a scrimmage game on Saturday. Sorry!" He gave Trino a wink. It seemed like he thought he was smart for getting out of the library trip.

"Then we'll go on Sunday—in the afternoon," Lisana said. "Jimmy can come with us, too."

Trino was relieved that Lisana picked a day when he wouldn't lose any money. But he wasn't so sure he wanted to spend Sunday afternoon in the library, either.

"I guess we should go, Trino. There might be books we can use for our report."

Hector sounded so serious that Trino just stared at him. "And then we'll get the girls to write the report for us, huh?" He gave his goofy grin and cross-eyed look to Lisana and Janie, then laughed at their reaction when both girls started to complain loudly.

Trino smiled, not because Hector was funny, but because he knew that as long as Hector said dumb things, Lisana might like Trino more.

When Jimmy came back with his food and brought the boy named Albert along, they kept joking around, talking and laughing. None of the guys made fun of Trino like they did each other. But when they did make a joke, they didn't seem to mind that Trino laughed with them. By the end of the lunch period, Trino still felt like someone standing outside a window looking in. Did he have a chance to become just another one of the guys?

Excerpt by Diane Gonzales Bertrand is reprinted with permission from the publisher of *Trino's Time* (Houston: Arte Publico Press–University of Houston, 2001, pp. 88–90).

QUESTIONS FOR STUDENTS TO CONSIDER

1. How does Trino negotiate his different "selves" in this passage?
2. Why is it difficult for some adolescents to speak up about who they are?
3. Can you be different in some contexts without losing a sense of your true self?
4. In what ways does Trino defy stereotypes? In what way does he confirm them?

By questioning static and stereotypical character representations within literature, middle-level students come to realize—become conscious of—the complexity of individuals, regardless of dominant traits, behaviors, or appearances. In different contexts, people may act in ways that may seem inconsistent with the ways in which we first defined them (Morgan, 1997). Through critical consciousness, students may become more tolerant, empathetic, and knowledgeable.

Critical Literacy

Critical literacy blends the skills of critical thinking with an attention to social justice and the political aspects of power and language in texts. Alvermann (2002) contends that the diversity of adolescents' interests in various types of texts

suggests the need to teach youth to read with a critical eye toward how writers, illustrators, and the like represent people and their ideas—in short, how individuals who create texts make those texts work. At the same time, it suggests teaching adolescents that all texts, including their textbooks, routinely promote or silence particular views. (p. 198)

Neutrality or objectivity is impossible to achieve. Attempting to accomplish such a goal convolutes the information to the point of inaccuracy because all readers maintain certain perspectives about the world.

In relation to the young adolescent novels available to middle-level students, critical literacy attempts to "further [students'] negotiation with the written word and [their] engagement and critique of the social world" (Rogers, 2002, p. 773). Critical literacy is the practice of resistant reading by teachers and students working together to discover language patterns that promote particular ideas about power and oppression based on race, class, or gender, or a combination of these three. By engaging in a critical read of a novel, students learn to challenge dominant ideologies that may limit their potential and possibilities, or those of others who may fall outside the expected norm. Students can learn to resist the expected interpretation of a text by questioning the author's intent, the representation of character types within the text, or the dominant message implied within the story.

This type of resistance is vastly different from the resistant reading often found in schools when students resist reading entirely. Through a critical lens, resistant reading is engaging a text with a questioning stance. For instance, *A Perfect Snow* (Martin, 2002), a book about a boy who decides to join a white-supremacy group in Montana, allows students to question what they read, the language used to persuade or manipulate others, and the purpose of a text. In the following excerpt (see story pp. 10–12 for a more detailed excerpt), Ben comes home to the family trailer to find his dad sitting in their old recliner. He knows his dad has been job hunting at the local ranches near their Montana home. He asks his dad if he has any job prospects. Ben does not want to upset his father, so when his father asserts that some racial and economic groups are privileged over another, Ben joins his father by making fun of immigrant workers.

> "Not so much as a bite," Dad said. "This town has no use for an old cowhand like me. Investment brokers and art dealers are the only guys that can get a job now. The Jew boys running everything make sure of that...."
>
> "You'd have a better chance if you were a Mexi wetback," I joked. "Then they'd jump to hire you. Maybe you should fake being a wetback, Dad. Dye your hair black and shuffle into the job saying, '*Sí, señor*, twelve kids, give job.'" Dad and David [Ben's brother] finally laughed.

Excerpt from *A Perfect Snow* (Martin, 2002), pp. 10–12.

QUESTIONS FOR STUDENTS TO CONSIDER

1. Where did you find yourself resisting the information you were reading? Why?

2. What did you feel as you read?

3. Where else do people who feel this way live besides Montana?

4. What would make you continue or stop reading this book?

We believe that issues of language and literacy are also elements of critical literacy. For example, students who have difficulty reading realize how often they are silenced in a reading or language arts classroom where the very nature of that subject area should be about always learning to read and reading to learn. Through the investigation of language with middle-level students, teachers can encourage students to become critically aware of how some groups are described in ways that privilege them over other groups, how some points of view are encouraged over others, and how some ideas are promoted over others. Hynds (1997) asserts that "the common wisdom in most American classrooms is that today individuals are able to make choices and are not held back by race, gender, or other factors over which they have no control" (p. 248). Yet, there are still students who do not feel welcome to express their opinions in classrooms, nor do they feel welcome in school.

By learning about language through young adolescent novels, middle-level students realize that the materials and messages they encounter daily contain biases that empower some groups while oppressing others. By using materials such as young adolescent novels and picture books that are relevant to adolescents, teachers can create opportunities for their students to become familiar with the use of language and, in turn, to extend this knowledge by investigating how this language affects them and their ideas of the world. They also can investigate other texts, whether they are print or nonprint, produced by others or written by themselves.

Coming to understand the usefulness of critical thinking in correlation with critical consciousness within a critical literacy framework requires the persistence of teachers as they attempt to help middle-level students reconsider some of the patterns of thinking that allow the inequity of power and privilege to go unchecked in society. By assisting middle-level readers as they learn about language, social justice, and literary understandings, teachers become the cultural workers that can transform society.

Addressing Social Justice

The concept of social justice is complex and often ambiguous. What is social justice? How do issues of culture, gender, class, or race and ethnicity relate to social justice? Can social justice also address diversity and tolerance? What about equity and equality, fairness and injustice, difference and sameness?

All of these questions address aspects of social justice, which in the larger sense is about disrupting the status quo and the myths that blame the victims of the dominant culture's historical and contemporary ideas about race, class, gender, and literacy. Comber and Nixon (1999) suggest that social justice is the "ongoing commitment [of] exploring the effects of our institutional and discursive practices" (p. 322) in connection to issues of race, class, and gender. Questioning the way in which some practices are assumed to be more natural than others, and thus are spoken through formal laws and informal functioning in a society, is one way of viewing social justice. Examining the beliefs a culture holds as "natural" about women, men, the poor, the wealthy, and people of color may not be not natural at all. Rather, the reified ways a culture has defined these groups and then made policies or social practices that fit those myths or ideas are central to discussions of social justice.

Other theorists suggest that social justice involves critical literacy and challenging state and federal mandates involving a society's language- and literacy-learning policies and practices that push only one way of learning and knowing (Allington, 2002; Coles, 2003; Edelsky, 1999; Shannon, 1992).

These ideas of social justice—and by extension, the actions they call for—often cause us discomfort because they demand that we become more reflective in our teaching practices as well as our mannerisms and attitudes toward the content we teach, the methods we employ in our teaching, and the relationships we establish with our students. Social justice, when viewed from a more comprehensive perspective, disrupts our ideas of the world and who we are as teachers. When asked to reflect on ourselves as teachers within a social justice framework, we find that we have not always advocated for all our students, a distressing thought when juxtaposed with our ideas of teaching within a democracy.

In connection to literacy learning, most of the teachers with whom we work can better understand a commitment connected to allowing students to learn in multiple ways and, by extension, learning to address individual needs rather than a "one size fits all" mentality that seems to accompany the teaching to particular standards. Edelsky (1999) suggests that the focus of teaching and learning within a social justice frame is "to promote democracy, justice, and equity" (p. 9), which would mean that all our middle-level students have a right to our time, our attention, our best teaching. We also have interpreted Edelsky's remarks to include dialogue with our students about what they are learning in our reading and language arts classrooms and important personal goals they wish to attain. Thus, meaningful participation had to become an element of our classrooms where our students bring their whole selves and experiences to the conversation. They do not leave parts of themselves on the doorstep. They make personal as well as broader societal connections to the content taught in our classrooms.

Social justice, then, involves the understanding of injustice as well as conditions that may create justice. Such discussions would necessarily involve "unpacking the knapsack of white privilege" (McIntosh, 1998), which most white teachers resist because this process causes confusion, fear, and anger, not to mention disbelief within them. Value systems run deep, and so do the myths about individuals and groups. One such myth is that individuals and groups earn their status, and if someone is underprivileged, he or she just needs to work harder to be successful.

Another aspect of social justice that is particularly salient for classroom teachers involves who participates in classroom discussions or interactions and how (Moll, Vélez-Ibáñez, & Greenberg, 1988). The subtle and not-so-subtle discriminatory acts that allow some students to dominate in classroom interactions while relegating other students to silence are an aspect of social justice that teachers need to consider, especially when coupled with student resistance to the traditional methods and textbook materials often used in schools to "teach." As schooling practices marginalize particular students based on language, sex, race, or economic disadvantage, the equal opportunities premised on education are nullified. The loss of opportunity is often the precursor to the loss of voice, the loss of self, which creates conditions that produce injustice and oppression. Oppression is often the result of schooling where issues of diversity and social justice are not acknowledged or understood.

Young (1990) identifies five factors of oppression: (1) exploitation, (2) marginalization, (3) powerlessness, (4) cultural imperialism, and (5) violence. When students become the unwilling victims of cultural imperialism, which suggests that the dominant group of any society is normal and renders those outside the dominant group silent or invisible, the oppressive factors of marginalization, powerlessness, and emotional and symbolic violence are manifest as well. Thus, teaching for social justice involves knowing the factors of oppression and finding ways to disrupt them. We believe that this can be accomplished through young adolescent literature and the elements of critique and pleasure.

Pedagogies of Engagement for Middle-Level Learners

Freire (1994) suggests that teachers need to enter into dialogue with their students about concrete situations or students' actual experiences. By providing middle-level students with opportunities to talk about what they learn in school and connecting this knowledge with the world outside the classroom, we give them the instruments and strategies with which to engage the world. A curriculum that allows students to discover their own thoughts about issues, situations, or events that affect their lives creates possibilities and desires for deep engagement and deeper learning. The theories that underlie the following pedagogies are based on social justice and democracy, and suggest that educational institutions might serve to create societies where all citizens are valued.

Pedagogy of Possibility

Simon (1992) has written extensively on critical pedagogy and a "pedagogy of possibility." He asserts that such a pedagogy "requires the situated refusal of the present as definitive of that which is possible" (p. 30). He suggests that what people could be, either as individuals, as members of particular groups or institutions, or in general life, has not yet been fulfilled, but could be. We understand a pedagogy of possibility to be putting into practice our hopes for the world, our students, and ourselves, and we believe that schools can be transforming institutions where teachers and students can change themselves and the world.

Furthermore, a pedagogy of possibility also embraces the vision that aspects of schools that regulate human potential can and need to be disrupted. Schools can be places where students do not necessarily have to mold their lives to accommodate the interests of a culture that privileges particular cultural, racial, ethnic, gender, language, or class norms over others. A pedagogy of possibility allows for diversity and the freedom that allows all students the opportunities to grow toward their own potentials as individuals who have something worthwhile to offer.

Giroux (1990) contends that "the language of possibility...can be developed as a precondition for nourishing convictions that summon up the courage to imagine a different and more just world and to struggle for it" (p. 41). Teachers, with such a commitment, become cultural workers who wish to see a social transformation that would create a society that is more tolerant, more just, more diverse, more open to the potential that all kinds of people bring to a democratic society.

Teachers, however, do not work alone in this work toward possibility. They work with others outside the education system who also wish to see social change. For instance, in the United States during the late 1950s and into the 1960s, people from different class locations, different ethnic and racial heritages, and different geographical and professional areas all came together in the Civil Rights movement. They worked across their differences to come together to create social change. Thus, a pedagogy of possibility includes political awareness and the realization that schooling is political because it has to do with power and who has it.

Issues about curriculum, teachers, and the types of schools built in a district or state all fall under the politics of that area. The values one community reinforces over others is ultimately about power and who gets to decide what is best for the community. Some groups have power in certain areas, while other groups have power in other areas, and what type of education is implemented is decided by those in power. Those in power get to decide what will be valued, and with such decisions, some groups of people do not have the same types of opportunities as others—especially if they do not hold the same ideas as those in power. For instance, the standards movement that began for the United States in the 1990s was a political situation in which few teachers had the power to decide how and what their students should be taught. Those decisions were made by people who had the political clout to create change in schools. Students who could not keep up with the mandated curriculum were either labeled as learning disabled or failed. For many of these students, their opportunities for personal transformation were limited by the standards movement.

A pedagogy of possibility, then, is about learning, teaching, and justice. It is a pedagogy that is hopeful in its belief that people can work together to rid themselves and their communities of the oppression of others. Teachers must, however, work toward this goal and remain persistent in the belief that such a goal is worthy of our individual and collective endeavors.

This, then, is where we find the use of young adult literature for encouraging middle-level students to think about the possibilities of their lives and of the lives of others. From their discussions across different interpretations, different points of view, students learn that there are multiple ways of understanding a text, and of being in the world.

Critical Pedagogy

When teachers decide to embrace a critical pedagogy, they are deciding to bring a questioning stance into their classroom. Such a stance addresses issues of power and oppression, and advances the belief that all students should have access to skills that would allow them access to power within a society. Luke (2000) asserts,

From a sociological perspective, the work of literacy teachers is not about enhancing individual growth, personal voice, or skill development. It is principally about building access to literate practices and discourse resources, about setting the enabling pedagogic conditions for students to use their existing and new discourse resources for exchange in social fields where texts and discourses matter. (p. 48)

To create such an environment, however, we suggest that a teacher who embraces a critical pedagogy also attends to students' personal voices, individual growth, and skill development because all are needed or need to be questioned. Again, while middle-level students should be taught the skills and strategies needed to succeed in school and in the world, we also believe they should question some of the practices and requirements that accompany success. We also hope that students question the concept of success and what it means in their particular neighborhoods, communities, or cultures. These discussions can help create spaces where students discuss texts and ideas or discourses that matter to them.

Discourse can mean the actual language a person uses, or it can mean the way in which particular language is used in a specific content area or a specific place (like a research lab or restaurant). Gee (1999) suggests that different groups of people have different ways of being or acting. *Discourse* also can refer to the way things are done at a particular place, and the way people should or do behave in that place. For instance, visiting a doctor's office has a whole discourse style. Patients are generally quiet, wait for the doctor or nurse to see them, and in many cases, undress before the doctor enters the examination room. Doctors are the authority, and patients believe what they say. Visiting a doctor is a whole discourse that is rarely duplicated in any other circumstance.

Teachers can expand the classroom discourse from students' own beliefs and ideas to introduce the discourses of power in their society. By scaffolding student learning toward becoming critically literate, teachers can engage students in questioning texts, resisting the dominant reading, and becoming aware of how texts "work" on them.

Critical pedagogy also promotes student practices and actions that have the potential to produce a more just society. For instance, students might create a newsletter about how certain groups are represented in common texts, rewrite a story by placing a person of color in the role of the protagonist and exploring how that changes the relationships in the text, or create videos or dramas that highlight the relationships of power between the protagonist and the readers or the author and the protagonist. By working through such relationships, students come to realize the complexity of power and oppression that also is part of a critical pedagogy.

Discourse can mean the actual language a person uses, or it can mean the way in which particular language is used in a specific content area or a specific place.

17

A critical pedagogy situates learning in a context that often is over-shadowed by the dominant norm. Engaging students in the critical thinking that involves social, political, and economic realities increases the relevance of the learning that takes place in the classroom. Critical pedagogical practices also present situations and world events in ways that are relevant to students and in ways in which they can understand. Middle-level students are open to the discussions that are relevant to their lives. Just by asking students who are interested in music or art how much these topics are addressed or "allowed" in their school will help them begin to understand the power that decides what should be learned and how. Issues of race, class, gender, literacy, and language are relevant to them, as are issues of power and oppression. Critical pedagogies address such issues through materials middle-level students can understand and enjoy, even as they critique them.

Throughout this chapter, we have highlighted addressing the concept of being or becoming critical. This concept, regardless of whether it is used in the term *critical thinking, critical consciousness,* or *critical literacy,* is about questioning. Readers of all ages are asked to embrace a questioning stance toward the information they encounter in their daily lives. In the following chapter, we apply this theoretical understanding to the practical aspects of classroom learning and reading at the middle level.

"'Well, then we just have to be on the lookout,' [Lina] said. 'Some chance might turn up. We have to watch for it. I don't know what else to do.'"

From *The People of Sparks* (DuPrau, 2004, p. 284)

CHAPTER 2

Learning the Critical:
Moving From Theory to Practice

Understanding theoretical concepts begins the work involved in becoming critically conscious and critically literate. Knowing when and how to apply the concepts takes practice. Teachers at the middle level have the opportunity to "be on the lookout" for teachable moments that will bridge the gap between theory and practice for their students. Through classroom strategies that engage the developmental levels of their students, middle-level teachers invite their students to become more familiar with and adept at applying a questioning stance toward the texts they read.

Transforming Classrooms Into Places of Engagement

Two of the ways we most frequently ask middle-level students to critically interact with the texts they read is through our own reading aloud and through their participation in literature circles. We use other literacy strategies as well, but they are typically used in a literature circle format or as part of whole-class discussions following the daily read-aloud. By transforming classrooms to include literature circles and read-alouds, teachers have the opportunity to model their own critical thinking, consciousness, and literacy, and then give their students the opportunity to apply this learning to their own readings and discussions of texts.

Literature Circles

We address the importance of the social aspect of reading and learning throughout this text because to become critically conscious and critically literate, students need to be in conversation with others. When we use the word *conversation*, this is not about the superficial give and take in which many of us engage throughout the day but rather a deeper level of engagement that can expose us to other ideas, other theories, and other ways of being in the world. When any of us reads a text, we are in a conversation with the author, and when we watch a television newscast, we converse with the events of the world. We have opinions that matter, and we must come to the point of understanding that other perspectives—other viewpoints—matter, too.

Through the use of literature circles, students will come into contact with others' ideas and other opinions, and this exposure helps enhance students' understandings of the world. Literature circles are small groups of students who read either the same fictional book or a number of books that contain similar themes or content (Daniels, 2001; Peterson & Eeds, 1990). Literature circles support students' learning while addressing the teacher's desire for students to demonstrate and apply their learning in relation to the curriculum. When first working in literature circles, students usually talk for about 10 minutes and often need the teacher to scaffold their discussions through prompts or responsibilities. Eventually, students can discuss a text for as long as 45 minutes. Using picture books is a nice entry into literature circles with younger middle-level students.

Short et al. (1996) suggest that students come to literature circles with half-formed understandings and ideas about what they have read or experienced. Through their discussions with others, students have the opportunity to test those ideas and more fully form what they are thinking. Literature circles also give students the opportunity to reform or modify their ideas, often in the safety of a group of familiar people who will work with them on verbalizing and clarifying their thinking.

> Literature circles are small groups of students who read either the same fictional book or a number of books that contain similar themes or content (Daniels, 2001; Peterson & Eeds, 1990).

Read-Alouds

Students need to hear fluent and confident readers make sense of text. As teachers, we have the opportunity to model proficient reading that brings to life the words on the page. Reading aloud also is enjoyable for young adolescents, and it is especially helpful for those who have difficulty visualizing what they are attempting to comprehend. Teachers also can use read-aloud selections that have higher readability levels than students' independent reading levels because students' listening vocabularies are larger than their reading vocabularies. The use of language in a read-aloud also benefits students' vocabulary development (Richardson, 2000). Reading aloud to students also helps them get lost in a story and can build their pleasure in the process of reading.

Students have reported again and again how much they enjoy hearing a text read aloud. Ernesto, a 13-year-old struggling reader, explained that, "when the teacher reads out loud to us, I can understand it better. The hard parts aren't so hard anymore."

Often middle-level readers are caught between wanting to know what is in a book and being able to read it for themselves. When we read to our middle-level students, we purposefully selected texts that were a bit more difficult or on a higher reading level than many of those in the classroom. Through listening, they were better able to understand the content of the text, and with our reading, we knew we were scaffolding their comprehension development. We also used think alouds when reading aloud to our students. We would model our questioning of the information, we would address where we had difficulty believing the text, and we would highlight language we found especially salient or troublesome. From these demonstrations, our students learned to regard texts more critically. They did not just accept the information because it was in written form.

While we read aloud to our students daily, we did not always demonstrate our thinking aloud during the reading, but often waited to the end of the reading to discuss what we were thinking. Because we followed up the read-alouds with class discussions, our students had the opportunity to ask their own questions or present their own interpretations of the text. This sharing was beneficial because it meant misconceptions could be cleared up, if necessary. The class would revisit the text to examine the evidence found within it that supported one idea or other, or the language that could allow for multiple interpretations. Through read-alouds, students and teachers can enjoy the many materials available that support learning.

The Multiple Materials to Use With Middle-Level Readers

With the increasing numbers of publications available for teaching and learning at the middle level, teachers can benefit from using multiple materials with their students. Although we highlight the use of adolescent fiction in this book, there are movies, Internet sources, informational texts, and the everyday lives of people to "read" and discuss with young adolescents. Textbooks do a nice job of supplying superficial facts and impressions, but they rarely suffice when the readers of such texts begin to ask more challenging or complex questions. The use of trade materials that delve more deeply into a particular topic or idea allows middle-level students to become more deeply engaged. Through such engagement, they are bound to learn more. In the following section, we discuss the materials available for middle-level teachers and students.

The Appeal of Young Adult Literature for Examining Social Justice

For many students, understanding comes through the social interaction of dialogue. Social interactions that spark students' interests encourage them to ponder and use their own life experiences as stepping stones toward understanding the political conditions and conditions of power under which they live and learn. Through the codification of oppressive situations and conditions, all students can come to better understand the reality of justice and injustice. Young adult literature codifies situations of powerlessness through stories of abuse, situations of marginalization through stories of popularity and alienation, situations of exploitation through stories of inequity and discrimination, and situations of imperialism and violence through stories of bias and hate. Middle-level students know of such oppression, can connect to such situations, and can add to one another's understanding by sharing their own stories. Prompting middle-level learners' participation through discussion addresses some of Dewey's (1938) ideas about democracy and conjoined living between diverse groups, while also bringing Freire's (1973/2000) ideas about power and oppression to students' awareness.

By using particular pieces of young adult literature that reflect historical and current examples of oppression, inequity, and the actions that could rectify these conditions, teachers are better able to negotiate a dialogue about issues of social justice and injustice with young adolescents. A discussion of social justice, however, moves beyond the texts that codify instances of discriminatory practices or even practices that promote freedom. There are instances of "common sense" beliefs that litter young adult texts that can be disrupted by learning to question the representations within the text as well as the intentions of the author. While we would suggest that almost any piece of young adolescent literature could be used to address issues of social justice, we specifically look for texts that would be especially engaging for middle-level readers. (See Appendix A for examples of some of the texts we used in our social justice unit.)

We use young adult literature because we find that middle-level students comprehend better the texts that address their current experiences, prior knowledge, and life situations. As they become more adept at questioning texts, we move toward more complex pieces, including classics such as *To Kill a Mockingbird* (Lee, 1960), *The Children's Story* (Clavell, 1989), *The Adventures of Huckleberry Finn* (Twain, 1962), and Shakespearian plays such as *Othello, The Merchant of Venice*, and *Romeo and Juliet*. Regardless of what we read, we find that middle-level students become engaged in literature that touches their lives and their sense of justice.

The Appeal of Picture Books for Examining Social Justice

Although this book addresses fiction and novels specifically, there are other materials we use with middle-level students to create critical consciousness and to explore issues such as social justice. One such format is picture books. Picture books are often relegated to the sidelines once students reach the middle level, which is a mistake. Picture books are engaging, thought provoking, and completely appropriate for use in middle-level classrooms.

By working with picture books, teachers can engage middle-level students' visual and written literacies while inviting them to ponder—in a friendly and gentle manner—concepts that can be difficult to grasp. When children's literature is used to address issues of social justice, it allows readers to distance themselves, to "see" the stories that others tell.

Picture books also can create an accessible way for middle-level students to begin understanding the issues of social justice in relation to themselves as students, as citizens of a society, and as human beings sharing a planet with others who may not be like them. Through the use of picture books, readers more easily understand the "pictures" of how people's behavior toward the "other" occurs. In Shange's (1997) *White Wash* or Wiles's (2001) *Freedom Summer*, young adolescent readers are confronted with prejudice and the offensive behaviors that can accompany racial bias. With *Less Than Half, More Than Whole* (Lacapa & Lacapa, 1994), middle-level students can be introduced to the issue of identity and what that can mean to someone who may not feel as though he completely fits in. With *Farmer Duck* (Waddell, 1991) and *The Big Box* (Morrison & Morrison, 2002), young adolescents are able to ponder issues of power and oppression.

With picture books, readers use illustrations as a means to enter the lives and stories of young people like themselves or those who share their classrooms, their cities, their world. Through the use of child protagonists that are often the focus of picture books, young readers are able to live vicariously and examine their behaviors or attitudes toward others. And because picture books often use the perspective of the young to tell their stories, readers can better connect to young people's ideas of the world and those within it. The use of picture books that feature adults, however, also allows young readers to enter into the realms of injustice by reading about the lack of opportunities afforded to the less fortunate by larger society or through deliberate alienation of the underrepresented by the structures of power. Negotiating the meaning in *A Day's Work* (Bunting, 1994) or *A Chair for My Mother* (Williams, 1982) conjures the realities of limited resources and the circumstances of working for or for less than minimum wages.

Picture storybooks can be used as a means of discussing the realities that surround the issues of social justice, while also allowing young adolescents easy entry into the many topics that fall under the practices of social injustice that plague our nation. Ultimately, the use of picture books allows teachers to broach the hard questions that accompany the complex concept of critical consciousness and the accompanying issues of racism, sexism, class, and their connections to social justice. There are, however, other issues that teachers might also address when examining social justice with their students. These issues are more pragmatic in content but can be just as difficult to negotiate in the classroom.

Pragmatic Issues and Literature Discussions

There are several issues we have had to work through when teaching literature to middle-level students. These issues deal with logistics, personalities, and resistance. We consider these issues more practical in nature than the hard questions we addressed above because they relate to the time teachers have to cover material in their classrooms, to the personalities that teachers contend with in the classroom environment, and the resistance some students will bring to any of the content teachers attempt to teach in their subject area. Working through these issues, or at least understanding that others face similar problems, gives most teachers permission to think creatively about these dilemmas. Too often, teachers blame themselves or their students when classroom interactions are less than ideal.

Time Issues

In many school districts, teachers need to consider the time they have to discuss literature with their students when balanced against external factors such as curricular guidelines and testing structures. We work with middle-level social studies and language arts teachers who create global lesson plans that cover the entire year so they do have time to read multiple books during the school year. They also teach using thematic units so they can not only address the district's curricular guidelines but also include read-alouds and small-group readings in their curriculum. They start their classes with a read-aloud each day so that in a three- or four-week unit, they have completed a read-aloud that is similar in theme to the books their students are reading either individually or in literature circles.

We also know from our own teaching that middle-level teaching periods can be as short as 30 minutes or as long as 90 minutes. Thus, fitting in discussions to accommodate critical consciousness may not seem feasible, but we have found that when we implement an overarching theme for the year that addresses critical consciousness, each book we read addresses students' deeper thinking and critical literacy. One such overarching theme might be "Interdependence" or "Understanding Our Connections to Each Other."

At the beginning of each year, we would spend the first month helping students adapt to our expectations. Holly began the year by teaching a unit entitled "Knowing Yourself," in which students read and wrote autobiographical stories and poems. To enhance critical consciousness, she highlighted the importance of identity, and then she moved on to multiple perspectives using pieces of young adult fiction. Knowing her state and district curricular guidelines, she addressed state standards, while also addressing the issues important to her unit.

Through such planning, teachers can lessen their anxiety about time constraints while also highlighting the content and issues that brought them to teaching.

Access and Materials

Another issue teachers need to address involves materials and access to those materials. What we have found is that when middle-level teachers and students work together on developing students' critical consciousness, the world becomes a text for them to investigate together. We purchase the literature we use with students through grants written with other teachers, through our own resources, and through the use of funds that schools typically use to purchase textbooks. We find that most students need access to textbooks, but we do not recommend using those textbooks every day. Thus, we purchase only one class set of textbooks, rather than one textbook per student. This works because students read during class for particular units, and readings are staggered so not all classes need the textbooks at the same time. We also share textbooks with other teachers teaching the same grade. Thus, we can use some of the funds earmarked for textbooks to purchase trade materials.

Peripheral Participants

We have experienced that some students appear to not want to be involved in literature circles or the whole-class discussion of a text. We use the word *appear* here, not because there are not students who do not wish to become involved, but rather because there are times when students do wish to join in discussions but feel uncomfortable doing so.

Although we want students to become involved in discussions that investigate critical consciousness, we also know that some just cannot join us when we first address the issues involved. Therefore, we usually give these students the opportunity to watch for the first couple of discussions, and then we introduce an engagement activity where all the students in the class are given three buttons to use as speaking tokens. Students must use these three buttons during the small- or large-group discussion that day, but we ease them into the use of all three buttons by allowing them to use between one and three buttons the first time they attempt participation. The next time they must use two buttons, then three the following time. Using this strategy also limits opportunities for other students to dominate the conversation.

Other times, students do not have the confidence in their reading ability to enter into a discussion about a text. For example, Holly worked with Ignacio, an eighth grader who felt he was not a good reader and did not think he was comprehending the texts the class read. He was unsure of his ability to enter into even a small-group discussion, so Holly allowed him to travel the room like she did. As the year transpired, Ignacio became more and more engaged with the discussions, stopping briefly at each small group during discussion time.

Finally, Holly noticed that Ignacio was spending more and more time watching one particular group. He would perch on a desk so he could watch each of their faces as they would talk. If the group laughed, Ignacio laughed with them. Holly suggested that maybe Ignacio could sit with the group, but if he still felt uncomfortable, he could continue to watch. Ignacio agreed to this arrangement but found he did not want to remain uninvolved.

We have learned that although it would be nice if all of our students could feel comfortable in speaking, some students need time. They need to build trust in their peers and in their teachers. If we do not allow such trust to develop, we may jeopardize the critical consciousness and the awareness of social justice we wish our students to learn. They may, in fact, resist our ideas and thus not learn what we are attempting to teach.

Resistance

We have found that resistance comes in many forms. As we mentioned previously, peripheral participation can be viewed as a form of resistance to critical consciousness, but the form of resistance we believe may become more of an issue for middle-level teachers is the overt form of resistance where students will "just not learn from us" (Kohl, 1995).

One form of direct resistance may be refusing to learn; for example, students of color may feel it is "acting white" to learn from white teachers or to learn white history. We did not encounter this type of resistance primarily because the middle school students in the classrooms where we worked either had not begun to think in this manner or because they were hesitant to say something so confrontational in districts where "zero tolerance" rules were prevalent. Such resistance was rewarded with In-School Suspension (ISS) or other actions. Of course, going to ISS could be considered a form of resistance as well, but again, the students with whom we worked rarely voiced a willingness to leave the classroom.

One form of direct resistance we did encounter was students placing their heads on their tables and stating that what they were learning was too hard. Other times, students wrote only the bare minimum of what we would ask them to write in their journals. We countered this type of resistance through three actions:

1. Discussion, which became the primary learning mode of these classrooms when the topic was issues of social justice or critical consciousness.

2. Relevant analogies, which were used to help students connect the content they were learning with their own lives.

3. Personal inquiry projects, which were connected to critical consciousness and issues of social justice.

Because middle-level students are so social, we used discussions in literature circles as the primary mode of learning. Students read the books we selected and then answered prompts or questions—such as those provided throughout this book—to begin discussions to develop critical consciousness. Students who found the issues difficult or too complex were supported by others who could provide examples from their lives. This combination helped what we considered the gentle resistance that some of the middle-level students exhibited.

The direct incident of resistance Holly experienced came from a sixth-grade student, Priscilla, whose class was using picture books to begin exploring the concept of social justice. Holly was working with Ms. Mueller, the classroom teacher, on this project because Ms. Mueller wanted additional support while trying this unit for the first time. Priscilla stated, "I don't want to talk to you anymore," and she placed her head on the table. Understanding this as a form of resistance, Holly stated that it was all right for Priscilla to do this, and Holly continued to work with the rest of the class. Eventually, Priscilla reentered the conversation, but Holly and Ms. Mueller realized that other students may have felt the way Priscilla did. They decided to discuss resistance with the sixth graders. They used the word *resistance* with the students but then added words like *boring, difficult,* and *hard*. The students expressed that they were not bored, but rather social justice was difficult to talk about because it was, as 12-year-old Cole suggested, "everywhere once you started thinking about it." Understanding resistance, even if they were enacting it, was a difficult concept for some of these students. They could, however, express why social justice was difficult for them to understand. Another student stated, "Social justice is hard to talk about because even when you know what it is, you can't get it into words."

Students' comments indicated that the primary reasons for resistance were lack of relevance to their lives and the difficulty of the concepts. However, four months later Holly heard a student mention the word *justice* in a conversation about *A Girl Named Disaster* (Farmer, 1996). Ruben, an animated and thoughtful student, said, "*Social* justice...I still like the sound of that." Holly replied, "I like what it means." Ruben replied, "I like how it sounds...and what it means." Other students agreed.

The concept of social justice was something students had remembered, and in retrospect enjoyed. We believe that is because there was no pressure on them to "know" the knowledge for a test. That was never the original intent, and what we received from working with these students is a sense that they will continue to think about social justice and be more critically conscious in the years to come. We realize, however, that other teachers along the way also must be willing to build on this foundation. Without it, we are not sure students will find the concepts or their understandings of them valuable in the future.

Conclusion

When teachers ask students to think critically about young adult texts, they are asking students to become aware of themselves as social beings who have power—power to become more inclusive of others or to marginalize them, to construct themselves and others. Students also have the power to challenge what is presented to them as natural or cultural, and to disrupt or extend cycles of oppression or freedom. Through the practices of critique, teachers ask young adolescents to take pleasure in their development in becoming more critically literate. In the following chapter, we discuss the literary theories that we especially find engaging to middle-level students and through which they can become more critically literate.

"There was something wrong with the world, thought Kezzie, that most people seemed to have to break their backs for bread yet, day by day, in the newspapers and on the wireless all the talk of troubles in Europe meant that vast sums of money were being spent on building warships and making guns to prepare for a war against Hitler's Germany."

From *Kezzie* (Breslin, 1993, p. 57)

CHAPTER 3

Conflicts and Comparisons:
Using Literary Theory With
Middle-Level Learners

L ike the protagonist Kezzie in the book by the same name, students can become confused by the conflicting messages they receive from their community, society, and world. They are not afraid, however, to wonder about this confusion, and willingly do so aloud when given the opportunity. Just as adults attempt to find out the "truth" about what they hear in the media, in the books they read, or in the gossip they hear, adolescents sort through information, accept what seems to make sense, and reject the rest.

Yet the concept of making sense needs to be investigated by students. Teachers need to inform middle-level students that we all have a filter through which we view the world, but filters often lead to oversimplification, misconceptions, and stereotypes. What seems to be the truth—what makes sense—may not be the entire story. Discussing the reality of multiple perspectives may be the first step toward becoming critically literate and critically conscious, and may lead to deeper questions that can deter misconceptions and stereotypes.

Literary Theories as Multiple Perspectives

By learning and working with literary theories that develop critical thinking and critical literacies, middle-level students will come to better understand the world's complexity through the artifacts created by authors who either comment on the world or represent it in ways that seem to make sense to the authors. By learning literary theories, middle-level students can investigate the "truth" found in young adult novels from a number of differing perspectives, and thus come to better understand that truth to one person may not be the truth for someone else. Students also can become cognizant of how novels, written from perspectives other than their own, can broaden the sense they make of any phenomenon. Literary analysis, the interpretive study of literature, is one way middle-level reading and language arts teachers can help students use higher-order thinking to become more critically literate and more critically conscious of the world and literary works that represent it.

Literary theory involves the types of questions readers might ask in relation to four perspectives taken toward a text. Soter (1999) proposes that when working with middle-level students, literary analysis could be approached from the following perspectives:

- View relative to the reader: How the reader responds to and interprets a text.

- View relative to the author: Investigating the intentions of the author.

- View relative to the text: Scrutinizing the literary elements and how they work together to create meaning.

- View relative to the context: How the text reflects the culture in which it was written and is read.

We post these perspectives in our classrooms or use an overhead transparency to remind students of these perspectives as we discuss literature throughout the year. Each of these views corresponds with at least one literary theory but more often with two or more. We also highlight these four views as we read particular novels that seem especially suited to the theory we wish to address.

When teachers scaffold their students' learning of literary criticism by working it into what they are reading, teachers are able to gradually release the responsibility of learning to students (Pearson & Gallagher, 1983). As teachers scaffold knowledge from a foundation of what students already know, they can gradually hand over the responsibility of learning particular knowledge to students, who will be able to take on that responsibility. Too often students are not ready for what they are required to know because they do not have the foundation or prior knowledge on which to build. Teachers need to model the behavior or what knowledge is expected, then guide students toward that requirement. Once students can perform what is expected independently and accept the responsibility of this knowledge, teachers can release that responsibility to students. This is a cycle of modeling, releasing, and learning that benefits students over time.

Gradual release of responsibility is a cycle of modeling, releasing, and learning that benefits students over time.

Literary Theories for Middle-Level Readers

One of the most popular literary theories used in high schools is New Criticism, whose theorists assert that the meaning of the text resides in the text alone. From this perspective, then, students are expected to "find" the meaning of the text, and the possibility of only one meaning or interpretation is quite strong. This perspective often frustrates students, and they have a tendency to believe that they just cannot interpret text and that literary analysis is "hard." Thus, rather than using New Criticism with middle-level readers, we highlight four other literary theories that can lead them toward understanding the New Critical stance.

Students generally choose the books they read for our language arts classes, yet we also select books for the entire class at least four times a year so our students can experience some of the literary works we find especially engaging for young adolescents. It is during these times that we also highlight particular literary theories so students will become aware of a number of ways to look at and read a book.

At the beginning of each year, we begin with reader response theory because we find that middle-level students deserve the opportunity to respond personally to a text before they should be expected to view a text from another perspective.

Reader Response Theories

Reader response theories address the view relative to the reader since they focus on how the reader transacts with the text (Rosenblatt, 1978). Readers bring their own prior knowledge and experiences to the reading event and thus read through their own particular lenses. Beach (1993) outlines five perspectives that represent the different types of perspectives readers bring to the text:

1. Textual perspective: Understanding how text structures or genres work to help with interpreting a text.

2. Cultural perspective: Understanding how readers' cultural backgrounds, attitudes, or values shape their responses to the situations in a text.

3. Social perspective: Understanding how the social context in which a text is read influences how readers respond to a text.

4. Experiential perspective: Understanding how readers engage with the text or its characters through the connections readers make or how they come to interpret the "world of the text" (p. 8).

5. Psychological perspective: Understanding the reader's conscious or subconscious thinking dependent upon developmental level or personality.

Although the differing perspectives Beach outlines are helpful, we do not go into such detail with the middle-level students with whom we work. Rather, these perspectives give added insight into how readers respond to a text and can be of interest to teachers as they observe how their own middle-level students respond to the novels they read.

By becoming familiar with reader response theories, teachers can guide their middle-level students toward interpretations of young adult fiction that forefronts students' own perspectives. Then, when they are more comfortable with responding to literature, these students are better able to accommodate other literary analyses and how those analyses take other perspectives toward a text.

When interpreting a text from a reader response perspective that concentrates on the view of the reader, students look at their own responses to the text by asking the following types of questions:

- How do I feel about this text?
- How does this text connect with me or my life?
- Are my actions similar to the character's? Why or why not?
- What would I have done differently than the character?
- How did the different literary elements, such as plot, setting, or characters, make me feel?
- Why do I like or dislike this book?

We use an excerpt from *The Haunting* (Mahy, 1982; see story pp. 82–83 for a more detailed excerpt) to teach students that responding to a text from their personal perspectives is expected and encouraged in our classrooms. We first discuss the concept of the book—the idea of "haunting"—and what is necessary to create the mood. Then, we read the excerpt and invite students to respond to the idea of a haunting as well as to the situation of the protagonist, Barney. Because many middle-level students enjoy ghost stories, we have found this excerpt—and the book—to be a good way to introduce reader response theory to students. In this excerpt, Barney and his family have moved into a house that seems to be haunted. Two siblings hear footsteps and wonder what is going to happen next. Then, Barney feels a change in the air and feels like "something is rushing at him." He tells his sister that they must wait to see what will happen next, and as he speaks, those words the footsteps above them stop.

"They've stopped," said Tabitha. "They *have* stopped, haven't they, Barney?" Barney nodded. The silence fell again.

It was broken by the shrill cry of the telephone in the hall.

None of them moved, and at last Claire had to come through from the kitchen to answer it.

"It's for you, Barney," [his mother] called....

Slowly Barney walked down the hall. The hand that lifted the receiver was heavy with reluctance....

"Hello," he said in a small voice.

The phone sighed.

"Barnaby?" it asked, in the familiar, husky voice of his shadowy ghost.

"Barney! I'm called Barney!" Barney hissed.

"I've arrived," the voice said. "I'm here in your town."

Excerpt from *The Haunting* (Mahy, 1982), pp. 82–83.

QUESTIONS FOR STUDENTS TO CONSIDER

1. What do you think of this excerpt?

2. What feelings did it develop in you?

3. What would you do if you were Barney?

4. How does this connect with an experience from your life?

We find that by starting with literary criticism from a reader response perspective, students become more comfortable with the process of interpretation and the critical thinking that comes with it. Often, students who have not had the opportunity to respond to a text from their own perspectives become fearful of literary criticism because of an emphasis on a "correct" interpretation. Because reader response theories are based on the theory of transaction, there is no one correct view, but rather an openness to the text that allows for multiple interpretations. Once students understand that multiple interpretations are valid, they can more easily understand how others (in their classroom or outside it) may have different ways of looking at a text. From this comfort level, students can more readily move to other literary theories more restrictive in their interpretations.

Rhetorical Criticism

As we have mentioned, New Criticism is not one of the theories we highlight in the middle grades, but one way of asking students to look at the structure of a text, or how a text works, is through Rhetorical

Criticism. This theory asks readers to consider how readers, texts, and authors function in relation to one another (Burke, 1969). Those who are interested in Rhetorical Criticism address the following considerations:

- How the narrative structure seems to direct the reader to respond in particular ways.
- How the author uses language to elicit certain responses from the reader.
- How the author achieves certain intended results.

We have found this type of analysis quite entertaining for many middle-level students as they share their thoughts and responses to a text and then attempt to find where the author uses particular words, phrases, circumstances, or relationships to elicit certain responses from the reader. For example, when reading *To Kill a Mockingbird* (Lee, 1960) one of the elements a reader must consider is the author's use of Scout as the narrator. Scout, who is 6 years old at the beginning of the book, tells readers about the terrible events that occurred in her small Alabama town during the Great Depression. Of course, readers also must realize that the narrator is an adult at the beginning of the story, so through a child's voice, the author uses an adult narrator looking back on her childhood to present the story. Students might ask, What was the author's intent for using such a young narrator? Why not just let the adult Scout (Jean Louise) tell the story? What is it about the use of a child narrator that works on the reader?

The following excerpt from *If You Come Softly* (Woodson, 1998; see story pp. 75–77 for a more detailed excerpt) is another excellent way to introduce middle-level students to Rhetorical Criticism. In fact, most of Woodson's works would be suitable for exploring how an author uses gentle persuasion to bring readers to view the world from the author's perspective. In this story, Jeremiah and Ellie are beginning to fall in love, but their racial differences cause some discomfort to those around them. In this excerpt, Jeremiah is transferred into an advanced history class and sits next to Ellie. They discuss how the school "mistakenly" placed Jeremiah in a remedial class.

"Yeah—it just seems like more than a coincidence when it happens to me. Like what made them think I needed remedial anything. Nobody tested me. Nobody *asked* me. They just threw me in it then looked surprised when I knew it all. I mean, it makes you wonder—is it my *hair*" He smiled.... "Or the melanin thing?"

The melanin thing.... The world was like that a long time ago. But it wasn't like that anymore, was it? No. My stupid sister might be like that. And maybe my family sometimes. But not the rest of the world. Please not the rest of the world.

Excerpt from *If You Come Softly* (Woodson, 1998), pp. 75–77.

QUESTIONS FOR STUDENTS TO CONSIDER

1. What feelings do you get from reading this excerpt?

2. What ideas about the world does the author seem to express?

3. How does the author gently persuade the reader to think about inter-racial relationships?

Rhetorical Criticism also distinguishes between the author's voice and the narrator's voice, a difference that can be examined by middle-level readers. For instance, in *Whale Talk* (Crutcher, 2001), the narrator is T.J., a high school student whose racial identity is "Mixed. Blended. Pureed. Potpourri.... [A] UNICEF poster boy" (pp. 1–2). T.J. explores the issues of forgiveness, harmony, acceptance, and making the best of what is a less-than-perfect life. Throughout the text, however, the author's voice and beliefs are liberally sprinkled. They are expressed through T.J.'s thoughts, through the way characters interact with each other, and through specific situations. Yet, we wonder if middle-level students who are unfamiliar with this author's work would know this. The following excerpt is a good example of how the author uses the narrator to persuade readers to examine the issue of racism.

My parents have always encouraged me to be loud when I run into racism, but I can't count on racism being loud when it runs into me. Very few people come out and say they don't like you because you aren't white; when you're younger it comes at a birthday party you learn about after the fact, or later, having a girl say yes to a date only to come back after discussing it with her parents, having suddenly remembered she has another engagement that night. Not much to do about that but let it register and don't forget it.

Excerpt from *Whale Talk* (Crutcher, 2001), pp. 3–5.

QUESTIONS FOR STUDENTS TO CONSIDER

1. Does the narrator, T.J., sound like the typical high school student? Why or why not?

2. What part of this excerpt makes you think about racism?

3. How does the narrator reflect the author's ideas about the world?

Knowing about an author can help students with Rhetorical Criticism, and by asking students to do author studies—that is, research on the background of an author and comparing books published by that author—teachers can help their students come to better understand how authors use language, plot, and setting to accomplish specific intentions.

To begin literary analysis using Rhetorical Criticism, students can ask the following questions:

- What language directed my thinking and feelings?

- Why did the author use this particular narrator?

- How do I feel about this novel, and why do I feel this way?

- Did I accept without thinking what the author said? Why or why not?

- Why did or didn't I want to read this novel? What elements of the text might have influenced this decision?

- What would the author have had to do differently to get me to like or dislike this book?

These questions and others can help students address issues related to authors, the authors' work as writers and people influenced by their own value systems and social contexts, and the ways authors' use their work to speak to readers. By addressing such questions, middle-level readers become more adept at interpreting not only whole pieces of literature but also particular language usage within texts. These questions also allow students to contemplate what kind of readers they might be when they begin reading a book.

As we have noted, Rhetorical Criticism is about authors and narrators. Authors actually write the book, while narrators are the characters telling the story. Middle-level readers can readily understand this difference when teachers explicitly teach it. There are, however, multiple types of audiences that may be a bit more difficult to understand, and because these distinctions are highlighted by this literary theory, we list the four major types of audiences authors consider when writing:

1. Actual audiences: Real readers who may or may not be influenced by the author's work.

2. Authorial audiences: Readers who enter the world constructed by the author in an attempt to understand the author's viewpoint.

3. Narrative audiences: Readers who enter the book's constructed world and connect and affiliate with the characters.

4. Ideal narrative audiences: Readers who uncritically accept what the author has to say through the narrator, fill in gaps between them, and assume the author's value system.

Attempting to figure out to which type of audience they belong can be difficult for middle-level readers, yet it is a giant step toward becoming more critically conscious of how authors work, use language, and present scenarios that influence us in particular ways. Having this knowledge does not preclude a reader's own proclivity toward certain behaviors, beliefs, and actions; however, understanding how texts, authors, and readers all connect is a positive move toward becoming more responsive and more responsible readers and citizens. In addition to novels, students can begin to look at advertisements, commercials, and other media in more critical and sophisticated ways. We also find that once middle-level students begin to see how texts work on them, they are more willing to explore the ways in which they perceive a text based on their own ideas of the world.

We use the following excerpt from *Trino's Choice* (Bertrand, 1999), a novel about a Mexican American boy in southern Texas, to ask students to think about the way the text works, the way they respond to it, how the author uses language, and to which kind of audience they think they belong.

By the time Trino rested his tired black eyes on his family's white trailer house, the sun had melted into an old bruise on the horizon. The trailer park was noisy with Tejano tunes crackling from somebody's radio, a lady yelling "Mari-lena" like a howling cat, and some kid crying between whacks of a belt. Cartoon music blasted through the torn screen of their trailer door as Trino opened it and walked inside.

Gus, Beto, and Felix sat on the torn red rug in front of the TV, sharing a head of cabbage between them.

Excerpt from *Trino's Choice* (Bertrand, 1999), pp. 15–17.

QUESTIONS FOR STUDENTS TO CONSIDER

1. How does this excerpt make you feel?

2. How does the author use language to create a feeling, mood, or world?

3. In terms of audience, what kind are you (see list above)?

4. How does this text connect with your life?

Using Rhetorical Criticism, teachers provide their students with language study that can deepen their students' understandings of how texts work, and how those texts work on them. Another theory that also will have students reflecting on how a text works and how they are affected by a text is culturally situated response theory, which is examined next.

Culturally Situated Response Theory

One of the newer literary theories that middle-level students might find of interest is culturally situated response theory. This theory suggests that authors, their texts, and readers all are situated within particular social, cultural, and historical contexts. These contexts, then, influence authors' beliefs and their literary works, including what is written as well as how it is written. Thus, readers' responses are culturally situated and readers' contexts influence how they perceive texts. Because readers bring individual values, attitudes, and histories to their readings, they must be aware of how these values, attitudes, and histories may influence the transactions they have with a text.

How often do we read something and say we don't "get it"? How often, when reading a piece of literature from a culture unfamiliar to us or outside our experience, do we suggest that the situations in the text are unrealistic? Culturally situated response connects to reader response theory, especially Beach's (1993) cultural perspective, but in a culturally situated response, the emphasis is on the reader interrogating the self, not the reading material, with regard to the disconnect or connect between the reader and the text. This theory also addresses specifically the cultural perspectives and backgrounds of the reader and the text, which is not always the case in reader response theory. Thus, this theory is used when readers want to explore cultural connects or disconnects, knowing that they will exist because of the particular reader and reading material involved.

Two elements of this theory involve insider and outsider perspectives. An insider perspective generally means that the author is a person who comes from a background similar to that in the story. For instance, Gary Soto, who was born and raised in California under conditions similar to those that he writes about in *Baseball in April and Other Stories* (Soto, 2000), would have an insider perspective to the Mexican American culture of California. An insider perspective also can be accomplished through research and spending time within a culture to learn its nuances. An outsider perspective is when the author is writing from outside the culture or experience of the people or context of a given story. This phenomenon was more prevalent in the past when authors from the dominant culture would frequently write about underrepre-

An insider perspective generally means that the author comes from a background similar to that in the story.

sented groups in their respective communities or countries. Often such authors did not understand the importance of another group's language or traditions, thus rendering their descriptions of those groups inaccurate at best. What was lacking from accounts that did not include an insider perspective was authenticity or the nuances and information that would paint a realistic and often more subtle and complex picture of a group and its culture. There are instances, however, when an author cannot help but write from an outsider perspective. Genres such as fantasy, science fiction, and historical fiction are good examples of this.

Culturally situated response theory intentionally considers author perspectives and how such perspectives influence the writing and reading of texts. The other issue concerning insiders and outsiders is the question of who the audience is for a particular story or text (Sims, 1982). Can readers also inhabit insider and outsider perspectives? Theorists using culturally situated response theory suggest so.

In a study of authenticity, Holly asked her eighth-grade students to read pieces of realistic fiction as outsiders; that is, she asked them to find and read books from a cultural perspective or context dissimilar to their own. This was her initial way to examine how young adolescents approach a text from outside their own cultural perspective, thus broaching some of the issues addressed in culturally situated response theory. Thus, some Latino students read books from an African American perspective, and some Caucasian students read books from a Latino perspective. In addition, students read books from other nations, novels that address living in an urban environment, and novels with protagonists from other religions or economic situations that are not familiar to them. Most of Holly's students found books that address situations outside the dominant white mainstream. After reading the books, the students wrote in their journals about the reality of the situations portrayed.

By interviewing her students, reading their journals, audiotaping their literature circle meetings, and discussing some of the novels in whole-class discussions, Holly found that her students questioned the reality of the situations in the young adolescent novels they read because they could not connect with the protagonists' viewpoints, the characters' situations, or the plot development. Many of her students asserted that the novels they read weren't "real," or authentic. They did not share enough in terms of values or experiences with the situations in the novels to make the cross-cultural connections needed to understand the realistic nature of the young adult fiction they read. If they knew about culturally situated responses, however, Holly's students could have attempted to understand these other cultures and learn from the books they read. Because they did not have this background when

An outsider perspective is when the author is writing from outside the culture or experience of the people or context of a given story.

they read, they could not accommodate the story or even question why they could not connect with the novels.

For instance, Holly asked her students to read *A Girl Named Disaster* (Farmer, 1996), a book about Nhamo, a young adolescent girl in Mozambique who flees her village rather than marry a cruel, older man to appease a vengeful spirit. She thought that readers could be drawn into the book by this adventurous girl's spirit and fight for survival as she takes a canoe and travels to Zimbabwe. These students, however, did not find the story realistic or current. They could not imagine the situation in which Nhamo found herself, nor could they imagine people marrying because of spirits. The students found this book to be a fantasy, rather than the reality that many young girls face in another part of the world. The students voted to abandon the book, and Holly felt they missed out on a wonderful reading and learning experience because of their resistance to Nhamo and her situation. Based on this experience, we use the following excerpt from *A Girl Named Disaster* (see story pp. 11–13 for a more detailed excerpt) to teach culturally situated response and to directly discuss situations that are realistic—although unfamiliar to many students in the United States. Nhamo has just returned to her village after collecting firewood, but her aunts wonder where she has been and suggest that she is lazy.

> Nhamo didn't say anything.... Not far away, other women knelt by other outdoor hearths, preparing the evening meal. The men, tired from fishing, farming, and hunting, had gathered in the *dare*, the men's meeting place. Now and then, laughter reached her on the cool evening breeze.
>
> Soon the air was full of the comforting smell of food. Nhamo's mouth watered, but she didn't dare help herself to anything. First, the men must be fed, then Grandmother and the small children.... They ate mealie porridge, called *sadza*, with tomato, onion, and chili sauce; boiled pumpkin leaves; and okra with peanut butter. Everyone had a piece of boiled fish with some of the water for gravy. It was a good, full meal.

Excerpt from *A Girl Named Disaster* (Farmer, 1996), pp. 11–12.

QUESTIONS FOR STUDENTS TO CONSIDER

1. In what ways is this excerpt realistic? In what ways is it unrealistic?

2. How does it connect to your life?

3. What elements seem foreign to you and why?

We have found that not all students dislike books from another cultural perspective. We are suggesting, however, that when students come to realize the diversity of the world, which includes their classrooms and their communities, they may connect with literature from other cultural locations with deeper engagement because they realize reality is not limited to what they know. Culturally situated response theory focuses on learning across cultural boundaries, and middle-level students, once they are given the opportunity to ponder diversity, are much more willing to step outside the boundaries of their own cultures for enjoyment, interest, and understanding.

Some of the questions that culturally situated response theory address include the following:

- What does it mean to be an insider or an outsider?
- Can readers fully engage in pieces of literature when they are outside the culture?
- Are we really insiders of the literature we read that supposedly represents our culture?
- How should we read literature from outside our cultural experience?
- What do readers miss in the literature from other cultures when they are outsiders to that culture?

Of course, these general questions provoke other questions about cultures being stagnant, and about the universal experience of being human. They also evoke questions about the idea that any one novel could represent an entire cultural experience, and why, as readers, we might think this way. Do readers perceive texts to be representative of cultures and, if so, in what ways? How do we avoid such generalizations? Middle-level students also might explore their resistance to certain texts because of their ideas about another culture. Teachers can also have students examine the idea of understanding another experience or cultural situation, rather than being dissuaded from it when they do not feel as though they share any of the values or practices represented in the text. Finally, middle-level readers might explore the assumptions they bring to a text that cause them to connect or disconnect from the experience being presented.

Theorists using culturally situated response promote the idea that readers can learn to accept the unfamiliar and subsequently honor the plurality within particular nations, rather than expect differences only to appear across oceans or between nations. Although the students who read *A Girl Named Disaster* voted to abandon the text, we believe this provides an important aspect of culturally situated response that needs clarification. When asking students to read outside their cultural understandings, it would be best to frame the reading with the purpose of *learning* from the text rather than asking students to attempt to relate to the text. Given this invitation to the reading, Holly now wonders if the students would have responded differently to that text. We also know that other groups of students have enjoyed this adventure story and the information they learned about Nhamo's culture. Given the chance, middle-level students can learn how to remain connected to characters and situations that are unfamiliar to them, and thus culturally situated response becomes a model of learning rather than a model for expecting students to demonstrate knowledge.

Culturally situated response theory has much to offer the middle-level literature classroom, especially in light of the ever-expanding situations where cultures meet and coexist across the world. Another literary theory that would enhance understandings across cultures or groups is feminist response theory, which addresses key issues in relation to gender, gendered representations, and communication.

Feminist Criticism

Feminist criticism is not simply one theory; it can be combined with other literary theories for a combination of different literary analyses. For the sake of this discussion, we wish only to highlight some of the general observations that those interested in feminist criticism consider. One overarching concern of feminist criticism is the way in which females are portrayed in literature. Some feminist critics suggest that women, as a class, are exploited at all levels (economic, political, and social), and in literature that exploitation becomes apparent. One example of this is the character Celie in *The Color Purple* (Walker, 1982). Celie is abused by her father, told that her children died, married off to a man who abuses her emotionally and physically, and is generally underappreciated. Readers can see the exploitation of women on many levels in this novel, not only by white society but also by the black patriarchy as well.

Another concern of feminist criticism has to do with how women are represented in texts, often in stereotypical manners that represent them as weak, competitive with other women, overbearing, or too dependent. Furthermore, female protagonists are often portrayed as less dynamic than male protagonists. Thus, feminist criticism looks at several issues such as how women are represented in texts, how women read and transact with texts, and the writing produced by women.

Also involved in this literary theory is the representation of males and the expectations placed upon males and females about what they read (Barrs & Pidgeon, 1994; Simpson, 1996). Feminist critics contend that the way in which people read is influenced by a belief that the masculine is inherently better than the feminine, and that girls need to learn to read in a resistant manner so as not to accept the values that undermine women as people (Fetterley, 1978). Another perspective of feminist criticism is that women's writing has been underappreciated, and a revaluing of works by women needs to be considered. Questions that can help middle-level readers begin to think about male and female representation in the young adult novels they read include the following:

- How do the male and female characters act differently? Similarly?
- In what ways do the characters in this novel reflect how real males and females act?
- In what ways are the characters not like people in the real world?
- What would happen to this story if the main character were female? Male?

Questions that can help middle-level readers begin to look at their own reading habits and how they may be influenced by society include the following:

- What were your favorite books as a child?
- What do you read now for pleasure?
- Do you read stories about the opposite sex? Why or why not?
- What do you think your friends would say if you read books that were most often read by the opposite sex?
- What do we think about boys who read a lot? Girls who read a lot?
- Is reading one of your favorite activities? Why or why not?

Other examples of female exploitation include the character Cassie in *Roll of Thunder, Hear My Cry* (Taylor, 1976), who must deal with racism during the Great Depression, and the character Melinda in *Speak* (Anderson, 1999), who must wrestle with high school politics and injustice after she is raped at a party. In the following excerpt from *Speak* (see story pp. 194–195 for a more detailed excerpt), Melinda is again confronted by her rapist, and she begins to fight back. This excerpt from *Speak* might be difficult to use if students and teachers have not established a rapport that would allow such issues to be explored in their classroom. We use the detailed version of this excerpt because of the issue of power involved and the misconceptions and assumptions about rape that young people may hold. We also use it to establish how young men and women think differently about situations in connection to touching and sexual harassment. This is a riveting novel that is highly acclaimed by young people for its realistic portrayal of young people, teachers, and high school cliques. It is, however, seldom used as a classroom text because the issue is so difficult to address, which is unfortunate in respect to the current statistics concerning rape of girls and boys across the world.

Beast: "You're not going to scream. You didn't scream before. You liked it. You're jealous that I took out your friend and not you. I think I know what you want."

His mouth is on my face. I twist my head. His lips are wet, his teeth knock against my cheekbone.... My heart wobbles. His teeth are on my neck. The only sound I can make is a whimper. He fumbles to hold both my wrists in one hand. He wants a free hand. I remember I remember....

No.

A sound explodes from me.

"NNNOOO!!!"

Excerpt from *Speak* (Anderson, 1999), pp. 194–195.

QUESTIONS FOR STUDENTS TO CONSIDER
1. How does this passage make you feel?
2. How would this situation change if Melinda were a boy?
3. How are males and females represented in young adult literature?
4. How are they represented in this passage?

Author studies also can help create conversations in which students begin to think about feminist criticism. Author studies also can include searching for information such as how many males write for adolescents, how many females write for adolescents, and what types of books they write. The results can help get middle-level readers thinking about how they—and authors—are influenced by gender expectations in society. Inquiring into the gendered nature of reading and even how boys and girls talk about books can help produce more critically conscious readers at the middle level.

Feminist literary criticism invites middle-level students to ponder their own ideas of themselves as boys and girls, and how particular cultures or societies have parameters within which they must fit to be considered normal. This criticism also asks them to think about the way they read a text and how that can be related to their gendered location. Middle-level students are well aware of how girls and boys are represented in texts, and to disrupt that representation, the use of feminist criticism is an apt tool. The next literary theory we discuss—New Historicism—addresses the issue of context that can be combined with feminist criticism or used on its own.

New Historicism

Becoming critically literate involves not only asking questions about the representation of people, ideas, or individuals; transactions with text; and authors' intentions and language usage, but also learning about when books were produced, how the social context of readers and authors influences the way we read a book, and the values that are found within a text. Often, readers are instructed to not be critical of books written during a particular time period because they are only artifacts of that time. For example, readers might be expected to put aside their current beliefs about issues, such as the treatment of women, people of color, or children, because during the time period in which a book was written, the values of the society were different from our own. New Historicism rejects that way of thinking about a text.

New Historicism encourages readers to read from their current belief systems and societal values, and thus they are able to discuss how society has changed and comment on historical precedent without excusing it. For instance, owning slaves is illegal in most current societies. By reading a text produced in the 1800s or before the Civil Rights movement in the United States, students can gain insight into the values of American society during that time period; however, this still does not give readers permission to excuse the keeping of slaves. New Historicists also reject the idea that history is a unified story along one continuum. History is chaotic, and only certain texts were privileged; thus, we have only a partial view of history.

When working with a novel from a New Historicist perspective, middle-level students can ask the following types of questions:

- How do we really know how people acted during another era in history?

- Have human beings changed, or have the stories told about them changed?

- Is this book representative of the actual time period?

- In what ways does the protagonist represent how we think people would have thought and acted during a particular era?

- How has our society changed since that time?

- What do we think the author is trying to say with this novel about the issue presented?

- How does the author's time period reflect particular ideas about the world?

By asking questions such as these, middle-level students will find U.S. and world history an intriguing part of who they are and what they believe. They also may become more critical readers of the other texts that reportedly represent historical events accurately and authentically. These questions also can lead to more critical thinking about what has been left out of the history books or what has been represented misleadingly. Middle-level students will come to know that there is no objective story about the history of any nation, only people's ideas about what occurred in the past and their ideas about why it is important for the future.

Another consideration that middle-level students might find of interest when looking at novels from a New Historicist perspective has to do with when the novel was written. Authors tend to reflect their own time periods, even when writing about historical events. For instance, the book *Constance, a Story of Early Plymouth* (Clapp, 1991) presents the story of the early Plymouth colony and the lively and adventurous protagonist Constance, an adolescent attempting to adjust to life in the colony. Constance, however, is portrayed as a young woman with confidence and her own sense of self who does not blend well with her society. In many instances, she seems out of place with the behaviors and attitudes of girls in early Plymouth. Another book that has the same problem in relation to characters' language used for its time period is *The Primrose Way* (Koller, 1992). Set during the colonial period of U.S. history, this novel has characters that seem better suited to the present than the past. This does not mean, however, that the book should not be read or that it cannot be enjoyed. It has the potential for teaching adolescents about the colonial time period and reminding them that, perhaps, adolescents' attitudes since then have not changed so much after all.

We recommend *The Primrose Way* not only for the study of early American life but also for looking at behaviors and attitudes that seem inconsistent with a time period. Students can question not only the representation of young women within a novel such as this one but also the representation of women found within informational texts that might have readers believe that current attitudes would not have been found during a particular historical era.

The following excerpt from *The Primrose Way* (see story pp. 184–186 for a more detailed excerpt) shows how the character's language is used to express sentiments not expected from an early American time period. The narrator, who finds the indigenous people living around the colonial village docile and gentle, is confronted by Priscilla Braddock, another girl in the village who asserts that the indigenous people are savages because they collect scalp locks from their enemies. Priscilla suggests the Qunnequawese might attack their village and perform the "gentle art" of scalping. This passage allows middle-level students to see how New Historicism is relevant to their reading, regardless of the type of text involved. It addresses issues of context and how people behave in particular ways because of that context. There are times when readers are dissatisfied with a historical novel because its characters defy the context, or the plot does not fit the time period. When a novel is not consistent to the time period and the attitudes and behaviors of people from that time period and location, it has made the critical error of defying its own logic. While we enjoyed reading *The Primrose Way*, we also questioned the characters' use of language, and we remind students that it is all right to critique a work we find pleasurable.

> I was not anxious to lose a debate with Priscilla Braddock, however, and the more I thought, the more convinced I became that it was unjust to label Qunnequawese and her people savages because of such a custom. After all, war was a savage business, and if the truth be told, we English were no strangers to butchery.
>
> ...I bit back the words of anger that flooded my mouth. I wanted to tell Priscilla Braddock that Qunnequawese had more intellect in her great toe than Priscilla had in all her fat head, but I could not.

Excerpt from *The Primrose Way* (Koller, 1992), p. 186.

QUESTIONS FOR STUDENTS TO CONSIDER

1. What seems familiar about the narrator?

2. How does the narrator seem different from a typical girl from the 21st century?

3. How can you relate to someone from another historical time period?

From here, we encourage students to begin looking at other types of text, such as informational books, novels, and theatrical productions, in similar ways.

Conclusion

At the beginning of this chapter, we shared a quote from *Kezzie* about the confusing nature of Kezzie's society, in which most people had to work very hard just to eat, yet the government seemed to have a lot of money to build war machines to fight Hitler's army. Similarly, many times students feel like they are working very hard at understanding texts while their teachers continue to set higher and higher expectations for them without contemplating what students already are attempting to do. Teachers need to create opportunities to blend the learning of literary theory with enjoyment and satisfying engagement so that attempting these theories is a pleasurable activity for middle-level students.

Just as Kezzie had difficulty interpreting the conflicting messages in her world, middle-level students frequently question how they are supposed to enjoy reading when working with literature is an endeavor repeatedly filled with frustration and humiliation. Our answer is that through engagements that (a) allow students to wrestle with literary theories while applying these theories to texts that engage them, (b) do not diminish their fandom, and (c) encourage experimenting with the thinking involved in literary criticism, middle-level students can develop the skills for interpreting texts on multiple levels. Thus, they are blending critique with pleasure—pleasure in the sense that students will want to try their analytic skills again, or in their ability to name the conventions that influence their reading. We can never underestimate the pleasure middle-level students experience when they feel confident about what they know. Learning about literary theories and how they are used to interpret a text is knowledge that instills pride in most middle-level students.

Literary theories, like conflicting perceptions, can lead to confusion in students. Yet, teaching literary theories during the middle grades may be the best time to set the foundations of literary criticism in place. We have found that the literary theories we addressed in this chapter will help students become more aware of how critics look at literature, and how they, too, can become more aware of some of the ways literature can be interpreted and evaluated. By inviting students to learn the frameworks in which literature is often judged, we allow them access to the skills they will need to become better consumers of literature as they become older. We are not, however, solely concerned with preparing students for future endeavors. By learning about literary criticism as middle-level students, young adolescents also get a deeper engagement with literature as they read it. In addition, they feel a sense of accomplishment when they are able to discuss literature in ways similar to theorists in a particular literary field.

We find that when middle-level students think like readers, writers, and critics they become more involved in what it means for them to be literate in the field of literary criticism. Just as mathematics teachers desire that their students think like mathematicians, or history teachers teach their students to think like historians, we find that language arts teachers want their students to assimilate some of the ways to think like those in the field of English/language arts.

Literary analysis, and the critique that naturally comes with such an endeavor, can get in the way of students' reading pleasure. Literary theories are not difficult to learn, but many students do not enjoy the often tedious nature of learning how to interpret the text. However, if students are invited to think about how texts, contexts, authors, and readers work toward helping them understand themselves and the world in ways that are inviting and educative, and that address their sense of justice, the result can change. By learning about and using multiple literary theories to interpret texts, students can expand their repertoire of knowledge about the field of literary analysis and how novels do represent readers, authors, and the world. They can become members of a community of readers who draw upon the multiple literary theories available to them, choosing to examine a text from one perspective or another and finding pleasure in the variety. As they become more adept at viewing a text from different perspectives, they also can examine the historical contexts in which these theories were developed. From this rich heritage, middle-level students can continue to gain understandings of text throughout their education.

"Making fun like that gets me savage—
making fun of people because of the way
they talks and because I asked Harris a
few lousy questions. Everyone around
home talks like I do. What bloody odds do
it make anyway, so long as people
understands what you got to say?"

From *Hold Fast* (Major, 2003, p. 72)

CHAPTER 4

Identity and Representation: Becoming Critical of the Connection

I n *Hold Fast,* 14-year-old Michael, whose parents have been killed, must learn to live in a larger town where life is very different from the Canadian village where he grew up. One of the differences he faces is that of language. Michael uses a different grammar and dialect from those around him, and he feels alienated from everyone and everything. Other students make fun of him, and his new father intimidates him. Eventually, Michael becomes so angry that he decides to run away from his new family.

In this novel, Michael realizes that some groups possess the ability to name and judge other groups, and these more privileged groups often make assumptions about others based on their appearances and the way they speak. He realizes that people "read" the way he acts, the clothes he wears, and the way in which he speaks. He also learns that people make assumptions based on who they have decided he is. As the opening quote implies, Michael finds this practice unfair. He realizes, however, that within his own village and cultural group there is also safety. In his home village, he would have the advantage of fitting in.

Based on our experiences with middle-level students, we have found that they are able to address aspects of identity that give individuals and groups advantages over others. These aspects include race, ethnicity, gender, and appearance. Discussions that revolve around appearances and the advantages and disadvantages that come with assumptions about what someone looks like help middle-level students understand issues of identity and representation, and how the "natural" privileging of one group over another often is based on issues of identity, representation, and the assumptions that come with the way we represent ourselves and others.

Identity and representation are critical issues to address when discussing literature with middle-level students. Often students will go through high school and college without a real grasp on identity or representation or on their importance in the texts they read, whether those texts are advertisements, novels, or websites. When exploring these issues, we begin by discussing how students define identity and what representation means to them. We then lead them toward examining how the concepts are addressed in literary journals and political discussions.

Defining Identity

Defining identity has become more difficult than in the past because of the complexity of identity in terms of gender, race, ethnicity, class, and the fluidity of what used to be a more fixed journey toward adulthood and knowing the self as a unified entity. Currently, students have to negotiate multiple identities that can be connected to a variety of contexts and activities. When we discuss identity with students, we often discuss the more traditional ideas about who they are as adolescents and then move on to how those identities can change based on situations or contexts they may encounter. We also talk to them about the reality of "status" and how certain identities—either individual or group—may be more privileged than others.

Middle-level students often are overwhelmed by their changing bodies and the painful result of some of those changes. They also can speak to the issue of how having the "right" look or the "right" clothing will help them fit in with their chosen peer group. We have heard middle-level students share experiences about how the right shoes or the right logo or trademark on a piece of clothing is needed for them to be accepted. And we also are aware of how groups in and out of school reinforce their value systems or their allegiances to a group by wearing particular types of clothing. We have also heard their painful stories about how it feels when they do not fit in because of their clothing or the way they look. We often ask students to discuss how certain groups dress or "appear" different than other groups (e.g., athletes and nonathletes).

For example, when Holly and I were traveling in New Zealand, we boarded a ferry to take us from the North to the South Island and found places to sit within a seating arrangement for 12 people. Quickly, the other seats were taken by others boarding the ferry. Once the ferry was underway, we looked around and spotted a small group of women in one section. Holly leaned over to me and said, "They look like teachers." I agreed. After a few minutes, we began talking to some of the women and found that, indeed, they were teachers. We laughed and said they looked like teachers, and they mentioned that they had thought the same about us. How did we come to such conclusions? By the way we were dressed, the way we looked.

To begin discussing this concept of identity, we ask students to consider the following questions:

- How would you describe yourself to someone else?
- How would that description change if you were talking to the principal?
- How would your description change if you were talking to someone you were interested in dating?
- How would your parents react to some of your descriptions? Why?
- How do you think your parents would describe you?
- What do you notice about how these descriptions change or don't change?
- How do your behaviors change in relation to these descriptions?

By answering these types of questions, students can begin to realize that even their ideas and descriptions of themselves change according to whom they are talking to or who is talking about them. They also can discuss how their behaviors change according to whom they are with, the context of the situation, and how they wish to represent themselves. These discussions can then segue into discussions about representation, which is crucial to the concept of identity, and to the use of young adult literature for discussing the concepts of identity and representation.

However, before we discuss representation with students, we discuss identity using excerpts from young adult literature. We ask students to identify with characters or situations in which the characters might find themselves. We also use situations or characters to discuss our disconnections, which is again a form of identity development or understanding. The following excerpts work well in introducing the concept of identity. The first excerpt describes Kirby's first encounter with her uncle's family. Her mother, a victim of a nervous breakdown, asks her brother to take Kirby. Her uncle, who is part of a religious sect, introduces Kirby to his family as "Esther." Kirby struggles with this identification throughout the book *I Am Not Esther* (Beale, 1998; see story pp. 28–30 for a more detailed excerpt). The second excerpt from *The Real Plato Jones* (Bawden, 1993; see story pp. 6–7 for a more detailed excerpt) presents the sentiments of Plato Jones, a young man who is half Welsh and half Greek. Readers get a glimpse of Plato's family heritage and his role in the family. Readers also get a sense of Plato's identity through the language he uses and the way he talks about his life.

Caleb swept his gray glance around his family. "I want you to welcome Esther, your new sister."

I gasped. *Esther?* "I am not Esther," I said, keeping my teeth together so I wouldn't yell. "My name is Kirby."

Aunt Naomi said, "The women in our faith all have biblical names. As do the men." She smoothed back my wild hair and smiled at me. "We have given you the name Esther."

Excerpt from *I Am Not Esther* (Beale, 1998), p. 29.

QUESTIONS FOR STUDENTS TO CONSIDER

1. Why would renaming a teenager matter?
2. In what ways is our name part of our identity?
3. How would you feel if you were Kirby?

It's being half-and-half myself, I suppose. Half Greek and half Welsh-and-English...I live most of the time with my mother in England, and I can't see much difference between the people in our town near London and those in my grandparents' village in Wales. When I'm in Wales or in England I often feel very Greek. I think how funny and shut away these people are, living their indoor lives behind closed doors and curtains. [W]hen I'm in Greece I sometimes think there is quite a lot to be said for being private and keeping your true feelings hidden.

Excerpt from *The Real Plato Jones* (Bawden, 1993), p. 6.

QUESTIONS FOR STUDENTS TO CONSIDER

1. How is Plato's identity revealed through his heritage?
2. How is Plato's identity revealed through the way he talks?
3. What other ways is Plato's identity revealed in this passage?

Once students have an idea of how identity works and its complexity and fluid nature, which can take approximately two to four class periods, they can move on to discussions about representation and the issues that surround it. Because of the complexity, however, it may take longer for students to fully understand the fluid nature of identity. We move on to representation after students can describe their own changing identities in response to different contexts.

Defining Representation

Representation is closely tied to the concept of identity. As previously mentioned, most middle-level students will understand that they dress in particular ways that identify them as members of a particular group, whether a fan of a specific athletic team or as part of a particular club at school. They also recognize that they dress in particular ways to fit into a particular group or be identified as a particular kind of person. We use the following excerpt from *Kezzie* to begin a discussion of representation with middle-level students who understand the importance of appearance.

It was a strange thing, thought Kezzie, as she made her enquiries firstly at the station office and then the town hall, how one's clothes mattered. Lady Fitzwilliam had bought her the most expensive costume she could find, with matching shoes, gloves, hat and handbag. And it seemed to Kezzie that people *were* more respectful and attentive to her. It was unfair, she thought.

From *Kezzie* © Theresa Breslin 1993 (p. 196). Published by Egmont Books Limited, London, and used with permission.

QUESTIONS FOR STUDENTS TO CONSIDER

1. How does clothing work as a way to represent a person?

2. Have you ever had a situation similar to Kezzie's?

3. When does clothing matter? Should it?

Middle-level students can understand that they dress or modify their appearance as a way of representing who they are—their identity. What middle-level students might not understand, however, is that representation, especially in the media, is also used by groups to identify others, and frequently these representations are not flattering. Thus, when we talk about representation with students, we stress the symbolic nature of the concept and how we can represent anything through art, words, music, dance, or any other nonverbal sign system. Sign systems are communication symbols besides letters and words—art, dance, movement, mathematical symbols, sculpture, music symbols, and other texts and symbols—that have the potential to contain or transmit meaning to those who read them.

To show students what we mean about the symbolic relationship between appearance and identity, we have them create character sketches either individually or in small groups. The teacher generates

> Sign systems are communication symbols besides letters and words—art, dance, movement, mathematical symbols, sculpture, music symbols, and other texts and symbols—that have the potential to contain or transmit meaning to those who read them.

a list of six possessions—not personality characteristics—such as a basketball, necklace, or hair ribbons and writes them on index cards. Students then write a three-paragraph description of the character that comes to their minds based on these six possessions. For example, a teacher might ask students to create a character based on the following items: basketball, skateboard, swimming fins, chain necklace, MP3 player, and hair ribbons. Students share their descriptions and discuss the reasons they visualized this type of person based on the list of six possessions. The teacher then uses this information to address the concepts of identity, representation, assumptions, and stereotypes.

Through character sketches, students realize that we frequently define—and stereotype—people based on their appearance and activities. Students also realize that people can be stereotyped by the way others may describe them or represent them to the larger community. This activity provides a good opportunity to discuss how stereotypes can be negative or positive and what their effects—good or bad—may be on others. Students need to realize that through all types of symbolization they have the ability to stereotype others, represent them in negative ways, and produce unfair and inequitable power relations.

Teachers can extend this activity by using lists of descriptors for groups instead of individuals, which allows students to think about the way groups represent others. In addition, the activity can be modified to a visual representation. Using the same or different prompts, students can draw or create collages to visually represent what they see in their mind's eye when certain attributes are used to describe another person or group.

After character sketches, we present students with pieces of young adult literature to show them how authors use language to represent others and how that language may move or persuade us to think about the characters in particular ways. The issue of representation in literature for children and adolescents is ongoing. Who writes about whom, how individuals and groups of people are portrayed, and what books are available to students are questions that need to be considered as students wrestle with becoming more critically literate.

To begin a discussion on representation in literature, we ask students to think about words' connotations. Connotations are the emotional implications words can carry, and they can be personal or shared. If shared, they may be shared by a group or shared universally, meaning the implications are shared by most of those in the group or across groups. Denotations are the specific meanings of words without an emotional implication, often thought of as the dictionary definition. For instance, the word *cat* connotes particular ideas—either the description of an animal or, if students are familiar with jazz or the beat

A character sketch is a strategy that asks students to write a description of a character based on six items.

generation, a type of person. Thus, the word, either written or pronounced, may mean something different than the common representation of the animal found in many students' homes or neighborhoods. We want middle-level students to realize that language represents objects, yet may not do so in a one-to-one correlation. Understanding the complexity of language makes them aware of how seemingly "safe" language can be harmful to others.

The difficulty with representation comes not from common objects such as cats, tables, and chairs, but rather in the way people, groups of people, events, or situations are represented in any kind of text. This is where representation comes into contact with power. Whether in a magazine, TV commercial, famous speech, or young adult novel, people are represented in particular ways. As with stereotypes, sometimes those representations are positive, and sometimes they are negative.

Knowing that language is used not only to represent people but also to reveal thoughts and assumptions about others is an element of language that middle-level students need to learn to become more efficient and effective readers and citizens. We use the list of words in Table 3 to help students think about the connotations that come to mind when confronted with messages or materials that include these words. Then, we explore with students why they think they arrived at those connotations. Some questions that can be used to begin this process include the following:

- What particular words are used at your school to represent certain kinds of people or ways of being?

Connotations are the emotional implications words can carry, and they can be personal or shared. If shared, they may be shared by a group or shared universally, meaning the implications are shared by most of those involved.

Denotations are the specific meanings of words without an emotional implication, often thought of as the dictionary definition.

TABLE 3

What Ideas Come to Mind When You Think About These Words?

As you review this list of words that represent people, think of adjectives that come to mind. You may not wish to share your thoughts with others, especially if they are negative, but you can write down where you think these ideas about people came from.

Peddlers	Circus Performers	Salesmen	Homemakers
Girls	Women	Boys	Men
Latinos	Canadians	Asians	Americans
Arabs	Africans	Slaves	Landowners
Urban Dwellers	Farmers	Ranchers	Clerks
Freaks	Preps	Geeks	Athletes
Prostitutes	Gamblers	Alcoholics	Indians
Artists	Models	Actors	Poor
Teachers	Lawyers	Doctors	Surfers
Rappers	Cowboys	Mechanics	Newscasters

- In what ways are these words negative or positive?

- Where do you think these words came from, and what do you think they do to those who are called by those names?

Students discover that they often stereotype people based on ideas that have little merit. By discussing this list of words in Table 3 and their descriptions, students can develop alternative ways of viewing the world and people within it. Students will find that other students do not "see" people in the same ways, and thus they will be able to expand their view of the world. By attending to their own assumptions about people based on the connotations of the words that describe them and how they represent people in their own minds, students can become better able to see how unfair language or descriptions can be, and how they are used consciously or unwittingly by others. Students should come to understand that, through deliberate representations, some authors garner power for one group over another, and students' unconscious use of language to represent people can yield the same result. Thus, analyzing how language is used to represent people is a critical element when reading and discussing texts.

Another exercise that middle-level students can try when learning about representation is cubing (Neeld, 1986). Cubing is a strategy through which students analyze an object, character, or idea from six perspectives. These analyses include physical description, comparison, association, composition, application, and evaluation. Through cubing, students can analyze the way they use language in their writing and how that writing represents not only what they are describing but also how they feel about it. By asking the following questions, students learn to examine a situation, person, or element before dismissing it without much thought.

1. Describe the topic physically. What does it look like?

2. Compare the topic to something else. How is it similar to or different from something else?

3. Associate the topic to something else. What other thing does this make you think of? Why?

4. Analyze the topic. What is it made or composed of?

5. Apply the topic. How can this be used or what can be done with it?

6. Argue for or against the topic. Why is this thing good or bad?

The following example illustrates how running (as a human activity) can be examined from the six perspectives.

1. Physical Description: Moving quickly on two legs, mostly to cover a distance.

2. Comparison: Similar to walking or jogging but different from pacing or skipping.

3. Association: Running reminds me of the movie *Chariots of Fire*, treadmills, athletic tracks, and the summer Olympics.

4. Composition: Running consists of stretching, running shoes and socks, a water bottle, and running gear such as shorts and a T-shirt in the summer and sweat pants and shirt in the winter. It also consists of sweating, an increased heart rate, and, sometimes, shin splints.

5. Application: Running can be done to lose weight, for cardiovascular health, for escape, or as part of another sport such as basketball or baseball.

6. Evaluation: I think running is a good thing for most people—if they like it. There are other ways to become healthy, but it is definitely a necessary activity for basketball, football, or baseball.

By naming their beliefs, students are able to wrestle with them. It is through the conscious acknowledgment of their thoughts that students are able to disrupt their prejudices or unfair representations of others.

After students have discussed how they are able to represent types of people through descriptive language, they are more apt to recognize it in the novels they read. The following excerpts from young adult novels can be used to help students begin to critically think about how language is used to represent individuals or groups. These excerpts can be used to discuss why readers might be moved to think about the characters in particular ways, and they allow students the opportunity to discuss how characters are represented and how language has the power to produce images of people that can privilege them over others, or limit their opportunities to be full members of a community or society. Students also can explore how there may be times when these images might be beneficial and exploitive at the same time, which addresses issues of the interplay between privilege and oppression discussed in chapter 5 (see also Croteau, Talbot, Lance, & Evans, 2002).

In the first excerpt from the short story "Eleven" (Cisneros, 1992; see story pp. 8–9 for a more detailed excerpt), Rachel's math teacher forces Rachel to put on a sweater that does not belong to her and "smells like cottage cheese."

Cubing is a strategy through which students analyze an object, character, or idea from six perspectives. These analyses include physical description, comparison, association, composition, application, and evaluation.

"Rachel," Mrs. Price says. She says it like she's getting mad. "You put that sweater on right now and no more nonsense."

"But it's not—"

"Now!" Mrs. Price says.

This is when I wish I wasn't eleven.... That's when everything I've been holding in since this morning...finally lets go, and all of a sudden I'm crying in front of everybody.

But the worst part is right before the bell rings for lunch. That stupid Phyllis Lopez...says she remembers the red sweater is hers! I take it off right away and give it to her, only Mrs. Price pretends like everything's okay.

Excerpt from "Eleven" (Cisneros, 1992), p. 8. In *Woman Hollering Creek and Other Stories*.

QUESTIONS FOR STUDENTS TO CONSIDER

1. How does Rachel see herself?

2. In what ways does the teacher's language seem discriminatory toward Rachel?

3. In what ways is Rachel being unfair to herself? Is her teacher being unfair?

In the second excerpt from *Glory* (Lynn, 2002; see story pp. 6–8 for a more detailed excerpt), Glory's father suggests that 13-year-old Glory needs to start acting like a proper woman, rather than acting like a tomboy and getting involved in mischief.

"Could be I've been a bit too soft on you, Glory," Daddy continued. "You need to start learning the responsibilities of being a woman." He glanced at my coveralls and frowned. "Including wearing a proper dress."

I just stared at my fingernails. It was so unfair, calling me a woman and telling me I had to stop getting into mischief when [my brother] still got into loads of mischief and didn't get into trouble at all because he was *male*. And the coveralls—Daddy knew it was easier to work in pants than a dress!

Excerpt from *Glory* (Lynn, 2002), p. 7.

QUESTIONS FOR STUDENTS TO CONSIDER

1. Based on the description, what is Glory like?

2. How do you think the author feels about Glory?

3. In what ways is Glory different from you? The same?

By examining the concepts of identity and representation with middle-level students, teachers address a vital concern with which many young adolescents wrestle. As they reach adolescence, middle-level students become more conscious and self-conscious about who they are and how they are perceived by others. Understanding the issues related to identity and representation allows them the opportunity to become more aware of how these concepts may or may not be a critical part of who they are or how they behave in the world. The ability to define the concepts, however, is only part of this understanding. Students also need the opportunity to discuss these concepts and how they are used in literature and life with their peers.

Using Literature Circles to Discuss Identity and Representation With Middle-Level Students

Middle-level students can have a surface-level understanding of a concept or situation, but may not know how it works in their lives or in the literature they read. By asking students to participate in literature circles that specifically address such concepts and how foundational they are to people and to the literature that people write, teachers open up a venue for deeper learning and recognition of the issues related to identity and representation. Identity is such an important aspect of many young adolescents' lives that when we were middle-level teachers, we would start the academic year with a unit on personal identity. Now, when we work with middle-level students on the topic of identity, we use specific pieces of literature to address the concept and the issues that surround it.

We use an excerpt from *The Speed of Light* (Carlson, 2003; see story pp. 3–8 for a more detailed excerpt) during the literature unit on identity. Students read the excerpt and then form literature circles to discuss the issues. In this excerpt, the narrator is in gym class where the students are learning how to dance. As the boys arrange themselves in line, the narrator realizes that he has become one of the "bigger" boys, and not part of the gawkier or less acceptable kids—who still include his two best friends.

I look back of the line where, as always, the last guy is Witt Dimmick. The last five guys don't get a girl; they have to sit on the folding chairs by the phonograph. This is exactly Witt's plan. He sits there, arms folded, shirt untucked, the way it has been untucked for the six years he's been my best friend. I can see him eyeing the assemblage with a frown. He thinks of himself as a scientist, an observer, but when I ask him about dance class, he only says, "Human behavior. Man, that is trouble."

Excerpt from *The Speed of Light* (Carlson, 2003), p. 6.

QUESTIONS FOR STUDENTS TO CONSIDER

1. What language is used to represent Witt, Rafferty, and the narrator?

2. Because of the particular ways in which Witt, Rafferty, and the narrator are described, what feelings do you have about them?

3. Who are these characters, what do they care about, and how do you know?

4. In what ways would changing the descriptions of these characters make a difference in the ways you relate to them or feel about them?

Before we discuss the excerpt, we share our ideas about identity, what it means to us, and how their identities are changing as they grow older. We discuss the reality that many students "try on" identities as they learn more about who they are and who they are becoming. We also discuss the author–narrator relationship and the importance of understanding how an author might use a narrator to persuade readers.

In one eighth-grade classroom in which we worked for two years with Ms. S, as the students called her, we often joined literature circles to hear what students had to say and to take advantage of teachable moments. The following dialogue occurred during a literature circle meeting in which Ms. S discussed *The Speed of Light* with the group.

Andrea: I'm not sure I like this book.

Ms. S: Why not?

Andrea: It's about boys and it's sexist, and it's about science. Yuck.

Tad: What do you mean "sexist"? Just 'cause it's about boys?

Sharon: No! It's because of how they talk about girls.

Ms. S: Who are "they"?

Students immediately respond to the book and the representation of females within it. The teacher intercedes when the evasive *they* is used. She requires students to cite a particular reference or person; however, she does this in a conversational tone so the student who used the word does not get defensive. This question also helps remind students that *they* can be a damaging use of language that allows for inappropriate generalizing.

Sharon: OK, not "they," the way the narrator talks about girls.

Ms. S: But is that the narrator's feelings about girls?

Patrick: No! He says the other guys are like that.

Andrea: No, no, no. The fact that he uses that language to discuss girls says he feels that way, too.

Tad: Yeah, but doesn't he really sort of speak for the author? The author is the one who made up the words.

The teacher does not need to intervene often during this exchange, but she does challenge the use of the narrator as the particular sexist element to get students to understand the narrator–author relationship. Tad makes this connection, so the teacher remains watchful rather than becoming directly involved.

Andrea: My point! The book is sexist.

Patrick: Maybe the author just knows how boys think.

Sharon: So, the author is telling us that boys are just sexist and so we should just deal with it?

Ms. S: Wow! This brings up a couple of questions for me. Who should deal with it, and could it be possible that the author is not sexist but still writes this way? If so, why would he do that?

The teacher interrupts the discussion so the group members can think about the way they use language. Again the pervasive "we" can be challenged by asking students to explain who they think has to "deal with it." Then, students can think about how authors may use language as a device to persuade someone to read the book or respond a certain way.

Patrick: Maybe he is just trying to show us that he knows how lots of boys think and at the same time he sort of wants boys to uh, uh—

Sharon: Relate to his characters. It's like he wants to invite boys to read this book 'cause we are reading the beginning part.

Ms. S: Yes, this excerpt is at the beginning of the book and does address something Andrea started our discussion with about what this book may be about and who it might be written for.

Andrea: Boys! Science! Sex!

The teacher's questions prompt the students to think about who may be the ideal audience for this text and what the author does to produce his ideal readers.

Ms. S: But does it have to be? Who makes that decision?

Tad: Each of us can decide if we want to read the book. I mean, some boys aren't about science or sex. They might think the book is gonna be boring.

Patrick: They could be disgusted with the way girls are described, too, I guess.

The teacher asks students to think about their roles as readers and consumers of texts. Because the students articulate that readers have choices, she does not push further. Yet, Ms. S and Holly recognize that some students do not have choices about the texts they read, so this point could be more prominent in other discussions.

Andrea: OK, OK. So, if I had to make a decision, I might say to give it about 10 more pages, but if this is the way the book is, I don't want to read any more after that. But that's me. Not everyone would do that, though.

Sharon: I like the science stuff and, really, I sort of jumped that description of girls. I mean, I read it, but it didn't stop me because I wanted to know what was going to happen, and well, the way boys talk...well...

Ms. S: Talk about that, Sharon. What do you mean "the way boys talk"?

Sharon: You just hear that kind of thing a lot.

Ms. S: So, do you think that people would think it's normal or OK to talk that way about females, and that we should just not challenge it?

The teacher becomes more direct here. She offers her questions in a conversational yet serious manner, without being condescending to the students. Teachers also could use this opportunity to encourage Andrea's statement about reading more and reminding others that not all people would do that.

Sharon: No, we should challenge it in our minds. But at the same time, I don't think I wouldn't read something because of a word or two that, well, does seem kind of normal for boys.

Ms. S:	Hmmm, now it sounds like we are stereotyping boys, and shouldn't that be watched just like sexism in reference to girls?
Tad:	Look! Some boys talk that way, some don't. Some girls say things bad about boys, some don't. We just got to remember that. We don't got to believe it about all of us. I wanna read the book, if we have it Ms. S, because it sounds kind of fun. Those three boys are crazy, and they haven't said one word about chasing girls around. Can we talk about the crazy stuff they did, please?

(Laughter)

| Ms. S: | Lesson learned, I hope. We don't have to accept sexism, we can challenge it, and we can make decisions about whether we want to continue reading texts with such references in them. What I liked is that we discussed it. If the group agrees, Tad, we will move on. |

The teacher reminds the group that stereotyping can be applied to any group. Finally, she wraps up the discussion about sexism and representation and hands the direction of the conversation back to the students. She responds to Tad's burgeoning impatience but allows the students to decide if they are finished with the focus.

The discussion moved toward an exchange about the use of language to describe the characters' experiences with experiments and how this language usage further validated for this group that it was a book more boys would be interested in than girls. The group also expressed that the excerpt did invite readers into it because "you just want to know what those guys are gonna do next." The teacher continued to ask for clarification of ideas, yet challenged little after the initial topic of sexism. When asked about this, Ms. S admitted that there are specific elements of classroom life that challenge her, and watching for sexism is one of them. Because the dialogue shifted toward the antics of the characters and their experiments, she felt she did not need to be as directly involved.

Using the excerpts from this chapter, we realize that it may not be the representation of the characters that is problematic, but how these representations could be read that might be investigated. Through discussions of how groups of people are represented, middle-level students can learn that representation is not simply about how an author uses words, but rather a combination of the author's use of language, the connotations that can arise, and how readers bring their own biases to a text. Learning to reflect upon their own thoughts and the images that come to mind when reading is a valuable lesson for middle-level readers who are developing their critical thinking skills while also becoming more critically literate. Discussions about readers' prior knowledge and what readers bring to a text can help them with literary analysis and with the ways readers represent people from their own cultural group as well as those from other cultures.

After we have discussed the concepts of identity and representation, we problematize them further by discussing how certain groups may be more dominant or have more privileges in our schools, communities, and countries based on people's assumptions and stereotypes about what is better or more important in our societies. It is privileging certain people based on appearances that middle-level students understand.

Privileging and Appearances

Certain groups identify themselves by the clothing they wear, others by "the colors" they show, and others by the uniforms they don. In fact, we suggest that every person in one way or another advertises their affiliation by their clothing. For example, think about football fans and how they wear particular clothing to announce their link to one team or another. Or think about one profession or another. Many people expect lawyers to wear suits and elementary teachers to wear sweaters. Of course, not all lawyers wear suits nor all elementary teachers sweaters, but people do make assumptions about what these groups often wear, and when they meet lawyers or teachers who do not dress in the types of clothing they expect them to wear, they are surprised. It does not matter whether their expectations were realistic or not. They still make assumptions based on how people appear. When we use the character sketch activity (see page 60), students begin to notice how frequently they make assumptions about people based on their appearances or activities.

The problem with these expectations is that they often are connected to how we treat people. Frequently, people who do not dress in expected ways are treated rather badly. And it often does not matter where we are or what the current styles may be. We work with students who challenge the unwritten dress code of their schools, churches, restaurants, and other social institutions. They report that when they dress "down" they are often ignored, even at department stores where they are attempting to buy something "nice." This privileging of people based on their clothing is also apparent in the way people treat others based on race, class, or gender (Kidder, 1997). There are instances of bias throughout history and the media, and for adolescents, their daily lives, which could be attributed to how they appear racially, economically, or in terms of gender. We use the opening quote to discuss the issue of privileging with students. Then we ask them to think about the ways authors might privilege one group over another in their stories and how and why they would do this.

Privileging or "foregrounding" refers to the emphasis given to a particular perspective on a situation, event, or character (Moon, 1999). To privilege one perspective over another is not necessarily negative, but students must realize that in all texts one particular perspective is usually privileged over others. Students need to be taught to recognize the emphasis and what it means to the group or perspective privileged and what this privileging may mean to the perspective, events, situation, or characters not privileged.

For example, in young adolescent literature, the adolescent characters and their experiences are always privileged over the adult characters because this literature is written specifically for adolescents. Teachers can provide examples of further privileging in young adult literature by discussing whose perspective is more honored by the author. By discussing the question of privileging, students come to better understand how authors honor certain ways of being or living, and often a specific race, class, or gender. For example, *Belle Teal* (Martin, 2001) is a piece of historical fiction that presents readers with fifth grader Belle as she is confronted by her community's racism when African American children are integrated into the school. Throughout the story, it is Belle's incredulity, disbelief, and sadness over this racism that is highlighted. The author does not sympathize with the racist element of the community, but rather with those characters who are open-minded about integration and friendly to the African American children. Although many authors currently attempt to provide balance in their writing, there are still instances when an author emphasizes certain perspectives.

While often we all are reminded that we should not judge people by their appearances, many of us do this quite frequently. We judge people based on their race, age, or gender, and connected to those judgments are issues of identity and representation. When we connect middle-level students' interest in their appearance with issues of their identities and how they either represent themselves or are represented by others in texts, we explore an aspect of critical literacy that is deeply relevant to young adolescents. When we use literature to discuss these issues, we find that our students can readily express their ideas without appearing to be too critical of their classmates because the characters are not real, even if the issues are (Johnson, 1997). What we also need to help middle-level students understand, however, is that stereotyping and making assumptions are normal, but that they should be recognized and challenged.

> Privileging refers to the emphasis given to a particular perspective on a situation, event, or character (Moon, 1999).

Problematizing Assumptions

Assumptions help us function in the world and usually help us communicate with others. For instance, when people read the word *sale* at a department store, they assume that the products in the store are going to be less expensive than they typically are at other times. If they went into a store and did not see prices marked down, they would be surprised and wonder why the word *sale* was on the windows. Students might be advised that whenever they talk, they are allowing their assumptions to show. It is difficult for them, however, to know exactly what assumptions are. Our definition of an *assumption* is an unspoken belief that is taken for granted to be true and is shared by others. A *bias*, however, is a judgment or outlook that often is personal and prejudiced against or for someone or something. In becoming critically literate, we must be aware of both assumptions and biases so as to not limit or offend others.

Whenever we communicate with someone we make assumptions about what they know and what they believe. Sometimes we are surprised to find out that others do not share our same beliefs, knowledge, or values. Other times when we communicate, we assume that the person with whom we are speaking understands what we are discussing. When we find that we are communicating about two different things, we either laugh and try to discover where we miscommunicated or question why the other person thought something different from what we thought we were saying.

There are times when our assumptions are unfounded misconceptions that could lead to harmful associations or representations. When this happens, we are usually upset or embarrassed. Other times we function as though our assumptions are correct, and then we can cause harm or pain to others.

Literature, because it is language, can represent an author's connotations and denotations, and thus present the author's particular beliefs or assumptions about the world, things in it, or the peoples who inhabit it. Authors carry their own assumptions about the world, and readers, who also carry their own assumptions and beliefs, interpret literary situations or characters based on those assumptions and the authors' words. In fact, authors often expect their reading audience to have assumptions similar to their own and, thus, can leave gaps and silences in their work. They can assume that their readers will make inferences about what is said and not said, filling in any missing pieces. Harvey and Goudvis (2000) define *inference* as the ability to read between the lines, and it is through the practice of making inferences that readers "grasp the deeper essence of texts they read" (p. 23). They further suggest that when readers infer they draw conclusions about a

An assumption is an unspoken belief that is taken for granted to be true and is shared by others.

A bias, however, is a judgment or outlook that often is personal and prejudiced against or for someone or something.

subject or issue based on the clues the author gives in the text. Learning to notice our assumptions as readers and the assumptions of authors is part of critical literacy.

When students learn to name the assumptions by which they live, and which they take with them when they read, they become more conscious of how literature works to represent the world as well as comment on it. To help middle-level students name their assumptions, we ask them to participate in a short exercise that they first do independently and then do in groups of four. We invite students to look at pictures that we have taken from magazines, photo essays, or informational texts that show people, animals, or even interesting buildings in different contexts and then address some of the following prompts in their journals:

- Describe what is happening.
- Explain the relationship between the elements.
- Discuss the motivation of the people within the photograph.
- Explore the photographer's purpose in taking this photograph.
- Share your feelings about this photograph.
- Explain what this photograph reminds you of.
- Comment on how this photograph helps you understand people or the world better.

This exercise accomplishes two tasks. First, students realize how their prior knowledge, which contains their assumptions about the world, influences their interpretations of the photographs. Second, this exercise provides a direct link to reader response theory for literary analysis. By discussing these photographs with others, students realize that not everyone shares the same assumptions of the world, ideas of how it works, or the same values and beliefs about living in it.

To become more critical within reader response theories, we ask students to become "authorial readers" (Rabinowitz & Smith, 1998), which means that we ask students to engage the text by asking questions about who the author wrote the text for and how they feel about that (Wilhelm, 2001). With this type of question, middle-level students can begin to see the gaps and silences that fill texts—the assumptions under which we live, read, and make meaning.

These gaps and silences represent mutual understandings between authors and readers so the authors do not have to spend a lot of time explaining what they mean. They take for granted that their perfect audience would already understand. Authors make assumptions that they believe are held by their ideal audience, and those of us who do not

Inference is the ability to read between the lines; through the practice of making inferences readers "grasp the deeper essence of texts they read" (Harvey & Goudvis, 2000, p. 23).

understand what they are discussing may fall into the other types of audiences, not the ideal or perfect (see chapter 3 for a more detailed explanation of the types of audiences). We use the idea of a perfect audience because, as we all know, there are times when we read a text and do not understand its meaning. This may be because we do not have the prior knowledge to understand the material (a physics text comes to mind for us) or because we do not hold the same assumptions about the world, beliefs about human nature, or values as the author. When we encounter a text that just does not seem to make sense to us, we have to ask questions about the assumptions made. An example of this may be when someone makes a racist statement to their same racial group. They assume that because all their listeners are from the same racial origins that they all think or feel the same way. This is not true, but the assumption creates the possibility of agreement.

We also have to ask about who or what group is privileged and who or what is silenced in the text. Usually, we explain to students that when something is talked about, other things are not discussed. A simple example is when we talk about girls, we usually do not talk about boys, or when we talk about girls we may do so in opposition to boys—that is, boys' perspectives are silenced. We are not suggesting that this is wrong, but it should be a part of our thinking when we become critical readers—that when we explore one phenomenon, event, or situation, we may be silently comparing it to something else.

When we begin to think in this manner, we become more like the authorial readers we mentioned above. When students begin to think about the gaps and silences in a text, we ask them to think about the following:

- In what ways do you agree with the author and in what ways do you disagree?
- What seems to be missing from this text?
- Whose perspective is missing from this text, and why do you think it is missing?
- Who (or which group) is privileged in this text?
- Are there silent comparisons, or do you find yourself comparing the event, group, situation, or phenomenon to something else? Why do you think you are doing that?
- Look at the language the author uses that may lead you to comparisons.

By becoming aware of how all texts have gaps and silences, middle-level students can become more critically aware of what is being stated and what is left unsaid in a text. Often the unstated can be a crucial element of the concept, situation, or phenomenon being discussed.

Any book can be viewed through a lens that addresses the concepts of identity and representation, but we find some of the current horror books that many middle-level students like especially enjoyable to read and discuss. Other books such as *The Shadow Brothers* (Cannon, 1992), *Kim/Kimi* (Irwin, 1988), *Walk Two Moons* (Creech, 1994), and *Where We Once Belonged* (Fiegel, 1999) are also engaging, and can be insightful for middle-level students' own struggles with identity and how they represent themselves or are represented by others.

As students learn to think critically about identity and representation, they might also begin to ponder how their identity and how they choose to represent themselves, whether viewed or defined in a negative or positive way, is a perception and not necessarily the truth with a capital *T*. Reader response theory, which suggests that what a reader brings to the text is a crucial aspect of interpretation, addresses similar ideas about perceptions versus the idea of one truth for every reader.

Using Reader Response Theory With Middle-Level Students

As we outlined in chapter 2, reader response theories address the reader's connections to the text. Questions middle-level readers can ask when applying reader response theory to textual analysis include the following:

- How do I feel about this text?
- How does this text connect with me or my life?
- How am I like or not like the character?
- What did I think about the character's actions?
- What would I have done differently from the character?
- How did the setting make me feel?
- What did I like or dislike about this book?
- Why do I or don't I like this book?
- Why did I get angry at the protagonist?
- Why do I like the protagonist so much?

Although reader response theories allow for multiple interpretations of the text, we want to emphasize that not all interpretations are valid. Transaction (Rosenblatt, 1938/1995) allows for an openness of interpretation, but the text also guides the reader and offers constraints in terms of interpretation. We generally tell middle-level students that they cannot talk about a dog if the text was about a cat. In essence, we tell students that the text is a guide, not the dictator of their interpretations.

We begin using reader response theories with middle-level students with the first book they read in our language arts or reading classes. We introduce the idea of reader response using the excerpt from *The Haunting* (Mahy, 1982) that we discussed in chapter 3 (see page 37). We then read short pieces of traditional literature with students in a guided reading format, which allows them to practice responding to literature and recognizing the openness and constraints of the text.

Wilhelm (2001) asks his students to prove to him—to convince him of—their interpretations when they seem to fall outside the explicit text features (i.e., language, content, and so forth). When we ask students to prove their interpretations, they must refer to the text for support, and then it is the text that determines whether a student's interpretation is valid or invalid. Thus, students realize that reader response is not about allowing any interpretation to work, but rather a response that respects the text and what it presents to the reader.

Examining Identity and Representation Issues in Traditional Literature

Also considered "folklore," traditional literature is knowledge that was once passed down through word-of-mouth stories. Mitchell (2003) explains that "because these tales started as spoken stories, all are set in a time long ago, all have flat or stereotypical characters who generally represent specific human qualities, all have linear or single plot lines, and all are embedded with lessons or truths" (p. 228). Traditional literature includes folk tales, fairy tales, legends, tall tales, myths, fables, trickster tales, creation stories, pourquoi tales, and numbskull tales. Fractured fairy tales and current retellings of older tales also fall under this genre. Multiple versions exist of some of these tales, which reflect particular cultural, social, and political mores of the country of origin.

We use traditional literature when first working with reader response theories and critical literacy for four key reasons. First, traditional literature helps students understand binary opposites, as previously mentioned, and second, traditional literature is familiar to many students because they have prior knowledge of fairy tales and folk tales. We realize, however, that there are students who are not familiar with fairy tales and folk tales; thus, the use of this type of literature is a good way to introduce them to tales that reveal assumptions held by the

Traditional literature is knowledge that was once passed down through word of mouth.

dominant culture. Although accommodating tales from a dominant culture may sound like the antithesis of critical thinking, we have come to realize that students must know about something before they can challenge it. Through this type of classroom reading, teachers can help students learn the genre of traditional literature, its purposes in a society, and how students might question those purposes. We also recommend that tales from multiple cultures be used so students learn how traditional literature has been used across all cultures since the beginning of storytelling.

Our third reason for using this genre of literature involves predictability. Traditional literature often is overlooked as an excellent way to help struggling readers transition to more complex reading materials or literary genres. Finally, this literature also presents lessons or truths held by particular cultural groups, and thus, they are an excellent source for problematizing norms and assumptions, which helps our students on their route to being more able to think critically. In addition, traditional literature is engaging and enjoyable reading for most of our students, and we want them to take pleasure in reading and literary analysis and critique. Table 4 provides some examples of traditional literature to use with middle-level students.

TABLE 4

Examples of Traditional Literature to Use With Middle-Level Students

Alvarez, J. (2000). *The secret footprints*. New York: Knopf.

Brown, Y. (2003). *The 500 best urban legends ever!* New York: I Books.

Deedy, C. (2000). *The yellow star: The legend of King Christian X of Denmark*. Atlanta, GA: Peachtree.

Erdoes, R., & Ortiz, A. (1999). *American Indian trickster tales*. New York: Penguin.

Glass, A. (2001). *Mountain men: True grit and tall tales*. New York: Doubleday.

Hamilton, V. (1988). *In the beginning: Creation stories from around the world*. San Diego, CA: Harcourt.

Hamilton, V. (1993). *The people could fly: American black folktales*. New York: Knopf.

Hamilton, V. (1997). *A ring of tricksters: Animal tales from America, the West Indies, and Africa*. Troy, MI: Blue Sky Press.

Harper, J. (1998). *The legend of Mexicatl*. New York: Turtle Books.

Kipling, R. (1996). *Just so stories*. Ill. B. Moser. New York: HarperCollins.

Lobel, A. (1980). *Fables*. New York: HarperCollins.

Pope Osborne, M. (1991). *American tall tales*. New York: Knopf.

Wisniewski, D. (1996). *Golem*. New York: Clarion Books.

Strategies for Reading Fairy Tales With Middle-Level Students

When we work with middle-level students on critical literacy and issues of social justice, we highlight how people can be represented through stereotypes. Because traditional literature was originally used to teach values and cultural mores, we also want to show our students how we are taught—through stories—to think about individuals, groups, or cultures in particular ways. Using fairy tales is especially engaging because many students are familiar with the story structure and because they enjoy recent "fractured" fairy tales and other such variations of old favorites. For example, there are hundreds of "Cinderella" and "Little Red Riding Hood" stories available. Table 5 lists additional fractured and modern versions of fairy tales for middle-level students.

To emphasize identity and representation through the use of fairy tales, we address stereotypes, binary opposites, and language usage

TABLE 5

Fractured and Current Fairy Tales for Middle-Level Students

Picture Books

Huling, J., & Huling, P. (2002). *Puss in cowboy boots*. New York: Simon & Schuster.

Lowell, S. (2000). *Cindy Ellen: A wild western Cinderella*. New York: HarperCollins.

Pope Osborne, M. (2000). *Kate and the beanstalk*. New York: Atheneum Books.

Rosales, M. (1999). *Leola and the honeybears*. New York: Scholastic.

Scieszka, J. (1994). *The frog prince continued*. New York: Puffin.

Scieszka, J. (2002). *The stinky cheese man and other fairly stupid tales*. New York: Viking.

Spiegelman, A., & Mouly, F. (2000). *Little lit: Folklore & fairy tale funnies*. New York: HarperCollins.

Chapter Books

Block, F. (2000). *I was a teenage fairy*. New York: HarperCollins.

Block, F. (2001). *The rose and the beast: Fairy tales retold*. New York: HarperCollins.

McKinley, R. (1993). *Beauty: A retelling of the story of Beauty and the Beast*. New York: HarperCollins.

Napoli, D. (1994). *The prince of the pond: Otherwise known as the fawg pin*. New York: Puffin.

Napoli, D. (1995). *The magic circle*. New York: Puffin.

Napoli, D. (1996). *Zel*. New York: Puffin.

Napoli, D. (2001). *Crazy Jack*. New York: Turtleback Books.

Zipes, J. (1989). *Don't bet on a prince: Contemporary feminist fairytales*. New York: Routledge.

through strategies such as character sketches (see page 60) and understanding connotations and denotations (see page 61). Binary opposites are ideas, types, characters, events, situations, or feelings that are placed together to create an either/or categorization (Moon, 1999). Students can become more critically conscious of how authors use their texts to persuade readers to think in particular ways by recognizing how this persuasion is accomplished through language usage, privileging, or other rhetorical devices such as characterization and plot development that create sides that might easily be defined in opposition to each other (i.e., protagonist, antagonist). Binary opposites litter Western literature and are an essential element of traditional literature. Some common examples of binary opposites include the following:

Binary opposites are ideas, types, characters, events, situations, or feelings that are placed together to create an either/or categorization (Moon, 1999).

Good/Bad	Beautiful/Ugly	Brave/Cowardly
Hot/Cold	Young/Old	Cruel/Kind
Male/Female	Black/White	Rich/Poor
Happy/Sad	Wise/Stupid	Civilized/Savage

An exercise we use with middle-level students introduces them to the concept of binary opposites and then asks them to find more difficult combinations in their literature, their lives, and the world. Students typically come up with war and peace, happy and sad, male and female. One student suggested that mother and father could be binary opposites because of their different jobs in his family, while another said that democracy and autocracy could be binary opposites depending on how these types of governments really worked in nations. By addressing binary opposites, students become aware of how such oppositions are used indirectly in many pieces of literature in terms of assumptions, privileging, and representation by setting up artificial and competing viewpoints that pit characters or situations against each other.

There are, however, other strategies that we use so students can begin to see how authors are able to manipulate literary elements to represent characters and situations in a variety of ways. These strategies are Comparison Charts, Looking Through Another Point of View, and Character Quotes.

Comparison Charts

One of the first things we ask our students to do with fairy tales is work on Comparison Charts. A Comparison Chart includes elements, such as the portrayal of characters, the setting, or themes, across a series of stories. When we use Comparison Charts, we ask students to become more critical in the examination of language usage, point of view, binary opposites, and stereotyping. Table 6 is an example of a Comparison

TABLE 6

Comparison Chart for Cinderella			
Book Title (Year Published)	**Binary Opposites**	**Situations or Plot**	**Stereotyping**
"Cinderella"	Yes: Cinderella and stepsisters	Traditional story	Yes: Women as good or bad
Cinder Edna (Jackson, 1994)	Yes: Cinderella and Cinder Edna; Prince and Prince's brother	Neighbors of Cinderella, more modern	No
Cindy Ellen (Lowell, 2000)	Yes: Cindy Ellen and Stepmother	American West story, Cowgirl	Maybe idea of cowgirls; women as good or bad
The Rough-Face Girl (Martin, 1998)	Yes: Rough-Face girl and her sisters	Algonquin Indian story	Yes: Girls as either good or bad
Mufaro's Beautiful Daughters (Steptoe, 1987)	Yes: Nyasha and Manyara (sisters)	West African tale	Yes: Nature of girls as good or bad

Chart presenting critical elements about different versions of "Cinderella."

Once students begin to use Comparison Charts to look at issues of representation and stereotyping in relation to language usage and binary opposition, they become more proficient in identifying these issues in other reading.

Looking Through Another Point of View

Closely related to comparison charts is our point-of-view activity (see Table 7 for steps to follow to complete this activity), which invites middle-level readers to compare situations in two versions of the same fairy tale, written from different perspectives. In this activity, students must transfer their empathy from one character to another or explore how a story written in third person would be different if it was told from the first-person point of view. Examples of how stories change when this is done can be seen by comparing picture books to modern versions of the tales, such as comparing "Cinderella" to *The Rough-Face Girl* (Martin, 1998) or "The Three Little Pigs" to *The True Story of the Three Little Pigs by A. Wolf* (Scieszka, 1995). We also use to do this exercise when considering characters' differing perspectives on the same situation. Chapter books to include in a study of other points of view include *Zel* (Napoli, 1996), *Beauty: A Retelling of the Story of Beauty and the Beast* (McKinley, 1993), or *Ella Enchanted* (Levine, 1998), which allow for a more sophisticated look at some common Western fairy tales.

We target characters represented as binary opposites when first introducing this activity so students can begin to see the assumptions about individuals or groups that readers infer from character representation. As they become more accustomed to this way of examining texts and individual or group representation through characterization, students move away from the binary opposites often found in fairy tales and begin examining representations in other texts, including their textbooks.

Another way we use this activity is in comparing perspectives of similar tales written from varied cultures. For example, "Little Red Riding Hood" is very different from *Lon Po Po* (Young, 1996), the Chinese story about Red Riding Hood. By looking at folk tales and fairy tales that have derivatives across cultures and countries, students can gain perspective on how different cultures have differing points of view about the same story, issue, situation, or subject.

TABLE 7

Looking Through Another Point of View

1. Ask students to read a short story or text.
2. Form small groups, and have each group decide who or what is being privileged in the text.
3. Have small groups explore and list the binary opposites in the text.
4. With the information generated, have each small group select an alternative perspective and list how the story would be different if told from that perspective. For example, a young person is the protagonist who is complaining about his parents. How would the parents tell this story?
5. Have groups place their ideas on poster paper and present the information to the class.
6. Have a whole-class discussion about how this exercise changed students' ideas about how to read a book.
7. As a follow-up activity, have student pairs write a short story from two perspectives.

Holly introduced the concept of binary opposites to her sixth-grade class consisting of 10 boys and 6 girls, all of Mexican American descent. She then read both books to the students. She asked them to comment on the differences they noticed between *Lon Po Po* and "Little Red Riding Hood," paying special attention to binary opposites.

Christina: The Chinese book had the girls smarter than the other book.

Jorge: And the wolf was stupid because he was tricked by the one girl.

Aracelia: I noticed the mother left the house and the girls in the Chinese version, and in the American version, the mother had the girl go out by herself into the woods.

David: In the American book, the wolf just went into the grandma's house and ate her. In the Chinese version, the wolf had to get into the house with the girls. He didn't have it so easy.

Priscilla: The Chinese book had the girls tricking the wolf so he died. The American one, the wolf ate the grandma and Little Red Riding Hood.

Ruben: They had to be rescued from the wolf! The girls in *Lon Po Po* didn't need to be rescued.

Holly: What might be said about girls in the United States and girls in China from reading these two books?

Jorge: Girls in China are pretty smart and don't need to be rescued. They didn't have a guy come and rescue them.

Priscilla: Girls in America seem kind of easy to trick. They don't seem too smart.

Holly: What binary opposites did you notice?

David: Old and young. And smart and stupid.

Stefanie: Tricky and tricked.

Aracelia: The whole stories were alike, but different. The girls in China are left home and Little Red Riding Hood is sent away from home. Isn't that opposite?

These sixth graders were able to think about binary opposites and how they represent characters in a text. The class further discussed the idea of how traditional literature represents some of the ways in which members of a culture think or the assumptions they make about people, the world, and "normal" behavior.

By using these two pieces of traditional literature to discuss how girls are represented, the students began to think about how books, authors, and those in positions to publish ideas in a society can influence readers and formulate ideas of the world. In relation to "Little Red Riding Hood" and *Lon Po Po*, we wondered if students realized how the portrayal of girls in these stories can lead students to believe that in the United States, girls must be rescued and are silly, whereas girls in China can rescue themselves and are not silly. We think our juxtaposition of these two texts allowed students to gain insight into these portrayals and what they represent in respect to a society's beliefs and assumptions about females, while also problematizing the stereotypes the stories present.

Although we could have used a piece of literature from a culture more representative of the Mexican American students in the class, we felt that such a choice may have interfered with our intent to look at binary opposites. Students can have a difficult time speaking against their own culture (Johnson, 1997), so it often is easier for them to define a concept when they look outside their own cultural positions.

Character Quotes

Our third strategy, Character Quotes (Buehl, 2001), allows readers to develop insights into characters, their development, and their motivations. Students gather quotes from one character throughout a novel, and then based on these quotes, students have deeper insight into how characters develop or remain static. By understanding that characters reveal themselves through their oral or verbal expressions, students learn that people in the real world do this as well. Goffman (1974) expands this idea by asserting that people also reveal themselves indirectly through their actions, just as characters do through indirect characterization. Ultimately, middle-level students begin to realize how characterization helps develop a story's plot as well as highlight themes in literature. We have expanded Buehl's strategy to invite students to find their own quotes from their current reading and to present them to the class. (See Table 8 for steps to complete this strategy.)

We introduce character quotes by selecting evocative quotes from young adult literature that we plan to read with students. We do this for two reasons. The first reason is an incentive issue—we want students to think about the book in which the quote was found. The second reason is to activate students' prior knowledge and then find out what we may have to address about characterization, inference, or identity before students begin reading. There are times, however, when the entire class is not reading the same text. In these cases, we still use Character Quotes and have students attend to particularly salient quotes from

TABLE 8

Character Quotes

1. Using a book that the class is about to read, select a quote from three different characters.
2. Place each character's quotes on different sheets of paper.
3. Put students in small groups, and give each group one of the character's quotes. Ask the small groups to write a short character description from the quotes, explaining what the character looks like, in what activities the character is involved, and how this character would treat other people.
4. Have each small group share its ideas with the class, and then have the whole class work together to decide who will be foregrounded or privileged in the story and how this character will treat the others in the story.
5. Ask students to decide how the author feels about each of the characters and explain why they have predicted this attitude through the use of the character's own words.
6. Have students read the story and see if their predictions were accurate.

Adapted from Buehl, D. (2001). *Classroom strategies for interactive learning* (2nd ed.). Newark, DE: International Reading Association.

TABLE 9

Quotable Quotes From *Young Adult Literature*

"But life is slippery." (*Zel*, Napoli, 1996, p. 193)

"It's for their own good, Nadia, to protect them," Dr. Omayra Torres added. "They will be afraid of the needles, but actually, it's not as bad as a mosquito bite. Maybe the men would like to be first, to set an example for the women and children." (*City of the Beasts*, Allende, 2002, p. 345)

"How can they? How can they laugh, at this time? Don't they know what's happening in the world? Don't they know the war that's coming, haven't they seen those pictures of the great grey fleets gathering in the gulf? Of course they know, how couldn't they? They don't care, that's it…[t]hey just don't care." (*Wolf on the Fold*, Clarke, 2002, p. 141)

"I suppose part of me had known all along. The thought had been waiting like a scorpion at the edge of my mind. Now it stung me, and I nearly cried out with the pain." (*Homeless Bird*, Whelan, 2000, p. 121)

"Jeremiah was black. He could feel it. The way the sun pressed down hard and hot on his skin in the summer. Sometimes it felt like he sweated black beads of oil. He felt warm inside his skin, protected." (*If You Come Softly*, Woodson, 1998, p. 5)

"I turned off my light and lay back down on my bed. You have to think, Sam. It seemed like all I did was think. Because everything in my life, every single thing, was so hard to figure out." (*Hanging on to Max*, Bechard, 2002, p. 113) the various texts they are reading. Table 9 is a list of quotes we have used with students; we use them in conjunction with character sketches (see page 60) to discuss how we infer information from what people say but how one quote should not produce a stereotype.

Each of the strategies we highlight allows middle-level students an opportunity for pleasure as well as an opportunity to critique the texts they are reading. These strategies also require that students think more deeply about what they are reading and about the characters that may be used by authors to persuade them to respond in particular ways. Students also have the opportunity to ponder their own responses to the texts they read, and perhaps rethink their initial impressions.

Moving Beyond Personal Response to Become Critically Conscious: Examining Ideal and Resistant Readers

Using reader response theory with middle-level readers is the best way we have found to help them become acclimated to the world of literature and analysis. By beginning with a theory that asks them to think about the texts they are reading and their responses to it, we invite young adolescents to join in the arena of literary conversations that will be a part of their academic world for years to come. We want students to move beyond personal response, however, and become more critical of their responses to literature. In the same way we ask them to move beyond their own judgments and assumptions about others, we want students to read more deeply the literature that engages them. Before we introduce students to other literary theories (see chapter 3), we ask them to think about becoming critically conscious in connection to their responses by examining how they are either ideal or resistant readers.

Ideal readers are those whom the author envisions when writing, or they may be those who do not question the author's intent or value system. Narrative audiences fall within the category ideal readers because they connect with the narrator of the story and do not question the character's motivation or stance toward another character or a situation in the book. Resistant readers are those who make a stance against what they are reading. They may question the author's depiction of a character or situation. They might withdraw from the reading because of their value system, or they might not agree with what the author is saying. Knowing this allows us to consider two more aspects of being critically literate:

1. What we take for granted, how it may or may not be "normal" or true across all situations, cultures, or events, and being able to question this belief within ourselves.

2. What causes us dissonance when we read, and investigating why this dissonance may be a problem for us.

By examining ourselves as ideal or resistant readers, we allow more perspectives to be heard and to hold off our judgments and stereotypes of others. When we discuss these stances with middle-level students, we give them the tools to become more democratic and more tolerant of diverse perspectives.

Using the following excerpts from pieces of young adult literature, we explore the stances of ideal and resistant readers. The first excerpt from *Out of the Dust* (Hesse, 1997) describes the conditions of fields in communities across Oklahoma during the Great Depression. We use this excerpt to suggest to middle-level readers that if they are unfamiliar with wheat, crops, or farming, they cannot easily identify with the passage and the critical condition the dust bowl created for farmers. Middle-level readers are not the ideal readers, perhaps, for this excerpt. If they do identify with the harsh conditions of the dust bowl, they might not understand Billie Jo's comfort in the piano. If they understand how music can be a comfort, they might not be able to identify with the mother's anger. Thus, there are instances throughout this passage that allow for resistant and ideal reading.

> Beat Wheat
>
> County Agent Dewey
> had some pretty bad news.
> One quarter of the wheat is lost:
> blown away or withered up.
> What remains is little more than
> a wisp of what it should be.
> And every day we have no rain,
> more wheat dies.
>
> The piano is some comfort in all this.
> I go to it and I forget the dust for hours,
> testing my long fingers on wild rhythms,
> but Ma slams around the kitchen when I play
> and after a while she sends me to the store....
>
> *April 1934*
>
> ---
>
> Excerpt from *Out of the Dust* (Hesse, 1997), p. 39.

Ideal readers are those whom the author envisions when writing, or they may be those who do not question the author's intent or value system.

Resistant readers are those who make a stance against what they are reading.

QUESTIONS FOR STUDENTS TO CONSIDER

1. Who wrote this? Describe the type of person who would write this. What evidence does the passage give about who the author is?

2. Imagine if the person were black, white, Indian, Asian, male, female. What would change about this scene?

3. Is it difficult to imagine an individual from the city writing this? Why or why not?

4. Who is the ideal audience for this passage? What kind of audience do you think the author had in mind when writing this? Why?

In the following excerpt from *Memoirs of a Bookbat* (Lasky, 1994; see story pp. 22–25 for a more detailed excerpt), Harper has been reading a picture book by one of her favorite authors when her father becomes suspicious of the book because it may contradict his religious viewpoint. When Harper's mother tries to "smooth things over" for her, Harper lies that she does not really like the book anyway.

It was that guilty feeling nibbling at the edges of my brain that started me on a life of major lying and covering up. It doesn't really make sense. You feel guilty about lying so then you do it some more. You just get better at doing it, so it becomes easier to do and easier to rationalize. You begin to choose when you're going to lie and when you're going to be honest, and you figure out that the honesty outweighs the lies, or at least you tell yourself that.

Excerpt from *Memoirs of a Bookbat* (Lasky, 1994), p. 23.

QUESTIONS FOR STUDENTS TO CONSIDER

1. Who is the ideal reader for this passage?
2. Who would resist reading this and why?

Being an ideal reader and a resistant reader are stances we can encourage students to take toward a text, and reader response theories allow students to more closely examine those positions in relation to learning about the world, the human condition, or their own life experiences. Understanding how they can be ideal or resistant readers can work easily with traditional literature because most middle-level students voice resistance toward books they read when they were younger. When we use traditional literature with our students, which is often, we know that many of them resist the reading of what some of them have called "baby books." This does not mean that we do not use picture books; however, it does mean that we address upfront their resistance to illustrated texts. Using chapter books, such as Napoli's *Zel* (1996) or *The Magic Circle* (1995), allows middle-level readers the opportunity to see themselves as ideal readers when the content or the format of the book is targeted for their age group.

It is through their explicit knowledge that middle-level students become more adept at understanding their stances toward a text and the reasons for those stances. Realizing that they are often an ideal reader for one author and a resistant reader for another gives young adolescents more control over their reading and, in many ways, more control over their thinking about and understanding of the world.

Conclusion

By defining and then applying the concepts of identity and representation with middle-level students, we can help them become better critical thinkers when it comes to the texts they read, whether they are media texts, young adult novels, or the texts they speak when talking about or describing others. Through traditional literature and picture books, we find that middle-level students can easily accommodate the concepts of identity and representation. From these beginnings, we find the other genres of young adult literature can be readily accessed in addressing the same issues. Through activities that ask students to consider the issue of identity and representation, we give them the tools to be more critically literate and more considerate people.

"Now she knew what her father had meant when he had talked about the price miners' families paid for coal. Far from getting it cheaper than others they paid for it in blood."

From *Kezzie* (Breslin, 1993, p. 35)

CHAPTER 5

Power and Critical Literacy: Gaining Understanding of How Power Works

As we grow up we find that the world is much more complex than we imagined it as children. In each of our lives there are moments—"aha" moments—that frighten us, disconcert us, or make us older than our years. When these moments happen depends on our individual circumstances, but they do happen and they continue to happen to the students we teach. For the young protagonist in *Kezzie*, the world comes crashing down when her father is killed in a mining accident, and she comes to realize the danger and hardship of a mining life. Before Kezzie's father dies, Kezzie lives in a world where coal for heat is free and the danger of mining escapes her. Afterward, she knows the price her father and her family have had to pay for that coal, and what was once unknown or invisible becomes horrifyingly clear. Kezzie is now critically aware of some of the complexities, hardships, and unpleasant aspects of life with which she and others must contend.

Power is also invisible for many middle-level students. They do not always understand how it works or how it can be played out in their lives and in the lives of others. In Kezzie's story, her family eventually has to move out of their house because the mining company owns it. The power the company holds over their lives becomes more and more visible as Kezzie's life becomes more and more bleak.

Middle-level students are well aware of power once it is made visible, although they typically do not use this language when they talk about its issues. They realize that some students seem to be more popular, others are less so, and yet still others are ostracized for their appearances, their interests, or their traditions. Power seems to be out of their hands—it is just a phenomenon of the world. We do not agree with this assessment, but unless we discuss such issues with students, they will feel as though there is nothing they can do about their circumstances or place in the world. Teachers can expose students to the use of power littered throughout pieces of young adult literature, yet to see it, students must first be introduced to what we mean when we use the term *power*.

Defining Power

Power is a complex issue for many middle-level students because they do not quite know how it works. Some students suggest that power involves the "might equals right" ideology, whereby those who are the most persuasive either physically or mentally have the advantage over others who are not as physically strong or mentally capable. Others suggest it has to do with popularity or social positioning, which gives certain people the most power. Still other middle-level students might find that power is something only a few possess, such as teachers or principals, who are given their privilege and positions through legal methods.

In reality, power is something everyone possesses to a certain degree, and indeed there are instances of power that belong to people because of legal manipulations, popularity, or even physical capability. Most often, we talk of power when we discuss unequal advantages or privileges that only few people receive because of how they are located in a particular culture or society. We suggest that some power is legitimate power, while other kinds of power are illegitimate, abusive, or inappropriately privileging.

Another aspect of power that students need to recognize relates to language and how it is used. Fairclough (1989) asserts that through our use of language our assumptions are made visible, and it is assumptions about others, ourselves, and the way the world should be that predicate power relationships. For instance, in regard to teaching and learning, the way we as teachers express what should happen in classrooms allows our listeners to know what we assume teaching and learning should be. Many teachers and principals are concerned about classroom management because their assumptions about learning are that it only happens in an orderly, quiet manner. Thus, when classrooms appear too chaotic, they believe there is a challenge to teaching and learning in such an environment.

Holly experienced this situation firsthand. During her first year of teaching, she was told by a lead teacher—a teacher who had never visited her classroom, nor asked about the students' learning—to get her seventh-grade classroom under control. Because students worked in groups and were noisier than in other classrooms, the lead teacher and others assumed that learning could not be taking place. The lead teacher asserted her power by stating that Holly needed to bring the class to order. She used the social context of the school environment and the expectation of other teachers to assert the power of the institution and its traditions. Through the use of the language "get the class under control," the lead teacher revealed her assumptions about what learning should look like, what was happening within the classroom, and the authority of both the speaker and listener. If the roles were reversed, the first-year teacher could not readily have demanded that the lead teacher get her class under control. Although both women were teachers, there was an unequal balance of power that was used by the veteran teacher because she asserted her position as lead teacher without any evidence that learning was diminished in the younger teacher's classroom.

The use of labels, how language is used between people, and the assumptions underlying the discourse all have elements of power that middle-level students can learn to recognize and name so they become more conscious of how language is used to inflate the social status of some people and oppress or limit others. Fairclough (1989) asserts that the study of language and power can "help correct a widespread underestimation of the significance of language in the production, maintenance, and change of social relations of power....[and] help increase consciousness of how language contributes to the domination of some people by others" (p. 1). Thus, for middle-level students to become more conscious of how language works, and for teachers to invite students to look at language in a more social context—not just in isolated instances found on worksheets or in vocabulary studies—the use of young adult literature and a look at the ways that people speak to one another provides contexts that are more real and concrete than memorization of abstract concepts.

Discussing Power With Middle-Level Students

Middle-level students can discuss power in their own lives by looking at where they are positioned in society. We suggest that by asking students to complete a survey about power (see Table 10), you can help them begin to understand the concept of cultural or individual position as well as where they possess power and where they most often are powerless. By responding to these questions, students realize that with power comes control, and often people do not have the control they wish they had. Students also will discover that they cannot control every circumstance in their lives. There are times when they will feel powerful and times when they will not. Most often, students discover

TABLE 10

Do You Feel Powerful?		
1. I have control over what I learn in school.	Yes	No
2. I have control over what is taught in school.	Yes	No
3. I have control over the television at home.	Yes	No
4. I have control over what I eat for dinner.	Yes	No
5. I have ways of making spending money.	Yes	No
6. I decide when to do my homework.	Yes	No
7. I can do whatever I want on weekends.	Yes	No
8. I decide who I spend time with at school.	Yes	No
9. I am afraid of what people say about me at school.	Yes	No
10. I always get my way.	Yes	No

that the answer to many of the survey questions is "sometimes"; however, by discussing the contexts under which the answers are "yes" and "no" students can better grasp the element of power in their lives.

There are times, however, when the issues surrounding power are not a part of middle-level students' lives or are a part of their lives but remain hidden from view. As teachers, we want students to understand that power, while perhaps not affecting them directly, still may create situations in the world that are not just or that may develop into events or circumstances that ultimately could limit their freedoms or opportunities. Having students read about oppressive governments or historical events in which people were persecuted for their beliefs is one place to start. We do not want middle-level students, however, to subscribe to the misconception that power was only abused in the past. By reading excerpts from books such as *Shattered: The Stories of Children and War* (Armstrong, 2002), *Zlata's Diary: A Child's Life in Sarajevo* (Filipovic, 1995), and *The Freedom Writers' Diary: How a Teacher and 150 Teens Used Writing to Change Themselves and the World Around Them* (Freedom Writers, 1999), which present stories of young people and their losses of opportunity or freedom, middle-level students can get a sense of the abusive power that is currently happening in many places around the world. These texts, all true accounts of adolescents' lives disrupted by power struggles brought about at governmental levels, can help students who have not experienced such crises begin to understand that young people just like them must deal with power in unpleasant ways whether they wish to or not.

Reading and discussing true stories is one way in which teachers can engage their students in the study of power. Through the use of biographies, students can see how some historical figures we now admire wrestled with the abuses of power, or how they used their positions of power to create a more just society. Most middle-level students are familiar with the biographies of Rosa Parks and Martin Luther King, Jr.; however, many students do not know about the battles that Muhammad Ali and Mahatma Gandhi fought with oppressive governmental policies. Stories of union workers who wanted better conditions for miners in Appalachia and workers in the garment industry of the northeast United States also can be studied so students can come to understand how individuals and groups have had to struggle for social and economic justice. Table 11 lists additional information books that are excellent examples of how people have struggled for justice.

Reading about how people have struggled for justice can be complex, however. Students often have a difficult time understanding why books would be written about people whom they would consider negative role models. For instance, when Holly asked a group of sixth graders about heroes and what makes someone a hero, the students volunteered several U.S. leaders such as Martin Luther King, Jr., Abraham Lincoln, and George Washington. They also listed civil servants such as firefighters, police personnel, and members of the military. They had difficulty, however, with naming people who were not considered mainstream heroes. When Holly suggested people such as Muhammad Ali, Malcolm X, and Clara Barton, the students either did not see how these people were heroes or did not know them at all. We found similar results when we asked adults about their heroes, which suggests that if

TABLE 11

Nonfiction Books Containing Power Issues
Anaya, R. (2000). *Elegy on the death of César Chávez*. El Paso, TX: Cinco Puntas Press.
Bartoletti, S. (1999). *Growing up in coal country*. New York: Houghton Mifflin.
Freedman, R. (1998). *Kids at work: Lewis Hine and the crusade against child labor*. New York: Clarion.
King, C., & Osborne, L. (1997). *Oh, freedom! Kids talk about the Civil Rights movement with the people who made it happen*. New York: Knopf.
Kudlinski, K. (2003). *Sojourner Truth: Voice of freedom*. New York: Aladdin Paperbacks.
Myers, W.D. (1993). *Malcolm X: By any means necessary*. New York: Scholastic.
Myers, W.D. (2001). *The greatest: Muhammad Ali*. New York: Scholastic.
Smith, K.M. (1994). *New paths to power: American women 1890–1920*. New York: Oxford University Press.

students do not learn about unfamiliar examples of heroes, they may not learn about the many significant people who made extraordinary contributions to their nations or to history. We also found that students had difficulty believing anyone would find historical figures like Adolf Hitler and Osama bin Laden heroic. They could not understand that not all people in the world have Western standards for heroism. We believe this lack of understanding is because our students have always concentrated on and encountered only Western mainstream ideas about heroism and role models in their educational experiences.

As part of the unit on heroes we pursued with the sixth graders, we created a list of people who may not be considered heroic by Western standards, and we discussed how these alternate or unlikely people might be seen as heroes in their cultures. Using an overhead transparency with a list of these heroes on it, we then asked the students to generate a list of heroic characteristics. We then applied the characteristics to the people on the list by giving examples of how that characteristic was manifested in that person. We also suggested that we have heroes who might not be heroes in another culture. When one sixth grader asked if it was all right not to consider these people heroes, we affirmed that heroes may be linked to cultural standards, and that not all cultures or people agree on who or what is heroic.

In addition to nonfiction, we also use picture books to discuss issues of power with students. We introduce the concept with *The Big Box* (Morrison & Morrison, 2002), a short text that presents the cases of three young people who "just can't handle [their] freedom" (n.p.) and are placed in big boxes by their parents or other adults in their communities. Students meet in literature circles as part of their classroom routine, discuss the daily read-aloud, and then share their thoughts with other groups in whole-class discussions. In the following exchange, a group of sixth-grade students begin to talk about power issues in their literature circles after their teacher read aloud *The Big Box*.

David: That's weird that they were all in boxes.

Celia: The boxes meant they weren't free to do what they wanted. I don't think the kids were in real boxes.

Betio: It shows how adults make kids do certain things, or like, control them. This book is kind of scary because it shows how powerless the kids were.

Christina: And how powerful all those adults were. They, like, used that power against the kids and limited their freedom.

These students relate adults' power to control and to how power can render others powerless, which is an abusive use of power. This use of power also disconcerts and frightens them.

Celia: I wouldn't want to be in a box or even my own room where I couldn't get out when I wanted.

Betio: This reminds me of how power works with freedom, I mean against freedom because they took their freedom away. I would be mad about it, too, and those kids just seemed sad like they couldn't do anything!

David: I think the kids would feel bad about being in a box. They have a lot of toys but no friends. We got to treat people like we would want to be treated. I know that most people would want to be free.

Celia: It makes me mad because people judge people too much on their appearance and actions.

These students express what might be a typical outcome of abusive power—anger. While they may express that they do not have the power adults have, it does not mean that they are not angry about what they see as inappropriate use of power by adults to limit children's freedoms. The students also relate to how power is used against others based on misjudgments about appearance and actions—quite sophisticated thinking.

Christina: This connects to me because sometimes I get in trouble because I can't control myself, my mom says. Then I have to go to my room.

David: Yeah, me, too. And sometimes at school, people get in trouble for being out of control.

Betio: The school is like a box because of the rules and the punishment of what happens when you don't follow the rules.

Celia: It's like school because the teachers are always telling you what to do, and I am tired of being bossed around.

This aspect of the students' discussion serves to remind teachers that students and teachers should be partners in creating school regulations. Teachers can disrupt students' connection of abusive power to authority during whole-class discussions; however, teachers also must consider that sometimes school rules and punishments seem arbitrary to students.

David: But can't having too much freedom be a bad thing? Maybe the author is thinking about that, too.

Christina: I think the author is telling us not to take freedom for granted, but even with freedom we can't do whatever we want.

Problematizing the idea of too much freedom is another aspect teachers can discuss with students in a whole-class setting. The idea of freedom and power with responsibility is an aspect of critical thinking and social justice that teachers should highlight for middle-level students.

As evidenced in this literature circle discussion, we have found that middle-level students have a grasp of the issues related to power and how the abuses of power can create injustices that could become part of their lives. These students also made real connections to their own lives as well as to other issues such as responsibility and the balance between freedom and control, issues they see as related to power. We recommend holding follow-up discussions with the whole class in which students address the key ideas of freedom, control, authority, and responsibility in relation to power so they can begin to connect these related concepts.

Examining Power Issues in Young Adult Literature

Because young adult literature includes fiction, informational texts, poetry, and even picture books, many types of literature can be appropriate for teaching middle-level students about power. An effective way to talk about issues of power with middle-level students is through fiction, where characters represent types of people or situational realities in the world. With fiction, we have found that students are more willing to share their negative thoughts about how characters behave or the attitudes expressed in texts (Johnson, 1997), possibly because it is easier for students to confront negativity when it does not involve real people. Students can easily fault an adolescent protagonist who makes a mistake, but they have difficulty finding fault in themselves or in those for whom they care. Reading young adult fiction, then, allows students to work through some of the issues of power relevant to their lives without guilt or unnecessary condemnation of others.

Learning about power is an important concept in literature and literary analysis, especially when discussing aspects of social justice. Moon (1999) suggests that "the issue of power is crucially important to any study of literature and communication, because reading and writing are practices through which different groups promote their views of the world" (p. 123). Middle-level students can ask critical questions about who is being written about and by whom, and how authors represent different types or groups of people. Because power is typically about how people relate to one another, issues of power also involve who speaks, who listens, and what is being said. Thus, literature and literature discussions can be arenas for scrutinizing unequal power positions.

Middle-level students can study whole pieces of literature for an overall concept of power in relationships between people or they can look for how power presents itself through language in particular excerpts from texts. By studying excerpts within most genres of young adult novels, students can begin to see how language works as a tool of power and how power is imbued to particular characters who, in turn, use language as a way of maintaining their power. Many middle-level students know that when particular individuals use particular phrases, those phrases are not neutral or benign, even when they may sound like it. Young adolescents also are familiar with the use of sarcasm; they readily notice it in the texts they read. For instance, in *On the Bright Side, I'm Now the Girlfriend of a Sex God* (Rennison, 2001), the protagonist Georgia uses witty and sarcastic language to reflect on and respond to her life. Told in the form of a diary, this book is a best seller for adolescents around the world. One example of Georgia's sarcasm is presented in the following excerpt. Georgia is upset about her breakup with her current boyfriend, who has suggested someone more suitable for her. Georgia calls her friend Jas for advice.

On the phone to Jas. I was shaking with rage.
    Jas said, "Well, erm...if he's a good laugh, maybe you should meet him."
    "Jas, are you really saying that I should just stop liking one person and start liking another one, just like that? What if I said, 'Hey, Jas, forget about Tom, why not go out with Spotty Norman? He's got a really great-shaped head underneath the acne?'"

Excerpt from *On the Bright Side, I'm Now the Girlfriend of a Sex God* (Rennison, 2001), p. 76.

QUESTIONS FOR STUDENTS TO CONSIDER

1. How is Georgia using language for power?
2. How often do you hear this use of language in your daily life?
3. How does it feel to use this type of language? How does it feel to have this type of language used on you?

In this excerpt, Georgia is using sarcasm to control the situation. Although middle-level students tend to laugh at the sarcasm in the literature they read, they often have difficulty with it when it is directed at them. By investigating the difference between using language in a neutral way and in a sarcastic way, students can better understand how power can be used to control people or situations.

By recognizing how language is used and coupled with power, students eventually can disrupt the patterns of language that hurt or manipulate them and others by making decisions about their own language use and how it can be harmful to others. Or they can decide that what others say about them does not have to control them emotionally or physically. Also, students may find that the use of positive language can gain them entry into the paths they wish to take. When exploring issues related to language and power, middle-level students need to recognize that there are negative and positive uses of both, and that they can control their own thinking about how language and power can be used to their benefit or detriment. Students also need to realize that when a speaker uses the same language as another person, depending on the power structure within the context, he or she may be ridiculed. Middle-level students know about language and power, but they may not be conscious of this knowledge.

Learning to understand how words are imbued with particular meanings by the cultures in which students live also can help them begin to see how power and language are connected. Often, words in isolation can be damaging because of the negative connotations they derive from the culture in which they are used. Table 12 lists words that have various meanings depending on where students live. By discussing the words' connotations, students will begin to see how language can be used to empower the speaker while disempowering the object or person under discussion. Knowing that authors of all kinds of texts use words in particular ways will help students realize how language is subtly used in texts to stir up emotions or highlight particular ideas about events, situations, individuals, or groups of people. This knowledge can help students to think critically about how language can be used to manipulate others.

Students can continue to recognize how words can be used to exert power by discussing specific excerpts in literature circles. Students can first discuss the excerpts and the role of language and power within them in literature circles and then with the whole class. The following excerpts allow middle-level readers to work through how power is conveyed through language. For example, the excerpt from *Rag and Bone Shop* (see Cormier, 2003; story pp. 79–81 for a more detailed excerpt) can be used to show how language can be used to manipulate others. Jason, a 12-year-old suspected of killing a younger girl in his neighborhood, is being interrogated at the police station by Trent, a detective known for getting perpetrators to confess.

"Just relax, Jason. Think of this as a conversation, no more, no less." Trent was conscious of using his avuncular voice. "We'll talk about the events of

TABLE 12

Language and Power Activity

Look at the following sets of words and determine what you think about them. Are they negative, positive, or neutral? How can they be used in a sentence that would give a specific impression about a situation, event, person, or group of people?

Adjectives

Natural	Cute	Influential	Regular
Unnatural	Funny	Nimble	Yellow
Lazy	Large	Gay	Urban
Industrious	Tiny	Particular	Brash

Verbs

Force	Provoke	Blasted	Enthused
Manipulate	Allow	Boasted	Yelped
Persuade	Suggest	Weedled	Laughed
Skip	Paint	Whined	Slithered

Adverbs

Quickly	Sweetly	Energetically	Simply
Hesitantly	Deliberately	Lazily	Proficiently

Nouns

Gang	Family	Peach	Rose
Group	Cow	Jock	Apple
Village	Gorilla	Baby	Fruit
City	Dog	Grandpa	Pumpkin

Monday. What you saw and what you remember seeing." He was conscious of avoiding the word *murder*, would use soft words throughout the interrogation. "Memory is a strange device, Jason." The constant use of Jason's name was important, personal, avoiding the impersonal. "It plays tricks. What we remember or think we remember. And the opposite, what we've forgotten or think we've forgotten. We'll find out about it all together." Establishing them as a team.

Excerpt from *Rag and Bone Shop* (Cormier, 2003), p. 80.

QUESTIONS FOR STUDENTS TO CONSIDER

1. How does Trent use language to make Jason cooperate?

2. What language doesn't he use and why?

3. How do you think you would respond to Trent?

The second excerpt we use is from *A Single Shard* (Park, 2001), which received the Newbery Medal. This tale is about the journey Tree-ear, a young apprentice to a potter in 12th-century Korea, takes when he is sent to show the Emperor the potter's best clay work. Along the way, Tree-ear is abducted by two men who take him up a hill to rob him. In this excerpt, Tree-ear is on the mountain with the two robbers. We ask students to pay close attention to how a person can use language to humiliate another, and while this excerpt is a good beginning for the study of language, the whole book could be used to discuss how language is used as a tool of power. Another book we invite students to read is *Nothing but the Truth* (Avi, 1991), which can further develop students' understandings of language and power.

"Not rice! What is it you are carrying, idiot-boy?" At last, he drew out the first of the vases and his face grew purple with fury.

"Useless!" he screamed, gripping the mouth of the vase with one hand and waving it about. Tree-ear caught his breath with fear.

"We might sell it," said the second robber more calmly.

"Have you no eyes in your head?" his companion shouted back. "Look at it—can't you see, this could only be a gift for the palace! Nobody would dare buy it from us!"

"Keep looking. Perhaps there is something more."

The robber set the first vase down on the ground and returned to his search of the container. With more muttered curses, he pulled out the second vessel and threw the final handful of straw on the ground.

"Nothing!" he screamed. "All the way up this hill—and nothing!"

His companion shifted his grip and now had one arm across Tree-ear's throat, throttling him so he could barely breathe. With his other hand he pawed roughly at Tree-ear's waist pouch.

"Eh—here is something to cheer you up!" He held the pouch in his free hand and emptied the contents onto the ground. The flint stones and the little clay turtle fell out, followed by the string of coins.

"Something, anyway," grumbled the first robber, scooping up the coins. He kicked the *jiggeh* out of his way and headed down the path. "Come—we've wasted enough time here."

Tree-ear breathed a silent prayer of thanks. *Take the money—take anything. Just leave the vases alone...*

The second robber laughed. "Wait," he said. "Come hold this donkey for a moment."

The first robber retraced his steps. "What is it?" he asked impatiently, grabbing Tree-ear by the arms from behind.

"A little fun, as long as we're up here."

The robber picked up one of the vases. He stepped to the edge of the cliff—and flung it into the air. Peering over the edge, he put his hand to his ear in a pose of listening. After an agony of silence, the crash of pottery was heard on the rocks far below.

The second robber laughed again. "One more!" he said in a jovial voice.

"No!" Tree-ear screamed, an inhuman screech of utter desperation.

QUESTIONS FOR STUDENTS TO CONSIDER

1. How would you feel in this situation if you were Tree-ear?

2. What language is specifically used to humiliate him?

3. What body language is used for humiliation in this passage?

4. How is the robbers' treatment of each other humiliating?

After students have ample opportunities to explore power and language in young adult literature, they can progress to examining how language is used in the materials they read for pleasure, such as magazines, Internet websites, or novels. By understanding that language is rarely neutral, students can begin to recognize how language is used to persuade them, evoke particular feelings within them, or spur an action. Knowing about how language is used does not need to deter students' pleasure in what they read and enjoy, but this knowledge can help inform them by drawing to their attention the nuances involved with language and how it is used in different contexts for different reasons. Students also can become more cognizant of the negative and positive uses of language and how it is used to manipulate readers by influencing their responses to the information they read. Being informed can lead to changes in what students find pleasurable, and other times it can lead to rethinking their attitudes about people in the world and their relationships. We all are subject to language and its power over us. What we need to do is disrupt this correlation when it leads to negative thinking about others when there is no evidence to justify that negativity.

By asking questions that highlight power relations, students also can learn how language and power are contextualized in our social interactions. By looking closely at specific words, students can begin to address how assumptions lie beneath the actual words that are spoken. Through language study, students also can hypothesize about the relationship between the speakers and discuss where power is maintained or where it can be changed. Students need to become aware of how they are manipulated by language, how they may be humiliated by language, and how they utilize language to manipulate or humiliate others. It is in the manipulation and humiliation of persons that power is the most hazardous or harmful. By learning to recognize this potential danger, students can disrupt or challenge relationships of unequal power in their lives and in the lives of others. They also become better consumers of what they hear, what they believe, and what they are persuaded or asked to do.

Using Rhetorical Criticism With Middle-Level Students

The next step in studying the nature of how language is used to represent an author's intentions and investigating how power is produced in a text is studying a novel that combines a study of power and Rhetorical Criticism. By first using literature to show how language is a tool of power and used to influence readers' responses, teachers can then introduce their students to informational texts such as magazine ads, editorials, or public speeches to show how all types of authors use language to persuade their readers or listeners.

Table 13 serves as a reminder of the major elements of Rhetorical Criticism, and as a guide in teaching this literary theory to middle-level students.

We use *Big Mouth & Ugly Girl* (Oates, 2002), a novel that deals directly with issues of power and representation, for rhetorical analysis.

TABLE 13

Elements of Rhetorical Criticism

Rhetorical Criticism addresses the following three areas:

1. How the narrative structure seems to direct the reader to respond in particular ways, that is, the way in which the book or passage is written so that a typical reader will respond in the way that the author wants.

2. How the author uses language to bring about certain responses from the reader, that is, looking at the language the author used to make the reader sad, angry, sympathetic, and so forth.

3. Whether the author achieves certain intended results. Did the author succeed at attempts to make readers happy, sad, suspicious, angry, and so forth? How would you rate the author's success—excellent, fair, or poor?

In the beginning of this novel, Matt, an intelligent and witty high school student, is escorted out of his high school classroom by detectives for questioning. Eventually, Matt finds out he is accused of trying to blow up the school. Ursula, a female basketball player, knows what really happened, and she becomes involved in helping Matt work through his diminished status at school. By studying this novel, students discover how meaning is contextualized, for example, how overhearing a statement out of context can lead to misconceptions and unjust consequences. Through this story, students find they must question the way Matt is treated and the assumptions that led to his questioning by the police. In addition, we address the following elements in *Big Mouth & Ugly Girl* to discuss issues of language and power with students:

- Matt's friends and their reactions to his plight
- Ursula's decision to become involved in helping Matt
- The community's reaction to the rumor about Matt's plans to bomb the school
- The principal's position about handling the situation
- Matt's reaction to the accusation against him
- Ursula's ideas of herself
- The police and how they act

The first scene from *Big Mouth & Ugly Girl* (see story pp. 3–7 for a more detailed excerpt) can be used to introduce this novel to students. It draws students into the drama of Matt's life and creates a keen interest in the issues of power that pervade this story. In this scene, Matt is in his study period when two men appear at the door wanting to talk to him. They introduce themselves as detectives and ask Matt to come with them.

"Should I—take my things?" He meant his black canvas backpack...the numerous messy pages of his play script, and his laptop computer....

The detectives didn't trouble to answer Matt, and didn't wait for him to pick up the backpack; one of them took charge of it, and the other carried Matt's laptop.... They walked close beside him....

Matt heard his hoarse, frightened voice. "What—is it?"

The detective with the glasses regarded Matt now with a look of forced patience. "Son, you know why we're here."

Excerpt from *Big Mouth & Ugly Girl* (Oates, 2002), pp. 6–7.

QUESTIONS FOR STUDENTS TO CONSIDER

1. How is Matt represented to the reader? How does the author achieve this?

2. What feelings does a reader get about the police? How does the author achieve this?

3. What do you think the author is saying about adolescents and the police using these portrayals?

4. Who is the reading audience?

Additional questions we ask students after they have read the entire book address the issues of language, power, and representation:

- How does Matt's power change throughout the story?
- How does Ursula's power change throughout the story?
- Who has the most power in this story and why?
- How does this story make you, the reader, feel?
- How do you think the author wants you to feel?
- What language or words help you to feel certain ways about particular characters?
- How would you feel if you were Matt? Ursula? The principal? Matt's friends?
- What would you do if you were involved in a similar situation?
- What do you think the author wants readers to learn from this novel?
- Why is it important to learn this?

By asking these types of questions, teachers create spaces of opportunity for students to wrestle with how power is both positive and negative, how injustice can occur quickly based on the environment in which people live, how language is used as a tool of power, and how the author treats that power. Students also have the opportunity to discover how authors use language to create responses in the reader, how authors have intentions when they write, and how literature can reflect situations that real people may experience.

Because Rhetorical Criticism addresses author intention, the way authors use language or situations to evoke particular responses, and how audiences respond to text, *Big Mouth & Ugly Girl* is an excellent novel for scaffolding middle-level readers' understandings of this literary theory. We also find that it is an appropriate choice for discussing power, language, and representation in exciting and authentic ways.

Strategies for Discussing Young Adult Literature With Middle-Level Students

Power Graphs

One of the activities we ask students to complete while reading this novel is graphing Matt's and Ursula's power throughout the novel. Similar to creating a storyboard, graphing power allows students to see where major shifts in power occur and what events precede and succeed them.

Students first map out the story concentrating on five incidents where they see power shifts. To help students with this, teachers can generate a list of these incidents and then leave them on the board or on white paper so students can consult the list as they complete the activity. We ask students to consider five incidents when they first try this activity and then ask them to add more once they become familiar with it. (Another option is to ask younger middle-level students to work with five incidents and older students to work with more.) Once they have mapped the five incidents, students need to calculate what event led to the shift and then determine the result of that shift. Once they have completed the mapping, we ask them to think about showing the progression of shifts on a graph.

Character Journals

We also invite students to write character journals so they can better empathize with the protagonists as the plot unwinds. To do this, students read a few pages and then determine which character they would like to follow or embody for the duration of the book. Each day they attend to character motivations, feelings, or responses, and either expand on those emotions and actions or write what the character would be thinking, doing, and so forth. How students write in these character journals depends on the character they choose. If they choose a minor character, they may have more to respond to in terms of the relationship to the major character(s). If students select a major character that is highlighted in the text, they may have more to address in their writing in terms of why they behaved or said the things they did, and there may be little to say about minor characters.

Personal Log

A third activity students can take part in is keeping a log of their thoughts and feelings about a specific situation as the story progresses. Keeping a log allows students to see how their own thinking may involve misconceptions, assumptions, and biases. From this log, we ask students to write an essay about their own journey through this novel and how they were persuaded by the author to come to particular conclusions about power and justice.

Language Lists

Finally, we ask students to pay close attention to the language used within the text through language lists. These lists might be new vocabulary or new ways of saying something or the way language is used as a tool of power. Teachers can decide to discuss this language at the end of the class period each day, or ask students to write about the language used in one piece of literature after the students have finished reading and discussing it.

Discovering how words are used to create particular feelings or actions is an important lesson for all middle-level students. *Big Mouth & Ugly Girl* is a selection that middle-level students will find engaging and thought provoking. We also know that middle-level teachers and their students enjoy discussing the novel and its outcome.

Moving Beyond Textual Analysis to Becoming Critically Conscious: Examining Power in Classroom Literature Discussions

A final aspect of power, language, and representation that students benefit from learning about involves the issue of who speaks and who listens. Because power is manifested in most situations, including classrooms, students and teachers need to talk about how power—often invisible—is an element of classroom discourse. Classrooms are full of power dynamics, so by studying the relationships within their own classroom, students become directly aware of how power can work. An excerpt from *Slam!* (Myers, 1996; see story pp. 212–213 for a more detailed excerpt) presents how power is negotiated between a teacher and student. Mr. Parish uses his power to humiliate Greg "Slam" Harris, while also attempting to bolster his own power in the classroom.

> "So, Mr. Harris, just why are you taking up classroom space?" He was standing over me. "Why don't you just go out to your neighborhood and find a corner to stand on? That's what you want from life, isn't it?"
> "Don't be standing over me, man," I said.
> "Don't be standing over me?" he raised his voice. "Is that directly from your African background? Maybe from the We-Be tribe?"

Excerpt from *Slam!* (Myers, 1996), pp. 212–213.

QUESTIONS FOR STUDENTS TO CONSIDER

1. How does this excerpt make you feel?

2. How does the language in this excerpt represent power?

3. What other elements are necessary for someone to gain power over another?

We asked a group of eighth-grade students to read this excerpt from *Slam!* and then discuss the questions. The following exchange occurred during a literature circle discussion.

Candace: This is about power and how Mr. Parrish is trying to maintain his power in the classroom as the teacher.

Alex: Slam is trying to show his power by choosing to do his work or not do it.

Rosa: It's a power struggle because the teacher wants to be in control of the class and if his students don't do what he wants, he can't keep the power.

Lisa: Mr. Parrish uses Slam's language against him because he uses the "We-Be" to put Slam down. That is trying to make Slam feel like less of a person.

Alex: I think that might happen a lot. Do you think authors do that, though?

Andrea: I think the way they talk about some of the characters might be a way that would make a real person feel like less of a person.

Sam: Or maybe they would feel bad about themselves if they read it.

Lisa: Just like when the author treats a character who I like or who I think I might be like in a good way, I feel like it's a compliment.

Rosa: That fight between the teacher and Slam is definitely about power and it made me mad because sometimes teachers will try to use their power over you.

Alex: Yeah, and it makes me mad when I watch it in class because I can't do or say anything.

Lisa: I kinda liked that Slam just got up and walked out. That was pretty cool.

Andrea: He's older than us. Do you think you would do that in high school?

Alex: I hope if some teacher makes me mad or if they say those kind of things to me because I'm Mexican, I will walk out of class.

Lisa: I hope I don't have to do that—

Rosa: My mom would kill me! I mean, the teacher would have to report it, and then I am in more trouble.

Andrea: And it all started with the teacher who had a bad feeling about Slam.

From this exchange, we can see that students do have real thoughts and emotions about the power issues they encounter in schools and perhaps in their peer relationships as well. If the classroom teacher had been present during this literature circle discussion, she could have encouraged the discussion by adding information or challenging student thinking. For instance, the classroom teacher could ask for clarification about the following:

- The consequences of actions—students' and teachers'
- The impotence students feel when injustice is perpetrated
- The issue of age and power
- The persuasive use of language
- The necessity of maintaining power in the classroom

All too often students are well aware of the power differential between themselves and their teachers. We suggest that it is not the dynamics between students and teachers that should be solely investigated within a classroom. Students also should investigate the power dynamics between each other so they can begin to see how they use language to intimidate, honor, or anger one another. Classrooms are influenced by the emotions and relationships between students, and if relationships are negative, the conditions for student participation or learning are not optimal.

There are a number of ways students can investigate talk in their classroom and then interpret the process of interaction as individuals or groups. One way to start is to notice who talks when discussing literature. By consciously dealing with the conversations and the language used in literary discussions in their own classrooms, students will come into direct contact with power and how it can privilege some while limiting others.

Five questions students can ask about how discussion works in their own classrooms include the following:

1. How often do I talk in classroom discussions?

2. Why do or don't I feel free to talk?

3. Who doesn't talk during classroom discussions?

4. How can we find ways for all students to feel comfortable talking during class?

5. How does what happens outside of the classroom affect my interactions with other students and with teachers in the classroom?

Students can discuss these questions in their journals, in small groups, or as a whole class, depending on the dynamics of the classroom community. Initially, teachers can broach these issues in general so students can get used to the process of discussing potentially touchy subjects with others. The teachers with whom we worked held classroom meetings so students could bring up academic and social issues that were causing discomfort in the classroom.

Another way to allow students to think about talk in the classroom is through self-assessments. By pondering how they use talk in the classroom and how that talk might silence or engage others, young adolescents learn two important lessons. The first has to do with how we all hold power. The second is how we use that power to invite others into the classroom community or alienate them from it. We suggest that by reflecting on such interactions, students will have the awareness and the ability to alter the way the classroom community works for all its members.

A third way of addressing power in the classroom is through individual interviews. Students can be paired to discuss how power affects them in the classroom. By talking to peers, students can discover the multitude of perspectives that exist in their own classrooms and how those perspectives result in interpretations of reality, truth, and the questions of what happens and why. Students will find that the answers to these questions are as diverse as the number of individuals within the class. Students, however, must feel comfortable with one another before they will enter into dialogue about the nature of power in personal ways. We suggest that individual interviews occur after students feel they can reveal aspects of themselves with the class because of the close community they have formed.

Regardless of the effort teachers put into creating an open, inviting environment for student learning, there will be issues that arise because of the number of personalities within the classroom. Issues of power are often an aspect of this dynamic, and thus must be dealt with explicitly. Teachers can prevent negative interactions from escalating, and they can remind their students that power is not a limited quantity, but a condition or influence that can be shared among all members of the class.

Conclusion

Addressing the issue of power is a necessary component of an education that highlights social justice and critical consciousness. Young adolescent students can comprehend texts on many levels, and often they sense an uneasiness they cannot name when they know something is not fair or equitable. By becoming conscious about how power works in individual relationships, institutions such as schools and governments, and in the ideologies of cultures, students become agents in their own emancipation. They are able to name what hurts them and by naming it come to understand it and perhaps take some kind of control over it.

Through their personal reflections or individual interviews with other members of their classroom community, middle-level students can generate change within themselves and their interactions with people they know as well as people they have only read about or know indirectly. When students learn about power, they are handed some of the tools to break through the limitations that hold them in places where they do not wish to be and should not be forced to remain.

"If you lived in Kinship, you had your place."

From *Spite Fences* (Krisher, 1994, p. 34)

CHAPTER 6

Oppression and Critical Literacy: Becoming Conscious, Becoming Concerned

Often, forces that oppress individuals or groups go unopposed because people do not recognize these forces exist. Through reading and discussing literature that addresses what oppression is, middle-level students are better able to understand not only how the world works, but also why groups of people may oppose the government or other institutions by striking, holding demonstrations, or even rioting. Many students have experienced oppression in school or in their neighborhoods; they refer to it as bullying, a form of oppression that is not on an institutional level unless the school does not acknowledge it. The book *The Chocolate War* (Cormier, 1986) addresses such an instance when the school administrators allow a group of students to coerce other students into participating in a school fundraiser.

Often, adolescence itself can be considered an oppressive state because it is so often denigrated and prejudged by society. Understanding oppression is the first step to understanding how it works, and how subtle it can be.

Defining Oppression

While power is a primary force that students must understand in order to understand the world, another force directly related to power is also at work. The counterpoint to inappropriate power is often oppression, yet people often are hesitant to name it as such because it sounds more serious, more historical, and more global than what they are experiencing. Young (1990) suggests that oppression has five faces: (1) exploitation, (2) marginalization, (3) powerlessness, (4) cultural imperialism, and

(5) violence. These faces will be discussed in more detail in the next section. Many middle-level students are presented with at least one of these faces in or outside of school, yet few understand what is happening to them or know how to handle these situations.

Addressing oppression through literature circle discussions can be a way of naming what students experience when they are ridiculed, humiliated, ignored, or even beaten. Using questions, activities, and literary analysis enables middle-level students to connect power and oppression while also deepening their awareness of how language and representation both empower and oppress people. Knowing this information can empower middle-level students while also disrupting behaviors that are oppressive to them and to others.

Discussing Oppression With Middle-Level Students

As we suggested in chapter 5, we want middle-level students to discuss the difficult issue of power, but to do that, students may need to examine oppression in relation to power, which is the reason we often teach these issues simultaneously. We do not suggest that power and oppression are the two sides of one coin. In fact, power is frequently shared by people regardless of their positions, which can be the case in democratic classrooms. Other times, people may feel oppressed even when no power is exerted upon them. That is why discussing an issue such as oppression can be complex and convoluted. We begin by inviting students to explore the concept of oppression and how it is manifested in the world and in their lives.

Understanding the five faces of oppression as defined by Young (1990) is the first step in identifying and disrupting patterns that are oppressive to the self and others. For middle-level students, the following definitions along with age-appropriate examples serve as a springboard for learning about oppression and alleviating it:

- Exploitation: Using people or positions to gain an unfair advantage while limiting the advantages of others. Bullying is a form of oppression that is overt and is often perpetrated through violent actions. It also can be exploitative when it involves taking others' money, lunches, or homework.

- Marginalization: Deliberately working to keep someone out of a place of power. Students who often are demeaned for speaking or who do not fit in with the norm are frequently marginalized.

- Powerlessness: Creating situations where someone has no power. Teachers or student leaders who don't allow students a voice in classroom practices create a sense of powerlessness in others.

- Cultural Imperialism: Maintaining or privileging the power of one cultural group over another and in doing so, either marginalizing those not in power or creating situations where only the dominant group has power. Peer pressure can be seen as a type of cultural imperialism.

- Violence: Using power in a physical, emotional, economic, or ideological way that hurts others. Making fun or gossiping about others can be a form of symbolic violence.

Students can work with these concepts by keeping a journal about either their own lives or circumstances they have seen through media presentations. They can view films or newscasts about bullying, or share historical accounts from their families that can attest to the oppression some groups have experienced throughout time. We also ask students to think of ways of disrupting the oppression they have experienced, witnessed, or heard about and to note what issues are involved with confronting oppression. After they have defined oppression and connected the concept to their own lives and experiences, students can explore how oppression is presented in literature. Picture books, excerpts from novels, and entire novels can be used to examine the faces of oppression.

Through discussions of literature that presents oppressive situations, teachers can help middle-level students wrestle with this concept in concrete ways. Because oppression happens in many ways—physical, emotional, direct, indirect, empirical, and symbolical—it is both visible and invisible. Teachers also must remember that oppression is frequently not named as such, so we have a tendency to avoid using the word even when directly confronted with oppression. We know that many adults become defensive when they are confronted with their own attitudes or behaviors that could be labeled oppressive, and young people model adult behavior. By using young adult literature, however, teachers and students can grapple with oppression because no one person in the classroom is on trial—it is the situation or character in a book that is addressed, which allows us to experience oppression and oppressive acts vicariously, and then transfer the awareness to our own lives.

Using Picture Books That Represent Oppression

Picture books, because they contain short stories that students find easier to relate to, can serve as a way to introduce the topic of oppression to middle-level students. We begin with *Farmer Duck* (Waddell, 1991), a presentation of a farm duck that is overworked while the farmer lies around in bed bellowing, "How goes the work?" The responses of the duck and the other farm animals make this text an especially appropriate introduction to discussing oppressive situations and groups. Most middle-level readers can relate to this text because of their own issues with work, power, and authority. For example, the following discussion about *Farmer Duck* took place among a group of eighth graders in a literature circle:

Amanda: This is about power and justice because the farmer doesn't do anything and makes the duck do it all.

Rosario: And the duck does all the work. The other animals don't do anything.

Eduardo: It's like slavery.

Bryce: The farmer only picks on the one duck while the rest of the animals just do their normal thing.

Amanda: It's like the duck is really doing the farmer's work and doesn't get anything for it.

Eduardo: Like I said, it's like slavery, or even like the field workers today who don't get hardly nothing for their work because if they asked for more, they might get deported or something.

Rosario: Do you think the author is saying that everybody should help out those who are being abused?

Bryce: That's what the animals did, so I think it probably is the author's message along with the idea that power shouldn't be abused. Just because the farmer was the boss didn't mean he should make others do his work.

Amanda: It's like we should help out those in our neighborhood if they are being oppressed or abused.

Rosario: Helping out maybe more than our neighbors. The animals were all on the same farm, and that was like their world. It might be bigger than a neighborhood.

During this discussion, students made connections to history, to particular groups of people, and to their own actions. Although they may have wrestled with who should be helped by whom, they easily identified the oppressed as well as who was in power. The more difficult decision was deciding the relationship between those who are abused or oppressed and those who should prevent or disrupt that abuse. Yet, from this brief excerpt, we believe that students have the potential to realize that everyone should be disrupting oppression.

Many other picture books can be used to discuss oppression. The concept crosses cultures and genres, thus students can read traditional literature, realistic and historical fiction, or even fantasy in a picture book format to explore the many faces of oppression. Table 14 lists a few of the picture books available for discussing oppression with middle-level students. These books present various faces of oppression and help students discover how individuals and groups have been or still are oppressed.

There are also multiple ways to use these picture books with students:

- Teachers could use them to begin a unit on a particular type of oppression.

- Teachers can use them as read-alouds and invite the entire class to discuss the concepts.

- Individual students may use them in comparison studies of oppressive situations.

- Individuals can use them as models for their own creative writing.

- Pairs of students can write reviews of the texts for a local paper.

- Students can use these texts in individual inquiries about oppression.

- Students can read these texts in small groups and discuss the evidence of oppression in the stories.

- Small groups can dramatize the stories for another class or age group.

TABLE 14

Picture Books Presenting Oppression

Battle-Levert, G. (2003). *Papa's mark*. New York: Holiday House.
Best, C. (2001). *Shrinking Violet*. New York: Melanie Kroupa Books.
Coleman, E. (1996). *White socks only*. Morton Grove, IL: Albert Whitman & Co.
Kurusa. (1995). *The streets are free*. Toronto, ON, Canada: Annick Press.
Lorbiecki, M. (1996). *Just one flick of a finger*. New York: Dial Books.
Marsden, J., & Tan, S. (1998). *The rabbits*. Port Melbourne, Australia: Lothian Books.
Maruki, T. (1980). *Hiroshima no pika*. New York: Lothrop, Lee & Shepard.
Romain, T. (2002). *Jemma's journey*. Honesdale, PA: Boyds Mills Press.
Shange, N. (1997). *White wash*. New York: Walker & Co.
Wiles, D. (2001). *Freedom summer*. New York: Simon & Schuster.

Because oppression pervades the world, the use of picture books may be a gentle way to introduce how many oppressed people have lived or are still living in the world. We know that middle-level students enjoy reading and discussing the issues presented in these books and that, for them, the concept of justice cannot be explained without exploring injustice (Johnson & Miller, 2004). We believe that social action can begin with the reading and discussion of such texts, and young adolescents will respond to the call for a better world for all people that these books inspire. Through their awareness, young adolescents can begin the journey to envisioning a better world.

Using Excerpts That Present Oppression

When we first begin discussing oppression with middle-level readers, we use the following three excerpts from young adult novels and ask students to think about the following questions:

- What types of oppression are apparent in these excerpts?
- In what ways have you experienced similar situations?
- How is oppression a part of our lives and the lives of those in our nation and the world?
- How can we stop these kinds of situations from happening?

The first excerpt is from the book *Witness* (Hesse, 2003; see story pp. 74–76 for a more detailed excerpt), a story that examines what happens in a small Vermont town when the Ku Klux Klan begins recruiting there. The excerpt addresses an incident reported in the newspaper about a young black girl who rescued a Jewish girl from being hit by a train.

reynard alexander

wright sutter
received a letter
in the mail
warning him to leave town.

whoever wrote that letter said
they saw the article about leanora
saving the hirsh child from the train.
said,
they'd tie them both to the tracks next time,
make sure neither walked away.

fearing for leanora,

sutter took the letter to percelle johnson.

johnson asked the head of the local klan what they knew about such threats.

klan said,

we didn't send it.

Excerpt from *Witness* (Hesse, 2003), p. 75.

The second excerpt from *Lakota Woman* (Crow Dog & Erdoes, 1994) describes the narrator's understanding of how Native Americans were treated by white soldiers.

When the sun rose, after we had eaten our morning food and drunk the ice-cold water from the stream, I felt as I had never felt before. I felt so happy, so good. When I got home I blurted out to my mother that I had been to a Native American Church meeting. Mom was hurt. In the end she shrugged her shoulders: "Well, it's up to you. I can't tell you what to do!" But she also added something that I liked: "Remember, whatever, the Indian is closest to God." I understood what she meant.

Two weeks later I was staying at my grandmother's and a dream came to me. It was in the nighttime, toward morning. I tried to wake up but could not. I was awake and not awake. I could not move. I was crying. I opened my eyes once and saw my grandmother sitting on my bed. She was asking whether I was all right, but I could not answer her. In my dream I had been going back into another life. I saw tipis and Indians camping, huddling around a fire, smiling and cooking buffalo meat, and then suddenly, I saw white soldiers riding into camp, killing women and children, raping, cutting throats. It was so real, more real than a movie—sights and sounds and smells: the screaming of children that I did not want to hear, but had to all the same. And the only thing I could do was cry....

For a long time after that dream I felt depressed, as if all life had been drained from me. I was still going to school, too young to bear such dreams. And I grieved because we had to live a life that we were not put on this earth for. I asked myself why things were so bad for us, why Indians suffered as they did. I could find no answer.

Finally, the third excerpt from *In the Year of the Boar and Jackie Robinson* (Lord, 1986; see story pp. 56–58 for a more detailed excerpt) describes the treatment of Shirley, a young Chinese girl in her new U.S. classroom. Shirley is learning English as she attends school in California. Mrs. Rappaport, her teacher, creates an assignment where all the children are to find a poem and recite it in front of the class. This excerpt describes what happens when it is Shirley's turn.

At once, they were giggling. Even Mrs. Rappaport. There was nothing to do but gesture to the right and gesture to the left, exactly as she had practiced...

Now everyone was laughing openly...tears welled in her throat and she could only manage a weak smile...

Mrs. Rappaport was the first to notice that Shirley was no longer smiling, and immediately clapped for order.... "Thank you for a most remarkable performance.... Right here in our own classroom—the fabulous Donald Duck, Chip and Dale, and Mickey Mouse!"

Excerpt From *In the Year of the Boar and Jackie Robinson* (Lord, 1986), p. 58.

Students' initial reactions about these excerpts are always mixed. Some students are angry, other students do not understand the problem, and still other students become defensive. One student asked, "But what's wrong with laughing at someone who sounds like those Disney characters?" This is the question we wait to hear because it allows us to remind students that sometimes it is not the actual event that is the problem, but rather the way the person who is being ridiculed perceives the event. Because the character Shirley did not understand the reason for the laughter, she felt she was being made fun of and she was feeling marginalized because of her heritage and her language, not for her poetry recital.

Learning about how oppression can work directly or indirectly, as well as understanding how power is perceived by those in an interaction, is one of the critical lessons to teach young people when they are wrestling with the concept of oppression. By asking them to work through excerpts and then longer pieces of literature, middle-level students can begin to identify it in their own lives.

Disrupting Oppression Through Young Adult Literature

After students discuss these excerpts, teachers can use entire pieces of young adult literature that can further highlight oppressive behaviors as well as how oppression might be disrupted. Two of our favorite pieces of realistic fiction include *The Plague Year* (Tolan, 1991) and

Tangerine (Bloor, 2001). *The Plague Year* is the story of Bran, whose father is a serial killer. After his father goes to jail, Bran is placed with his aunt in a small town where people question where Bran came from and how he received the scar on his face. This novel turns the concepts of safety and goodness into questions about who people really are, the nature of neighborhoods as havens of safety, and what makes a person good or bad in respect to social mores and attitudes. *Tangerine* addresses family violence and secrecy along with marginalization and acceptance. *Stargirl* (Spinelli, 2002) and *Silent to the Bone* (Konigsburg, 2000) also are great examples of realistic fiction that address oppressive situations and are compelling stories that young adolescents enjoy.

In addition to the realistic fiction previously mentioned, there are a number of pieces of historical fiction that middle-level teachers and their students can use to address oppression. Throughout history, groups of people have been oppressed because of race, ethnicity, class, or a variety of other reasons. Historical fiction allows young adolescents to examine this oppression through literature written specifically for their age group, and often told from the perspective of someone near their age. *Roll of Thunder, Hear My Cry* (Taylor, 1984) is an excellent selection for discussing all five faces of oppression (Young, 1990) in relation to the cultural imperialism over and exploitation, marginalization, violence, and powerlessness of the black community during the Great Depression in the United States. *Number the Stars* (Lowry, 1989) addresses the violence and cultural imperialism toward and the powerlessness and marginalization of Jews in Europe during World War II. Historical fiction presenting the condition of Japanese internment camps, the Navajo Long Walk, and the plight of Mexican migrant workers also can be used to address the faces of oppression in relation to the history of the United States.

Another book that addresses the oppressive elements of marginalization, cultural imperialism, and exploitation is *Go and Come Back* (Abelove, 1998), the story of a young Peruvian girl who learns about cultural differences and misinterpretations across cultures when two U.S. anthropologists live with her tribe in the rainforest. The young protagonist relates how the two female anthropologists from the United States appear imperialistic, exploitative, and superior. Because the anthropologists do not know the customs of the culture they are studying, they are considered "not human" by other tribal members. By reading and discussing this book, students may realize that they also make erroneous assumptions about others and appear oppressive because of their lack of knowledge and their unexamined behaviors.

Few nations can boast that oppression has not been a part of their history. Some examples of oppression involve Canada and the French-speaking Arcadians, Scotland and the Clearances, the African tribes that sold members of other tribes to the Europeans as slaves, the Bataan Death March during World War II, the aboriginal peoples of Australia, the women of the Arab world, and the Maori of New Zealand. All these groups have stories to tell that confirm that oppression is a part of their history.

While history shows us that oppression is a part of the past, we do not want students to believe that oppression cannot be found today. Through small acts of prejudice, hatred, or gossip, and through larger acts of hate crimes and discrimination in hiring practices, oppression is still very much a part of the world and words we use in our social interactions. We want students to realize that oppression not only happens on a large scale to whole groups of people but also can be directed at individuals because of the oppressor's fear of difference or issues of self-esteem that are connected to this fear. Using young adult fiction often can help middle-level students see how oppression works in their present circumstances.

Often, young adult literature that comes from outside the dominant white mainstream addresses issues of oppression in ways that students can understand. For example, in *Just Call Me Stupid* (Birdseye, 1992) Patrick's friend Celia is Mexican American and Patrick is from a lower income neighborhood. Both Patrick and Celia are outside the dominant norm for their school. Patrick is ridiculed by his classmates because he cannot read, and because of his reading challenges, Patrick is marginalized by others while he also alienates himself and feels powerless to rectify his problem. Issues of cultural imperialism also are apparent in this text: Because the dominant ideology is that by fifth grade students should know how to read, the school culture has only limited alternatives to help Patrick. Students who read this text will come to understand how oppression can affect their lives not because of their color, their language, or their gender but because of their inability to perform as expected. The following excerpt helps students begin to understand how oppression can be subtle, underlying the assumptions people have about what is "normal."

> On Monday morning Andy Wilkinson was waiting for him on the soccer field. "How could you have written the best story in the whole school?" Andy demanded, striding toward him.... Andy kept on, this time loud enough to turn heads. "Who really wrote that story, huh? Your wetback girlfriend?"

Patrick stopped and swirled around, anger shooting up in him like a geyser. "She's *not* my girlfriend," he said between clenched teeth, "and *I* wrote the story."

Andy's laugh was harsh. "That's not your story. You couldn't have written it. Liar. Cheater."

Things began to close in on [Patrick], especially Andy's voice.

"You couldn't have written that story. You're too stupid."

Patrick began to panic. Stupid . . . Stupid . . . Stupid. The word echoed, and with that echo the weight bore down on his chest, the air pressed in like walls, the closet door began to slam shut.

"You can't even read!"

Excerpt from *Just Call Me Stupid* (Birdseye, 1992), pp. 147–149.

QUESTIONS FOR STUDENTS TO CONSIDER

1. How is Andy's behavior oppressive?

2. Why does academic success matter in terms of power and oppression?

3. How does Patrick internalize his oppression?

4. How can Patrick stop from oppressing himself?

5. How can schools disrupt oppressive cycles?

Another book to use when addressing oppression is *The Children's Story* (Clavell, 1963), a classic piece of literature that addresses the ideological power behind what students can be taught in school without question. Note that we are not suggesting that students should not be taught the pledge of allegiance, but rather that students should be conscious of what it means to say the pledge. In fact, reading this story can create a venue for discussing many of the ideological concepts that people, and often whole countries, embrace without thought. Reading and discussing this book can help students realize that their minds are vulnerable, and that vulnerability can be exploited. However, by becoming critically literate and critically conscious, students can disrupt oppression.

When we read *The Children's Story* in a literature circle group of eighth graders, it created a small stir within the group. Two of the students thought the story was unrealistic, while another student thought it was possible for a nation to be taken over and then the schools would change as well:

Brian: This seems kinda ridiculous to me. I mean, who is gonna let something like that happen without a fight?

Jason:	I think it probably already happened when the Nazis took over and a lot of the Jews didn't do anything about it. They thought they were safe even when the Nazis did some bad stuff to them.
Toby:	I think [the book] was so weird, too. I mean, wouldn't you do something if that happened here? Wouldn't we know about it? It would be on the news or something!
Jason:	I don't know, don't you think some parts of America could be invaded and we wouldn't know about it?
Brian:	No! How would those people get here? And then what would happen? We would just let them have like North Dakota or Florida?
Toby:	There would be a big war, so I don't think people will try to take over a school or something.
Jason:	I don't know. I think somebody might, but it probably wouldn't be peaceful.

With this interaction, we realized that students remained on the surface of the text, but the opportunity to go deeper was possible. If we had asked them to think about how ideas or trends become popular in a country or school and have the potential to become *the* way of thinking, we are sure the use of such examples would have helped make a point about how the same thing can happen with political or militaristic ideas.

Karen Hesse's book *The Music of Dolphins* (1996) leads readers through the "humanization" of Mila, a teenage girl "rescued" from her feral state as a member of a dolphin pod. Mila does not speak a human language, and as she begins to learn one, she is better able to express her unhappiness. She works to become human so she can be set free to return to her dolphin home. Through her attempts to become human, which are alien to her, Mila feels she will eventually be able to be free to return to who she is—a member of a dolphin family. Cultural imperialism is the major theme that runs through this text, and students will need to think deeply about the need to make someone like themselves, whether it is to "rescue" the "disadvantaged," educate the "disadvantaged," dominate the "disadvantaged," or make the oppressor feel safe. Students will enjoy discussions around the questions: What makes someone human? Why does Mila have to be human in the same way others are? and Why do the scientists feel it is necessary to make her human? This book explores the theory that with the learning of language comes socialization and ideological manipulation, concepts that will challenge young adolescents' thinking. When we use *The Music of the Dolphins* with middle-level students, some of the questions we focus on include the following:

- What should be done about Mila because she is a feral child? Why?

- How can the right actions according to the community be wrong for a person?

- Whose rights should be privileged—an individual's or a society's? Why? Is this always the case? What criteria should be used to make this decision and why?

- What should happen if a person does not fit society's rules or ways of behaving? What could be the result? Why?

- How does Mila's sex determine what should be done with her?

Through these questions and others about humanization, socialization, and oppression, middle-level students become more conscious of the way nations influence the behaviors of their citizens. This influence, however, can be questioned and challenged if we begin to think that perhaps this influence subtly or directly oppresses a nation's peoples. Students should also become aware of how texts, through the ways they represent people, might subtly oppress groups of people. Feminist criticism explores how gender may be one area in which people are oppressed in literary representations.

Examining Oppression Through Science Fiction and Feminist Criticism

The genre of science fiction is a variety of fantasy that is inspired by actual events in science. This type of literature includes space exploration, utopian societies that exist in the future, and survival stories that occur after an environmental or nuclear disaster. Science fiction has elements of the improbable, but these elements are not out of the realm of possible. At the time of its publication, *Frankenstein* (Shelley, 1818) was considered science fiction because of the clearly improbable events of creating life from parts of dead people. Yet today, with organ donation and cloning, many of the scientific principles that Shelley wrote about are no longer impossible. As another example, at one time space travel seemed impossible, but now space travel is quite common.

Often students do not see how science fiction pertains to current situations. To help them understand, we have pointed out to our students how we see "Star Trek" as cultural commentary and intercultural engagement. Once students begin to view science fiction from this perspective, they are better able to see how science fiction is related to the present. In this section, we wish to highlight science fiction because of its perceived distance from the present. We wish to show, however, that science fiction and fantasy also address the harsh realities of oppression and abuse of power.

We have found that *Harry Potter and the Order of the Phoenix* (2003), part of the Harry Potter series by J.K. Rowling, is ideal for discussing oppression. In this series, Harry is oppressed by his adoptive family; is a victim of physical violence at his school's athletic matches; and is a victim of symbolic violence through the use of language by his adoptive family, the school bully, and other members of his boarding school. Such incidents occur in the other books in the series, but what makes this text unique are Harry's reactions to the oppression and anger about it, which are more apparent. We find this realistic portrayal of reaction to oppression especially insightful and worthy of discussion.

We also wish to bring together feminist criticism with this genre because we have noticed that it is often young men who most often like science fiction. We want to challenge students to see how males and females are presented in this genre as well as to explore the issue of science fiction as a male domain.

As we mentioned in chapter 2, feminist criticism (a) can be combined with other perspectives for a combination of different literary analyses and (b) has the overarching concern about the way females are portrayed in literature. Some feminist critics suggest that women, as a group, are exploited at all levels and the dominant ideology suggests that the masculine is inherently better than the feminine. Another concern of feminist criticism has to do with how women are represented in texts, often in stereotypical manners that represent them as weak, competitive with other women, overbearing, or too dependent on men. In addition, this theory explores how female protagonists are portrayed and suggest that they are frequently less dynamic than male protagonists. Feminist criticism also addresses the representation of males and the expectations placed upon males and females in relation to what and how they read (Barrs & Pidgeon, 1994; Simpson, 1996). These perspectives could translate into the need for girls to learn to read in a resistant manner so as not to accept the values that undermine women as people (Fetterley, 1978).

Questions that can help middle-level readers begin to think about male and female representation in young adult novels include the following:

- How do the male and female characters act differently? Similarly?

- In what ways do the characters in this novel reflect how real males and females act?

- In what ways are the characters not like people in the real world?
- How would the story change if the main character were female? Male?

Teachers can ask students to look at their own reading habits and how they may be influenced by society's beliefs about males and females (see Table 15 for questions to get started). These questions can be followed by discussions focusing on whether students' answers are related to their sex. Students' responses often will lead to classifications of "boy" books and activities as well as "girl" books and activities, which then should also be discussed. Teachers can disrupt the idea that activities are either boy or girl activities by asking students to think about why a girl or boy couldn't participate in a particular activity. Giving examples such as men who cook and women who play soccer for a living, and explaining that both men and women fight in the armed forces, help disabuse young people of some of their binary thinking.

Connecting to the concept of oppression allows students to ponder how gender can be used as a target or tool of oppression. For instance, *The Music of Dolphins* (Hesse, 1996) can be used to explore oppression in relation to gender by asking students to consider how Mila is treated and whether or not boys would be treated in a similar manner. Students also can explore the idea of the language and concerns of Mila and whether or not a "feral boy" would wonder and feel the same way. We also wonder aloud with our students why the author chose to use two females as the "feral" children rather than boys. Through this type of thinking, students discover that authors might have their own biases about males and females, and that, as readers, they do not have to accept those biases.

TABLE 15

Questions to Begin Discussing Feminist Criticism
• What were your favorite books as a child?
• What do you read now for pleasure?
• How did you learn about your favorite books?
• Will you read stories about the opposite sex? Why or why not?
• What do you think your friends would say if you read books that were most often read by someone of the opposite sex?
• Who reads more—boys or girls?
• What do we think about boys who read a lot? Girls who read a lot?
• Why is or isn't reading one of your favorite activities?

As mentioned in chapter 2, students also can explore feminist criticism by investigating authors and how they write. Exploring how many males write for adolescents, how many females write for adolescents, and the types of books they write helps get middle-level readers thinking about how readers and authors are influenced by a society's expectations in relation to gender. It is in relation to these questions that we highlight science fiction and the representations of men and women in texts written especially for young adolescents.

Reading *The Keeper of the Isis Light* With Middle-Level Students

When we think of science, space travel, aerospace engineering, and medical advancements, we often think of those people who are involved in such projects. Quite often we think of men even though women also are involved in these ventures. Just as with the reading of science fiction, we must confront the stereotyping of science and science fiction as a male genre. Through reading *The Keeper of the Isis Light* (Hughes, 2000), written by a female author and presenting a female protagonist, we can create opportunities for all of our students to investigate this thought-provoking genre, which can be of interest to both young men and women.

We have found that middle-level girls are drawn to the female protagonist as well as the hint of romance in the plot. Boys find interesting the ideas of living on another planet and traveling through space.

In this novel, Olwen, the adolescent protagonist, is keeper of a beacon light on Isis, a harsh and alien planet. Her scientist parents brought Olwen with them to the deserted planet to maintain a rescue station with a beacon light for helping space mariners and settlers from earth who might eventually relocate to the planet. When her parents are killed, Olwen is left in the care of Guardian, a technological element that serves the family on their mission. Olwen is happy on Isis with her mountain pet, Hobbit, but is excited when a group of settlers relocate to Isis and begin establishing a permanent home for others from earth. Once the settlers come, however, Olwen discovers that suspicion and intolerance have accompanied them. It is upon their arrival that Olwen learns that, although she is human, she has been genetically changed to adapt to the harsh environment on Isis.

When we use *The Keeper of the Isis Light* with our students, we highlight a number of specific excerpts to discuss the five faces of oppression. The following excerpts explore how appearance is sometimes used by a dominant group as a way to oppress others. It is Olwen's response to her own difference that is interesting in this novel. She learns to embrace her difference, which may serve to inspire readers to examine their feelings about their appearances and how they treat others who may be different. In this excerpt (see story pp. 136–139 for a more detailed excerpt), Olwen learns that she has been genetically changed by the Guardian of the space station so that she would survive better on the planet Isis. She finds that her skin color has been changed, along with her bone structure and facial features. Olwen first responds with anger and sadness, and we use the excerpt to create empathy in middle-level students who may have picked on others who are different.

> Olwen drew in a sharp breath and looked down at her own hands. They were what they had always been, familiar, comfortable extensions of herself. Was there anything wrong with her hands? "Guardian, is that why there are no mirrors? Were you afraid that I couldn't even bear to look at myself? Am I...horrible?"
> "No, no. It is not like that..."
> "Am I...am I very different?"
> "Yes."

Excerpt from *The Keeper of the Isis Light* (Hughes, 2000), p. 139.

QUESTIONS FOR STUDENTS TO CONSIDER

1. If you were in Olwen's situation, how would you feel? What would you do?
2. How might Olwen feel about her changes if she were a boy?
3. If you met Olwen, what would you think?
4. With Olwen's changes, is she human? Why or why not?
5. Why did the author make the protagonist female in this story?

In *The Keeper of the Isis Light*, Olwen seems to readily adapt to her genetic changes and the distance created between herself and the settlers because of her appearance. In the next excerpt, we target the veracity of Olwen's belief about how others will treat her because she is different. She is on one of the planet's mountains reflecting on her plight when she meets another mountain Hobbit, a young pup like the pet she had that was killed by the settlers.

> A sudden agitation in the long red-grass brought her eyes back to the foreground. Bother! There was little Hobbit bounding towards her with that

same joyful trusting expression her own Hobbit had had. If only he had gone on sleeping until she was out of sight.

    She knelt down and put her arms around his neck and hugged him. "You can't come with me," she told him. "They'll only kill you, the way they killed my Hobbit. They don't understand, you see. They think that because you're ugly you must be dangerous. They're afraid of you."

Excerpt from *The Keeper of the Isis Light* (Hughes, 2000), p. 160.

QUESTIONS FOR STUDENTS TO CONSIDER

1. How does the little Hobbit symbolize Olwen herself?

2. Is what Olwen says to the little Hobbit true? Why or why not?

3. What advice would you give Olwen about who she is?

4. What advice would you give the settlers on how to treat the Hobbit and Olwen?

Throughout the reading of this text, students can ponder questions of gender and oppression, either as individual concepts or in combination. The following exchange took place among a literature circle discussion of eighth graders, who began to discuss the issue of gender in connection to the treatment of Olwen and the issue of author intent.

Charlene:	I gotta ask, did you ever think about how Olwen acted when she first saw herself in the mirror?
Lisette:	Yeah, I would have been freaked out. I mean, she looks like a lizard or something.
Dani:	Then she talks about how beautiful she is.
Brock:	But what I don't understand is how she didn't know what she looked like. She saw the other people there. Didn't she ever wonder about why she had to wear that suit?
Joseph:	The Guardian told her it was to protect herself. Geez, then she goes and finds out that she's ugly to those people.
Charlene:	And scary. And Mark fell off the cliff away from her.
Brock:	I would have flipped out, too.
Dani:	I wonder about if she had been a guy. Do you think some girl would have fallen in love with him?
Lisette:	Do you think he would have worn a suit so people couldn't see him?

Hector:	Yeah, would the Guardian made him wear the suit, or would he just let him go and greet the people like he was?
Joseph:	I bet he would have gone like he was.
Lisette:	Girls probably do care about their looks more.
Dani:	It is just that. Girls are expected to care more about their looks. We always wear makeup and check it in the mirrors between classes. Boys never do that.
Brock:	We don't have to!
Charlene:	So, the author made it like us. How we already are.
Lisette:	Yeah, so it is kinda real even if it is science fiction.

In addition to their comments about gender and gendered behavior, these students also wondered whether the settlers would have killed Olwen if she had been male. Other issues they covered addressed the gender of the protagonist, the gender of the author, and how these factors affect the plot and the way the book is written. We concluded the discussion by asking students about Olwen's response to the settler's treatment of her and why the author ended the book that way. Many of the students asked about a sequel because they wanted to know what happens, which we believe is an extremely positive response.

As a culminating activity, we asked the eighth-grade students to write a short essay focusing on three elements: (1) the genre of science fiction and the stereotype that it is a genre for boys, (2) their own ideas of science fiction and how the book may or may not have changed their minds about this genre, and (3) the relevance of science fiction to oppression today. From this type of essay, we typically discover that students find science fiction a reflection of reality, an aspect of the genre of which they often need to be convinced. We also see that it is a powerful way to look at gender issues and reading.

We would like to note, however, the gendered way in which these students read and discussed the book. They did not challenge each other on the belief that boys do not have to worry about their looks, a reality that indeed exists and plagues many young men who are not as muscular or as attractive as they think they should be. The boys remarked that they did not like this book as much as some of the others they had read because it was not as violent as they had hoped; the love story, while all right, seemed to the students to be something a female author would write about whereas a male author would not.

We also noticed students' avoidance of particular questions that asked them to think about how they would treat someone in their school who looked quite different from the rest of the student body or whether or not a man could write a love story in the same way as a woman. Some gendered questions were simply ignored as the students discussed the questions of their feelings about the book overall. The following issues should be addressed: what makes some questions more difficult to answer than others, how the delivery of a question in tone and body language might affect the students' reception of certain questions, and how the ethos of the questioner comes into play during literature circles. Students can address these issues with each other, individually, or as part of a whole-class lesson.

Finally, students also can address the connection of oppression to language and how language is used in young adult novels.

Examining the Language of Oppression in Young Adult Novels

As part of the exploration of *The Keeper of the Isis Light*, we also suggest that students examine the way the author uses language and ask themselves about "gendered" language and actions, and how language and plot relate to oppression. We often are surprised by how middle-level students can talk about language usage and gender, regardless of the plot and the characters highlighted. For instance, one literature circle of eighth graders commented on the use of the word *alien* in *The Keeper of the Isis Light* and how the word also is used to describe immigrants who are not citizens. In terms of gender, one student mentioned, "it's just the things the author seems to concentrate on that makes you know it's about girls or boys." The words particular authors use tell students of the gendered identity and language of the characters within a story. Holly also worked with a group of seventh graders on one story that was written by a male author and found that even when the characters were involved in what might be considered more female activities, the students said they thought the author was male because of the way the activities were described.

Although we begin by using science fiction, we want students to realize that representation is a key element of oppression in the novels they read as well as in the "literature" across billboards, newspapers, magazines, and other print and nonprint media. Thus, after they have completed their essays about *The Keeper of the Isis Light*, we continue our investigation of oppression by returning to the present world, reminding students that it is not just in science fiction and improbable situations that issues of oppression will occur. To help them understand that oppression is embedded in their everyday lives and current situations, we return to excerpts from realistic fiction to help them see how frequently oppressive events occur and how easy it is to overlook them.

When we think about oppression, we find that it is most apparent through language. Literature has been used as a tool of domination and oppression since human beings began to tell stories. When we explore oppression in literature with middle-level students, we find passages that show our students how language can be used to oppress others—to marginalize them, to render them powerless, and to dominate them. The following excerpt from *Jericho Walls* (Collier, 2002) shows two characters using language to oppress each other. The narrator arrives to float down the river with her friend Lucas and his dog Moses. The pair hopes to avoid members of the community because they have to hide their interracial friendship.

Lucas and Moses were waiting when I got to the river. Lucas stood and brushed off his overalls. "Ready?" he asked.

I nodded. A lump of excitement welled in my chest. "Ready." I stowed my towel filled with provisions in the middle of the raft. It was a good-looking raft, I thought. Just the right size for Lucas and me and even Moses, if he sat down and didn't move too much.

"Let's go, then." Lucas licked his lips. I guess he was excited, too.

Lucas put Moses on the raft first, with a firm warning to lay down and not move. Lucas and I grabbed hold of the raft, then pushed it into the shallows of the river. We waited until it was floating and even, then climbed on. It wobbled, but Lucas and I steadied it with poles that we'd fashioned from branches. Soon we were in the middle of the river, floating away on the current.

"We're moving!" I hollered. Lucas gave a whoop. Moses barked.

Lucas and I looked at Moses in fear. "Sit, Moses," he commanded. Moses was our biggest concern. If he got to barking and jumping, he could tip us right over. Moses sat. Lucas and I grinned, then floated in silence. The raft seemed to want to spin, so Lucas and I had to pole to keep it straight.

We floated past the colored swimming hole, both sighing with relief that it was deserted this early in the day. I had been ready to jump overboard and swim underwater if we'd seen any people there. That was our last obstacle. Now we were home free.

"Reckon I'll be Huckleberry Finn and you can be Ole Jim," I said when we were sufficiently under way.

Lucas whirled around to look at me, causing the raft to wobble. "I won't!"

I looked at him in alarm. "Why not?"

"I aim to be Huckleberry."

"You can't be Huckleberry," I said, trying to talk reason. "You ain't white. You're colored, so you have to be Ole Jim."

"Well, you ain't a boy, and Huckleberry's a boy. So there." That remark stung.

"You shut up, Lucas! I say you gotta be Ole Jim."

"Well, I say I ain't! Simon says colored folks can be most anythin' they want."

"Can't be white," I muttered. I glared at Lucas, and he glared right back. I swear Lucas was the most stubborn person I'd ever laid eyes on. "You gotta be Jim!"

Pages 78–80 from *Jericho Walls* by Kristi Collier. Copyright © 2002 by Kristi Collier. Reprinted with permission of Henry Holt & Co., LLC.

QUESTIONS FOR STUDENTS TO CONSIDER

1. In what ways does the narrator marginalize and dominate Lucas?

2. What type of relationship do they have in this passage?

3. How can language be used to create problems in friendships?

4. In what ways can people of different races be friends when there are issues of oppression that exist between the races?

Middle-level students can be guided toward thinking about language and how it is used to oppress or empower people, either individually or as members of a particular group. We use Hinton's (1967) *The Outsiders* to show how an author can use language to represent a type of person in a positive or negative way, which can lead to marginalization or violent behavior toward members of that group solely on the basis of their group affiliation. We use the following excerpt when we talk about representation and the treatment of character types in literature because *The Outsiders* is such a powerful story about group affiliation and rivalry that can be oppressive. It is also a relevant and engaging story for middle-level students. In this excerpt (see story pp. 52–55 for a more detailed excerpt), Johnny and Pony Boy thought they had outrun the group of "Socs" that were following them. The Socs were angry because Johnny and Pony Boy had the audacity to talk to a couple of the girls the Socs dated. Johnny tells the Socs they "better watch it" because they are "outa their territory" when they entered Johnny's neighborhood. The Socs, however, decide to use the concept of territory differently.

"Nup, pal, yer the ones who'd better watch it. Next time you want a broad, pick up yer own kind—dirt."

I was getting mad. I was hating them enough to lose my head.

"You know what a greaser is?" Bob asked. "White trash with long hair."

I felt the blood draining from my face. I've been cussed out and sworn at, but nothing ever hit me like that did. Johnnycake made a kind of gasp and his eyes were smoldering.

"You know what a Soc is?" I said, my voice shaking with rage. "White trash with Mustangs and madras."

Excerpt from *The Outsiders* (Hinton, 1967), p. 55.

QUESTIONS FOR STUDENTS TO CONSIDER

1. How does the author use the characters to define each other?

2. In this passage, who are the "good" guys and who are the "bad" guys? Why?

3. In what ways does the author use language as an element of oppression?

With the study of the language used in a text, students come to understand how their use of language can be as oppressive as the examples they find in literature. Yet, it is not only language that teachers can address with their students but also the behaviors that may or may not accompany the words students can direct toward one another or others outside the classroom. Classroom behaviors are often more oppressive than the words students use toward one another, but frequently these behaviors are ignored or only discussed in a reactive rather than proactive manner.

Assessing Oppressive Behaviors in Classroom Literature Discussions

Through the use of literature and the situations they encounter within it, students can explore the negative effects of oppressive elements within communities, personal interactions, and government ideologies. Middle-level students also can address oppression by questioning the idea of literature as oppressive per se. Another way to study oppression is by examining the interactions that occur in the classroom and school community. Remembering that oppression consists of the five elements of exploitation, marginalization, powerlessness, cultural imperialism, and violence, students will be able to find evidence of such practices within their own school (see pages 115–116). Bullying is a form of oppression that is overt and is often perpetrated through violent actions.

It frequently happens "during school hours in areas where there is limited or no adult supervision" (Espelage, 2004, p. 6). As teachers we must constantly be aware of what is happening in our classrooms and encourage our students to openly discuss bullying behaviors in and out of the classroom. Bullying is oppression in any one of its forms: marginalization, violence, cultural imperialism, powerlessness, and exploitation. Not all bullying will employ all these types of oppression, but all can be a result of bullying. By building a trusting environment, we hope that students will feel free to disrupt the bullying they see when it is happening, or at least contact an adult in the school community to stop or prevent such behaviors. (See Marano, 1995, for more information about bullying.)

Bullying is only one of the issues that typifies oppression in classrooms and schools. Other oppressive behaviors can occur in classrooms during literary interactions. Three elements of classroom interactions that could be deemed oppressive if they are not discussed and understood by middle-level students include discourse styles, who talks and when, and literature circle dynamics.

Discourse Styles

As we mentioned in chapter 4, discourse style refers to the manner in which people speak, the language they use, the words they choose, and the grammatical patterns they follow. Other times discourse, often referred to with a capital *D* (Gee, 1996), is not only language but also other areas of representation such as clothing, activities, and behaviors. In middle-level classrooms, students can oppress one another through their discourse styles. Sometimes, students talk in ways that intimidate their peers—through word choice or mannerisms or tone of voice that accompany otherwise "harmless" words. Other times, the Discourse of one group of students can be intimidating to others because of social privileging that exists in the community. This could be considered a form of cultural imperialism, where certain Discourses are privileged over others. As teachers, we must be aware of the way students interact with one another, and disrupt oppressive actions so that all our students have the opportunity to learn.

Who Talks and When?

Another aspect of classroom interactions that teachers need to be aware of is turn-taking and who talks when. Although on the surface it might not appear oppressive when we have enthusiastic students who are willing to share in class, this situation can be intimidating to students who are not comfortable with speaking in class. These students then could be marginalized from classroom interactions.

Tannen (2001) suggests that males more often interrupt women in discussions than females and that they take more turns speaking in discussions than females. Classroom practices may encourage this pattern of behavior. Thus, we must be sure that our classrooms are not gender biased, with girls left to the margins of classroom discussions.

Literature Circle Dynamics

Some of the above behaviors are manifested within the classroom without forethought or an oppressive agenda. We believe that most of the time students are not thinking of oppressing others through their mannerisms or classroom behaviors, especially when discussing literature. There are times, however, when students' behaviors are explicitly about oppressing or dominating others. Talking about these issues allows students to become aware of how their behaviors may be oppressive to others.

When we use literature circles, we must be extra vigilant about these behaviors because they can be produced in small groups without our knowledge (Evans, 1996). We suggest that teachers move around the room as much as possible so that all groups are observed and held accountable for the social interactions that occur between members.

Students can use their power to silence others or to demean them, and thus oppressive factors are at work within the classroom even during legitimate activities condoned or encouraged in school. By observing how the interactions progress in literature circles, teachers take a small step toward understanding oppression because learning to recognize these behaviors will help students overcome them.

Oppressive Literature?

When reading literature with middle-level students, we consider not only what pieces of literature they will read but also how they might read them. In reality, any book could be thought of as oppressive, and thus it becomes crucial that teachers know not only that there are all types of literature available to use in the classroom but also how to select appropriate materials to use with particular groups of students. When selecting literature, teachers might consider the developmental and literacy levels of their students along with their interests and prior knowledge of the topic under study.

Teachers might also want to gauge their students' social identities in relation to the topic. Depending on the stance of the reader, a book that we might consider "safe" or "harmless" could be quite damaging. This dilemma pushes us to know students, their life experiences, and their living conditions. We talk with students and their parents about the contents of a book that might be considered problematic before we use it as a read-aloud or whole-class text. We also have spoken with particular students and their parents about texts that could make them feel alienated because of the way texts use language about their cultural group. Table 16 lists some of the issues we consider as we select books for use with students.

When considering a particular piece of fiction to use with students, we always ask ourselves about issues of power and oppression, representation and balance. We also consider the nature of our students and how we might best approach issues of social justice and cultural consciousness. We know that we may have to use different materials with particular groups because of their prior knowledge, their resistance, or their abilities to engage with the materials we choose. We do not, however, back away from these issues. Students have the right and the willingness to work through their own ideas of the world and how to make it a better place for all people.

As teachers, we have no control over students' transactions with literature, but we still find that through discussion and individual reflection, our students can come to terms with their biases and stereotypes. For instance, when Holly read and discussed *Make Lemonade* (Wolff, 1993), *Among Friends* (Cooney, 1988), *I Hadn't Meant to Tell You This*

TABLE 16

Issues to Consider When Selecting Texts
1. How are people from diverse cultural groups represented in the text?
2. What seems to be the author's message about members of a specific cultural or gender group?
3. When I use texts about a specific cultural group, is there diversity in the representation?
4. What would someone else—from another cultural group—think about this text?
5. Does this text balance my collection?
6. How does this text represent the time period involved?
7. How does this text represent the genre involved?
8. What prior knowledge would I have to teach before using this text?
9. What issues are highlighted in this text?
10. What is my purpose for using this book, and does this book adequately do the job?

(Woodson, 1994), and *Humming Whispers* (Johnson, 1995) with middle-level girls in grades 7 and 8, she found that their ideas of themselves and of others changed through dialogue about issues of race, class, and gender (Johnson, 2000). This change, however, does not happen without discussions focused on issues of oppression and power. It also helps when we select pieces of literature that address concrete situations of oppression or situations that the middle-level students with whom we work are familiar. Thus, the selection of literature in teaching about oppression is a delicate and deliberate endeavor.

Conclusion

When teachers are willing to discuss the issues of oppression and power with middle-level students, they create opportunities for change and for students to become more critically conscious. Not only can teachers change the dynamics of their classrooms but also they can make positive changes in individual students who either have been intimidated or used intimidation as a tool for their own privileging or power. Beyond the classroom, talking about oppression and power with middle-level students has the potential for changing the world they and we live in. Students whose knowledge includes understanding power and oppression and how they work will not be held captive to limiting ideas of the world. It is our hope that students will not use excessive power that can oppress others, but rather use their new understandings to create a more tolerant and just world. A more just and tolerant world, however, cannot exist without understanding that there is more than one way to look at the world. In chapter 6 we discuss the importance of multiple perspectives, from which students can learn about the variety of ways to live in and view the world.

"Vinny breathed deeply and looked up and out over the island....

He had never seen anything like it.

Had it always been there? This view of the island?

He stared and stared, then sat, taking it all in.

He's never seen anything so beautiful in all his life."

From *Island Boyz* (Salisbury, 2002, p. 19)

CHAPTER 7

Multiple Perspectives: Addressing and Understanding Differences

L
ike Vinny, who had lived in Hawaii his whole life but never really thought about the multiple ways in which the island could be seen, many people get accustomed to seeing the world from only one perspective. It is when they are given the chance to view their world from another standpoint that they have the opportunity to expand their understandings of the world and become more critical, and often more appreciative, thinkers. Teachers have the unique privilege of showing students that there are many ways to view the world—other filters through which to view the world and other perspectives that must be considered.

Each one of us has a filter through which we view the world and the people within it. We are socialized by our parents, the media, our schools, and our government to "see" in certain ways. Often, we do not question our filters because others around us are using the same filters and thus validate our perceptions. Yet, there are many times when the filters we use do not serve justice. Filters have a way of creating generalizations in people's ideas of the world. People use their filters to paint broad strokes that may cover the innuendos that also contain the various ways of being human and living in the world. By realizing that others may see the world differently, middle-level students can begin to understand that there are multiple ways of living and multiple ways to interpret behaviors and ideas.

Defining Perspective

By using texts that allow for different perspectives—different points of view—middle-level students can grow as readers and consumers of the world and its differences. When discussing multiple perspectives, we introduce or review literary point of view. This is especially helpful when students engage in cross-cultural communication or readings. Point of view refers to the narrative perspective—who is telling the story. Typically there are three common points of view:

- First Person: Story told through the "I" voice.
- Omniscient Third Person: Story told through the narrator who knows and sees everything.
- Limited Third Person: Story told through a narrator who has limited knowledge about other characters and their feelings or motives.

By first learning point of view, middle-level students learn that information depends on who is narrating the story. Thus, when we discuss issues of race and class—and who most often tells the stories in one culture or another—students can begin to see that what story is told and how it is told depend on the position of the storyteller, narrator, or author. Students also learn that the "truth" depends on the storyteller's perspective and even his or her value system.

When we use literature in class, we also want our students to question the perspective of the narrator and/or author and to examine that point of view. We want students to realize that stories can be read from another point of view other than the one given to them by the author or narrator. When readers read "against the grain," they attempt to understand another perspective, and they hold in abeyance the point of view privileged in the text. We want students to learn to read this way, regardless of what they read. We especially want students to do this, however, when they read cross culturally and when they explore issues of race and class in the literature they are assigned.

Discussing Perspective With Middle-Level Students

Most of us understand that when we agree with something, we typically do not question it or our ideas about it. For instance, when we are told that we need laws to guide our daily living—laws such as speed limits, having driver's licenses, or disallowing child labor—we do not question these legalities. There are times when we may not like these laws, but we understand that we need them for the common good. There are other times, however, when we hear about laws in other nations that we do not understand. We cannot comprehend why people would live that way or not rebel against that government. It is at these times of dissonance that we can explore the reality that there are multiple perspectives about living in the world and the laws people follow.

Middle-level students also can become conscious of multiple perspectives, whether it is a law or just a common practice that may not make sense to them. By addressing how a situation or idea can be viewed from different perspectives, and how perspectives are frequently based on value systems, students can begin to wrestle with the diversity of the world. They also can critique their own thinking in relation to this diversity. Learning to realize that our thinking is just one way of looking at a story, situation, or culture allows us to view the world with a depth that often might be missing when we attempt to understand others in the world.

A number of books written for young adolescents are written from more than one perspective. By reading such novels, students can begin to understand how each person's telling could be a type of truth, which creates a more whole picture of the situation. Often we notice details that others may not, and so when each of us can tell our part of the story, a bigger picture is painted that deepens everyone's understanding of what happened. There are five texts we find especially suitable for addressing the concept of multiple perspectives. One book that we use is the young adult classic *The Pigman* (Zindel, 1968), a story told in the alternating viewpoints of the two main characters—John and Lorraine. They befriend a lonely old man, Mr. Pignati, when they make prank phone calls to him. Readers discover that while the story is generally the same according to the two characters, the characters do have differing ideas about some of the details. We also use *Flipped* (Van Draanen, 2001), the story of two young people growing up across the street from each other. Their differing perspectives about their relationship from year to year are made explicit through alternating chapters told from one character then the other. Through their reflections about one another, they begin to appreciate or understand one another better. Another text we use to address multiple perspectives is *Nothing But the Truth* (Avi, 1991), a story about following school rules and the perceptions of a school and community that get out of hand once the media gets the story that students supposedly cannot sing the national anthem. In addition, *The Wanderer* (Creech, 2000), a Newbery Honor–winning book, is about Sophie, a young girl who sails with her family from New England to the United Kingdom for a reunion with her grandfather. Again, chapters alternate voices and clarify the relationship Sophie has with the rest of her family—accounts that are drastically different from one another. Finally, we use *Seedfolks* (Fleischman, 1997), which is told in a variety of voices and presents a diverse neighborhood, its community garden project, and the individuals who grow toward tolerance through their communal endeavor.

Before reading these texts, however, we use the following excerpts to introduce middle-level students to how one situation can be seen through different perspectives. The first excerpt is from *Heartbeat* (Creech, 2004; see story pp. 77–81 for a more detailed excerpt). Annie, the main character, has been given an assignment in her art class to draw the same object 30 times. In wondering how to do this, she realizes that the same object can be looked at from a number of perspectives.

PERSPECTIVE

Apples, apples, apples
thirty drawings of one apple.

The first ten looked pretty much alike
which was starting to bother me

and then one day when I was
out running
I glanced at budding branches overhead
and was thinking about spring
and the coming of the new leaves
and how I usually see the undersides of leaves
and I would have to climb trees
to see the leaves from the top

and I thought about my apple.

I could draw it from the top
looking down on it
and from underneath
looking up at it.
I could put it on its side!

Excerpt from *Heartbeat* (Creech, 2004), pp. 77–78.

QUESTIONS FOR STUDENTS TO CONSIDER

1. How would you now define *perspective*?

2. How did this excerpt help you understand perspective?

3. What similar situations have you had with differing perspectives?

Through this excerpt, students have made connections to their own experiences. For instance, one seventh grader explained that the passage helped her understand that "anything could be looked at in different ways, if we wanted to." And learning to want to is the attitude teachers can help instill in their students.

The second excerpt is from *Kezzie* (Breslin, 1993). In this scene, Kezzie is staying with the McMaths during her search for her sister, Lucy, who was shipped from an orphanage in the United Kingdom to Canada.

> One day Kezzie was helping Mrs. McMath put the winter quilts on the bed. They were in the small attic room where Jack slept, when on turning the mattress they discovered a vast quantity of food crushed under the bed. Most of it was rotten or had mould growing on it. Mrs. McMath sat down heavily in a small chair.
> "Lord, Lord" she said. "What does that tell you, Kezzie?" she asked.
> "That he is a thief," said Kezzie reluctantly.
> The older woman shook her head. "It tells me that at some time he has starved."

Excerpt From *Kezzie* (Breslin, 1993), p. 231.

QUESTIONS FOR STUDENTS TO CONSIDER

1. How does this connect to your idea of multiple perspectives?

2. In what ways have you experienced a situation similar to this?

3. Why do you think people make such judgments about others?

This excerpt causes middle-level students to rethink their initial ideas about incidents in their own lives. They ponder when they have reacted to a situation before they completely understood the circumstances or when they have misspoken in response to a comment before they understood the speaker's intent. When asked by their teachers to connect to these passages with experiences from their own lives, middle-level students have their own stories to tell.

Examining Perspective in Connection to Culture

The concept of culture can be difficult to discuss with middle-level students, not only because they are sensitive issues for many people but also because figuring out what we mean when we talk about specific issues such as race and class can be complex. Often middle-level students have prior knowledge that gives them an idea of what is meant when the terms *race* and *class* are used, but we like to explore these definitions with students when we start to read about these issues in literature that addresses the concepts of culture, racism, and class differentiation.

Often, culture and ethnicity are used as parallel terms to race, but these are three distinct concepts. *Culture* refers to patterns of behavior, thought, tradition, or values that can cross racial categories. *Ethnicity* is often geographical and connected to family heritage, which also crosses racial categories. *Race* is a social construction or category often based on physical attributes such as skin color, hair texture, and facial features. Race is an artificial distinction between people based on physical features, and historically, negative actions and behaviors have accompanied distinctions between races, such as segregation, separation, or different treatment (Howard, 1999; Wardle & Cruz-Jansen, 2004). Throughout the chapter, however, we often use the terms together, but any discussion of race or ethnicity or culture in connection to literature could be expanded to include all concepts.

Class refers to social standing, socioeconomic status, or privileged ways of being in the world. Often discussed in terms of upper, middle, or lower class, the concept of class also can include educational levels, language usage, behavior, and so forth. In many Western nations, it is assumed that people can change their class distinctions. Often, gradations of treatment accompany class distinctions, with upper classes being treated as dominant over lower classes.

Based on these definitions, we understand why teachers might have questions about why they would want to address issues of culture, and specifically race and social class, with middle-level students if such categories are superficial or artificial. Although racial and class differences might be considered arbitrary or socially constructed, they are still very real. People make life decisions about how to treat people, what to believe about certain groups, and what attitudes to hold about those outside their own racial, class, or cultural groups. Students need to understand race and class, and they need to understand the arbitrary nature of these distinctions. Teachers can highlight, through young adult literature, how these artificial distinctions are made real in students' everyday lives.

As students realize that each person has a filter—their perspective through which they view the world—they readily allow that each person's filter is a valid way of viewing the world. Validity does not need to mean right or best or even understandable, but rather respectable because each individual is unique and a member of the human race. With this sense of validity it is a small step to the reality that there will necessarily be multiple perspectives on any one situation, person, or event. It is then another step to examining how perspective is connected to backgrounds, identities, cultures.

> Race is a social construction or category often based on physical attributes such as skin color, hair texture, and facial features.

> Class refers to social standing, socioeconomic status, or privileged ways of being in the world.

Examining Cross-Cultural Engagement and Critical Consciousness

Based on our experiences as teachers, students typically want to believe that life is fair and that people generally work and are able to live on what they earn. They also believe that people who may not have the same luxuries as others lack these things because of less work and effort. There are some students, however, who come from situations where they see their parents working and yet they still do not have the latest CD or sneakers that their peers have. When these different livelihoods interact, there can be conflict or anger because students do not understand one another's lives, perspectives, or frustrations. When we talk with students in an open discussion about issues of race and class, they all make assumptions about each other or others in the world who are not like them either ethnically, racially, or in terms of socioeconomics. By addressing some of the assumptions, as well as the realities, that students bring to the classroom, students can begin to understand one another and learn to communicate more openly about social justice, inequities, and diversity in more critically conscious ways.

Teachers must first, however, get students to a place where they are able to recognize how intercultural communication can be problematic because of the different values the speakers may hold. By using the following excerpt, we are able to broach the topic of intercultural communication and how people may think they are talking from the same perspective, when they really are not. The excerpt from *Where We Once Belonged* (Fiegel, 1996; see story pp. 135–136 for a more detailed excerpt) highlights intercultural engagement between an American Peace Corps volunteer and a student from Samoa. The volunteer came to teach and wanted the students to write an essay about one of three topics. The essay prompt that each student avoided was titled "What I saw on my way to school." The excerpt reveals that in Samoa, the singular possessive of "I" is used infrequently at best. In the United States, the first person possessive is used often and the thinking behind the collective "we" of Samoa would be difficult for many students to understand. Yet the differences between countries and cultures are something students can more readily understand; it is the differences between those of us in the same community, city, or country that seem especially complex to students because they come to expect that if we all live in the same place, we must all think alike.

WE

You were *always* with someone. I didn't go to school alone. I went to school with Moa and five, maybe even ten, other girls at the same time. We all woke up when the sun woke up...rolled our sleeping mats...washed our faces...put on our school uniforms...ran to the store to buy bread...made tea...drank tea.... We all took the same road to school...rode the same bus.... Nothing was witnessed alone. Nothing was witnessed in the 'I' form....

'I' does not exist, Miss Cunningham. 'I' is 'we'...*always*.

Excerpt from *Where We Once Belonged* (Fiegel, 1996), pp. 135–136.

QUESTIONS FOR STUDENTS TO CONSIDER

1. What is the problem in this situation?
2. Why does the author italicize the word *always* in this passage?
3. What assumptions did the narrator and the teacher make about the understanding of the other?
4. How could this misunderstanding be cleared up?
5. Who should clear up the understanding and why?

When we ask students to think about this excerpt, they are incredulous that the characters in the novel would not think of themselves in the singular. The middle-level students we have worked with use the "I" pronoun so often that they are unaware of it, so we also ask them to try not to use that pronoun for one day. They have great difficulty with this activity, but laugh about it when they say they tried to use "we" instead. Students also express their dissonance with the group mentality that comes from the "we" pronoun, but once we explain that it is just another way of viewing the world, they want to discuss why that view would be held by a group of people. Teachers can have interesting discussions about economics, history, and philosophy if they wish to extend students' thinking about this excerpt.

The intercultural situation in *Cuba 15* (Osa, 2003; see story pp. 44–47 for a more detailed excerpt) can be used to address issues of language, intracultural understandings, and the differences between ages, generations, and traditions of one family. In this excerpt, Violet Paz is considering a quinceañera, a traditional coming-of-age party, to celebrate her 15th birthday. Violet must find out what a quinceañera is, what it means, and how it connects her to her cultural traditions. When Violet brings up her quinceañera to her parents, they resort to speaking in Spanish. Violet becomes angry and runs to her room.

I had finally blown up over something that had been boiling inside me for as long as I could remember. Mom and Dad had always used their shared language to discuss whatever they didn't want me and Mark to hear....

Spanish was currency. Currency I didn't have.

"That must be how it sounds to a dog," I said to Chucho, who was snoring now. I thought of a comic strip I once saw about what dogs really hear when you talk to them: "Blah blah blah, Ginger, blah blah."

I had known there wouldn't be any easy answers.

Excerpt from *Cuba 15* (Osa, 2003), p. 44.

QUESTIONS FOR STUDENTS TO CONSIDER

1. What does Violet mean when she says "Spanish was currency"?

2. In what ways does language separate people? Why is that separation difficult to overcome?

3. Why does communicating with your parents or even your grandparents seem difficult sometimes?

Teachers and students also need to discuss intercultural communication or engagement in situations where people from different socioeconomic classes are involved. The following excerpt from *Esperanza Rising* (Ryan, 2000; see story pp. 116–120 for a more detailed excerpt) shows how differences in class situations can cause frustration, anger, sadness, or misunderstanding. Esperanza's situation changes dramatically when her family moves to the United States during the Great Depression. As a young girl in Mexico, she had known only wealth; she was taken care of by servants. In the United States, however, she becomes a servant. In this scene, Esperanza tries to sweep the floor of the cabin where she is living, but she does not know how. As she tries to sweep, the other migrant workers start to laugh at her and they call her "Cinderella." She is humiliated and attempts to explain the situation to another migrant worker, Isabel.

Esperanza sat on the mattress and patted the spot next to her. Isabel sat down.

"Isabel, I will tell you all about how I used to live. About parties and private school and beautiful dresses. I will even show you the beautiful doll my papa bought me, if you will teach me how to pin diapers, how to wash, and..."

Isabel interrupted her. "But that is so easy!"

Esperanza stood up and carefully practiced with the broom. "It is not easy for me."

Excerpt from *Esperanza Rising* (Ryan, 2000), p. 119.

QUESTIONS FOR STUDENTS TO CONSIDER

1. How would you feel if you were Esperanza?

2. What would you do if you found yourself in a situation where people laughed at you?

3. How are class differences apparent in your community?

4. Why do people treat others differently because of their working or class situation?

In the next excerpt from *The Last Book in the Universe* (Philbrick, 2002; see story pp. 202–204 for a more detailed excerpt), again people are separated by class, abilities, or tribal allegiances. This futuristic novel portrays life after a horrific disaster. In this scene, Lanaya, a young girl who is a "proov," which means that she has access to technology that can prevent her from being sick or genetically inferior, lives in Eden, a garden-like community outside the destroyed "Urb" or inner city. On one of her travels to the city to help those considered "normals" by the people of Eden, she meets a young man who is trying to get the medicine he needs to cure his sister's leukemia. She brings the boy and his sister back to Eden, where the sister is cured, but then the people of Eden find out about the situation. Lanaya tries to persuade the people of Eden that they should help those in the Urb.

> "As you can see, she was easily cured by our technology. We have the means to cure almost all of the diseases that plague the Urb, and yet we don't bother trying! We let them sicken and die. We let them starve; we let their latches burn. Is that right? Is that proper? I say no! I say we must remember that the people we call 'normal' are not so different from ourselves!"
>
> Heckling comes from the crowd on the hill. Lanaya has gone too far. "Look at them!" someone cries. "They're ugly! They're hideous! They're stupid! They're *normal*!"

Excerpt from *Last Book in the Universe* (Philbrick, 2002), p. 204.

QUESTIONS FOR STUDENTS TO CONSIDER

1. Why does Lanaya have to make this type of statement?

2. In what ways are Lanaya's and those outside Eden's lives alike? In what ways are they different?

3. Why is socioeconomic status such a barrier for people?

We use this excerpt to point out to students that multiple perspectives or ways of looking at the world, as well as the problems that can result of these differing perspectives, occur in all genres of literature, not just realistic or historical fiction. Other books we use to discuss class distinctions are *Make Lemonade* (Wolff, 1993), *Silver* (Mazer, 1991), *The Pictures of Hollis Woods* (Giff, 2002), *Kezzie* (Breslin, 1993), and *Trino's Time* (Bertrand, 2001). These texts address the issue of class in ways that allow middle-level students to understand how the treatment of students from lower socioeconomic circumstances can be blatant or subtle, but still damaging to students' self-esteem.

The next excerpt is a good way to transition to a discussion of social class in connection to peer treatment at school. Middle-level students understand social standing in relation to their peers, and this excerpt creates a nice bridge to the concept of social class and how students may treat each other because of socioeconomics. In this scene from *Stand Tall* (Bauer, 2002), Sophie is responding to the treatment she has gotten from a group of girls at her new school. She approaches the girls in the lunchroom and makes the following declaration.

"I'm not here to make trouble. I just want to know how come, ever since I showed up at this school, you look at me like I fell off a garbage truck."

A gasp rose from the popular girls assembled as Amber, their leader, looked at all of them like she *couldn't* believe this...

Sophie gripped her tray. "I just want to get one thing clear. You're not better than me. I'm not crawling with bugs or have green slime running down my neck. I'm a person just like you."

Excerpt from *Stand Tall* (Bauer, 2002), p. 50.

QUESTIONS FOR STUDENTS TO CONSIDER

1. Why aren't students as honest as Sophie?

2. Why do you think Sophie said this?

3. Have you ever felt the way Sophie does? When? What did you do about it?

Learning to confront their own weaknesses in relation to their peers and the just or unjust ways they treat their classmates can be a difficult endeavor for middle-level students. Most of us do not look at ourselves from the perspective of those whom we hurt or have treated unfairly or stereotypically. Few students have had encounters where the injured, as in the case with Sophie and the popular girls at her middle school, refuse to go away, and thus students have been allowed to remain unconscious of their treatment toward others. If students are confronted more frequently with their mistreatment of others, however, they might be more mindful of how "others" are treated by the dominant mainstream. Students can become more critically conscious of their own shortcomings in terms of opportunity, access, and equity. Students have the opportunity to become more aware of how damaging such treatment can be, to learn such lessons through the use of literature that asks them to look at "othering" those who are different, which is the creation of a situation where a person feels that he or she is not part of the group but rather is outside it.

One last way we talk to students about cross-cultural interactions is by looking at race and how people from different racial identities, backgrounds, or perspectives may come to a discussion differently than their white peers. The following two excerpts open a dialogue with middle-level students about different racial identities and the cultural perspectives that are a part of those identities. The first excerpt from *Maniac Magee* (Spinelli, 1990; see story pp. 158–159 for a more detailed excerpt) highlights how race can play a part in a communicative act. In this scene, Maniac brings Mars Bar, a kid from the neighborhood across the highway, to a party given by the McNab boys. The McNab boys are racist and Mars Bar, who does not take any foolishness from white people, is considered to be "the blackest of the black." The two "breeze into" the party before anyone can say anything, which was Maniac's goal because he realized how little the people from each neighborhood knew about each other.

> Thinking of the McNabs' wrong-headed notions. Thinking of Mars Bar's knee-jerk reaction to anyone wearing a white skin. And thinking: *Naturally. What else would you expect? Whites never go inside blacks' homes. Much less inside their thoughts and feelings. And blacks are just as ignorant as whites. What white kid could hate blacks after spending five minutes in the Beales' house? And what black kid could hate whites after answering Mrs. Pickwell's dinner whistle?* But the East Enders stayed in the east and the West Enders stayed in the west, and the less they knew about each other, the more they invented.

Excerpt from *Maniac Magee* (Spinelli, 1990), pp. 158–159.

QUESTIONS FOR STUDENTS TO CONSIDER

1. In what ways besides words are attitudes and feelings communicated in this excerpt?

2. What is Maniac Magee communicating between races in this excerpt?

3. What two messages are communicated in this excerpt?

4. How can the use of one simple question such as "What's he (or she) doing here?" cause anger, mistrust, and racial tension?

The second excerpt from *If You Come Softly* (Woodson, 1998; see story pp. 134–136 for a more detailed excerpt) creates a venue for students to think about racial identities and cultural understandings, and how knowing themselves culturally can bring about a difference in the way they live and act with those who may not have the same ideas they do. In this scene, Miah, a high school junior, is talking with his father, who brings up the difference between black people and white people.

"Thing about white people," his father was saying…. "They don't know they're white. They know what everybody else is, but they don't know *they're* white." He shook his head and checked his rearview mirror. "It's strange…."

"Maybe some of them know."

His father eyed him and smiled. "When they walk into a party and everyone's black, they know it. Or when they get caught in Harlem after nightfall, they know it. But otherwise…

Excerpt from *If You Come Softly* (Woodson, 1998), pp. 134–135.

QUESTIONS FOR STUDENTS TO CONSIDER

1. What does this excerpt mean to you?

2. How can this excerpt be interpreted from someone outside Jeremiah's racial group?

3. In what ways is this excerpt valid, and in what ways is it not accurate?

There are many ways to look at intercultural communication—across educational levels, language, race, class, gender, age—and middle-level students can understand these issues once they are shown how cultural differences can affect a conversation or discussion. Books such as *Dakota Dream* (Bennett, 1994), *Maata's Journal* (Sullivan, 2003), and the short text *The Gold-Threaded Dress* (Marsden, 2002) address the various issues students face when attempting to fit in or interact across cultural lines. Another text we use to discuss such issues while also engaging students in the narrative poetry format is *Foreign Exchange: A Mystery in Poems* (Glenn, 1999). Using texts such as these with middle-level students allows teachers to work through the issues in sensitive ways that can invite students to reflect on their thinking and the ways they might change their behaviors in similar situations.

Picture books also can be used in conjunction with literature units to explore issues of race and class within the larger concept of social justice. Table 17 lists the picture books we use with middle-level readers when discussing multiple perspectives and the concept of social justice. By using these short texts, teachers can help their students begin to

TABLE 17

Picture Books Used for Discussing Social Justice

Altman, L. (1995). *Amelia's road*. New York: Lee & Low.
Bishop, G. (1999). *The house that Jack built*. Auckland, New Zealand: Scholastic.
Bradby, M. (1995). *More than anything else*. New York: Orchard Books.
Bunting, E. (1989). *The Wednesday surprise*. New York: Clarion Books.
Bunting, E. (1993). *Fly away home*. New York: Clarion Books.
Bunting, E. (1994). *A day's work*. New York: Clarion Books.
Bunting, E. (1999). *Smoky night*. New York: Voyager Books.
Clark, T. (1992). *The house that crack built*. San Francisco: Chronicle.
Conrad, P. (1996). *The rooster's gift*. New York: HarperCollins.
Daly, N. (2003). *Once upon a time*. New York: Farrar Straus Giroux.
Gregorowski, C. (2000). *Fly, eagle, fly!* New York: Margaret K. McElderry.
Jiménez, F. (2001). *La mariposa*. Boston: Houghton Mifflin.
Lacapa, K., & Lacapa, M. (1994). *Less than half, more than whole*. Flagstaff, AZ: Northland.
Lionni, L. (1967). *Frederick*. New York: Knopf.
Littlesugar, A. (2001). *Freedom school, yes!* New York: Philomel.
Lorbiecki, M. (1996). *Just one flick of a finger*. New York: Dial Books.
Lorbiecki, M. (2000). *Sister Anne's hands*. New York: Puffin.
Madrigal, A. (2001). *Erandi's braids*. New York: Penguin Putnam.
McGovern, A. (1997). *The lady in the box*. New York: Turtle Books.
Morrison, T., & Morrison, S. (2002). *The big box*. New York: Hyperion/Jump at the Sun Books.
Rahaman, V. (1997). *Read for me, Mama!* Honesdale, PA: Boyds Mills Press.
Raschka, C. (1998). *Yo! Yes!* New York: Orchard Books.
Stanek, M. (1989). *I speak English for my mom*. New York: Albert Whitman & Co.
Turner, A. (1998). *Drummer boy: Marching to the Civil War*. New York: HarperCollins.
Waddell, M. (1991). *Farmer Duck*. Cambridge, MA: Candlewick.
Wiles, D. (2001). *Freedom summer*. New York: Simon & Schuster.
Williams, V. (1982). *A chair for my mother*. New York: Greenwillow.
Woodson, J. (2001). *The other side*. New York: Penguin Putnam.
Woodson, J. (2002). *Visiting day*. New York: Scholastic.
Yolen, J. (1992). *Encounter*. San Diego: Harcourt.

name justice and examine the complexity of the conflicts that revolve around discriminatory acts based on race, class, and gender. Other texts in this list present the consequences of discriminatory acts that may not be directly named as racist or sexist, but which can be identified by students as they contextualize the situations or juxtapose what they believe to be true with what may be reality.

When teaching a unit on social justice and the varying perspectives through which it can be viewed (see chapter 1), we also use novels such *Belle Teal* (Martin, 2001), *The Jumping Tree* (Saldana, 2002), *Roll of Thunder, Hear My Cry* (Taylor, 1976), *Any Small Goodness: A Novel of the Barrio* (Johnston, 2003), *Stargirl* (Spinelli, 2002), and *The Giver* (Lowry, 2002). (See Appendix A for a more detailed description of the social justice unit we created.)

Exploring Different Perspectives Through Young Adult Literature

Aspects of social justice that are particularly salient for classroom teachers at the middle level involve some of the issues we have already discussed in this book, such as who participates and how. The subtle and not so subtle discriminatory acts that allow some students to dominate while relegating other students to silence are an aspect of social justice that teachers need to consider. As students and teachers marginalize particular students based on language, gender, race, or economic disadvantage, the equal opportunities of education are rendered moot. The loss of opportunity is often the precursor to the loss of voice and the loss of self, which creates conditions that produce injustice and oppression. When students ponder these issues and use their own life experiences as stepping stones toward understanding the political conditions and conditions of power under which they live and learn, they develop their critical consciousness (Freire, 1973/2000).

One of the most powerful lessons we can teach middle-level students is the importance of understanding and exploring situations, events, language usage, behaviors, and value systems from different perspectives. We begin with reader response theory (see chapter 4), which we use to scaffold their learning toward understanding culturally situated response theory. We use literature to scaffold students' learning of different perspectives because literature gives them the distance to reflect upon their own thinking. Through the use of literature in which young protagonists wrestle with the same issues and concerns as students do, teachers can help their students become more aware of the diverse world in which they live and more conscious of the ways they can interact within it.

Using Culturally Situated Response Theory

As we discussed in chapter 2, culturally situated response theory asks readers to examine their responses to literature through a cultural lens. This theory also addresses how written works are artifacts of a particular social, historical, or cultural situation, and thus can be explored through a lens that addresses these considerations. The questions readers might ask when reflecting upon or interpreting literature via this theory would include the following:

- What does it mean to be an insider or an outsider of a culture?

- What do readers miss in the literature from other cultures when they are outsiders to that culture?

- Can readers fully engage in pieces of literature when they are outside the culture depicted in the texts?

- Are we really insiders of the literature we read that supposedly represents our culture?

- How should we read literature from outside our cultural experience?

These general questions provoke other questions about culture itself, about cultures being stagnant, and about the universal experience of being human. Generally, culture can be viewed as patterns of thought, values, ideas, beliefs, and assumptions a particular society or group holds. Easier to see in other societies, individuals, or groups, the cultural mores we hold are more difficult to see in ourselves. We hold our cultural assumptions as the norm because they are a part of everything we do and are in our ideas of what is common sense or common practice.

Students must question more than the meaning of culture, cultural stagnation, and their own cultural backgrounds. They also must question the idea that any one novel could represent an entire cultural experience, and why as readers, they might think this way. Do readers perceive texts to be representative of cultures, and if so, in what ways? How can readers avoid such generalizations? The literature teachers can use to get students to ask and answer these types of questions is typically identified as multicultural literature.

What is multicultural literature? Defining this term for middle-level students requires that we make decisions about what multicultural literature is using wider parameters than most literary theorists.

> Culture can be viewed as patterns of thought, values, ideas, beliefs, and assumptions a particular society or group holds.

In the broadest sense, multicultural literature could include every book because every book comes from the point of view of a culture and every book can be read from multiple points of view based on gender, socioeconomic class, ethnicity, and so on.... In the interest of diversity and equity...[it] is literature about and/or by historically underrepresented groups, whose faces and stories and histories are missing from much of our literature. (Mitchell, 2003, p. 200)

By asking students to accept the idea that all literature is multicultural, we create an opportunity for them to see themselves as cultural beings—whiteness or European American heritages cannot be invisible or used as reference points for "other" cultures or racial and ethnic locations. Literature written from any cultural, racial, or social perspective parallel to literature written from any other perspective can be considered multicultural literature. Once students understand that any piece of literature can be seen as a cultural artifact, they can begin to see how they are located as cultural beings and as readers who come from a cultural perspective. This ability to locate themselves as readers with differing cultural perspectives helps middle-level students better understand and utilize culturally situated response theory.

Reading *Monster* With Middle-Level Learners

Reading *Monster* (Myers, 1999) with young adolescents is an amazing experience to have because using it to explore and utilize culturally situated response theory is an adventure that middle-level students enjoy and wrestle with. We use *Monster* with seven- and eighth-grade students for a number of reasons. First, the story line of the text is complex in relation to our reading audience. We have worked with a predominantly white student body in our careers as teachers, but we also have worked with Mexican and African American students. Most of our students would agree that the protagonist's experience in *Monster* is not their own. Steve, the main character, is accused of murder and is telling his story from the time he is placed in jail until his trial. Most of the students with whom we have worked have not had this experience, but students of color can relate to the racial stereotypes and thinking addressed in this text. White students also can confront their stereotypes about black males, and all students can ponder their own cultural situations in response to this text.

Second, when first using culturally situated response with middle-level students, we find that using a piece of literature that presents a more common racial or ethnically situated positioning expedites their understandings of the theory because we can then ask them about the validity of the characters' perceptions in relation to students' own racial or ethnic backgrounds. In *Monster*, the author places Steve, the protagonist, in the position of being a black youth accused of murder and explores how that looks to dominant white culture. Through this story, the author has his reading audience confront the stereotypes so often implicitly conveyed on television and in other media. Teachers especially can address issues of cultural bias in readers' perspectives through this text.

Third, we use *Monster* because middle-level students also must wrestle with the format of the text. We want students to learn how authors use text formats to convey their values and to advance the plot. Myers uses screen play adaptations to tell this story, making explicit what often happens when students read: They make movies in their heads. Steve, the main character in this book, is interested in filmmaking and is aware that the news is broadcast over the television and his story is making the news, thus to write his story as a film fits the media event that has become Steve's life. The screenplay style of Myers's text makes the story more accessible to students by making explicit what happens with the movie that is in readers' heads when they read.

As in chapter 6, we highlight particular scenes or passages to evoke students' responses, and then we ask students to think about those responses from their particular cultural perspectives or backgrounds. Because we introduce culturally situated response theory after students have accommodated reader response theories, they are able to respond more quickly than if they had not been familiar with responding to literature.

We begin by looking at the following excerpt from the beginning of *Monster* (see story pp. 1–5 for a more detailed excerpt). It brings readers directly into the action of the text, and it creates an opportunity for students to wrestle with their own feelings and assumptions based on their cultural identities, perspectives, or understandings.

The best time to cry is at night, when the lights are out and someone is being beaten up and screaming for help.... If anyone knows that you are crying, they'll start talking about it and soon it'll be your turn to get beaten up when the lights go out....

They say you get used to being in jail, but I don't see how....

Sometimes I feel like I have walked into the middle of a movie...about being alone when you are not really alone and about being scared all the time.

Excerpt from *Monster* (Myers, 1999), pp. 1–4.

QUESTIONS FOR STUDENTS TO CONSIDER

1. Could you find yourself in such a situation? Why or why not?

2. What type of person could end up in such a situation? Why do you think that?

3. What is it *about you* that makes it difficult or easy for you to relate to this situation?

We typically ask students to read silently in class, but because of the format of this text, there is the opportunity to invite the students to dramatize, so throughout the week we alternate dramatizing the story, reading aloud to students, and having students read silently to build their reading independence, confidence, and stamina.

The following excerpt highlights and allows teachers to apply culturally situated response theory without overemphasis on theory. Thus, neither the story nor our students are overwhelmed by the literary criticism; the emphasis is still on the reading event.

PETROCELLI
Mr. Bolden, have you ever been arrested?
BOLDEN
Yeah. For B&E, and possession with intent.
PETROCELLI
Possession is obviously drugs and the intent to distribute. Can you tell the jury what B&E means?
BOLDEN
B&E. Breaking and entering.
PETROCELLI
Can you name the person involved in the robbery?
BRIGGS
Objection! He can testify to the conversation—not the robbery, unless he was there.

Excerpt from *Monster* (Myers, 1999), pp. 47–49.

QUESTIONS FOR STUDENTS TO CONSIDER

1. What is the setting of this scene?

2. What helps you understand this scene?

3. What is it about your cultural background that helps you understand this scene?

4. Why would it be difficult for someone who didn't have a television to understand this scene?

5. How do you connect to this scene? What about your cultural background enables you to make that connection?

Other scenes in the text allow us to ponder the media and how it is a cultural influence. The media is used throughout this text, so we select particular scenes and ask students to think about some of the following questions:

- How are the television scenes similar to or different from what you know about the television news?
- What is considered "news" in this culture?
- How does the news reflect the cultural values of a society?
- From what you know about how crime, young people, and the way news works, what would you predict is going to happen next?
- What part of our culture influenced your prediction?

When reading *Monster* with middle-level students, we also explore the literary device of character. Steve, the main character, is complex, reflective, and dynamic. Other characters are much more static or stereotypical. Questions we ask about character include the following:

- Why is character so important to a society?
- How is character judged? Is the judgment always accurate? Why or why not?
- On what basis do people from other cultures judge each other?
- From the description of Steve throughout the text, what would you say about him? Could he still be guilty of the crime? Why or why not?
- Through examining your answers to these questions, how much do you think your cultural background and understandings of the world influence your ideas?

Finally, we examine the last scene of the text, which reveals whether Steve is found innocent or guilty. As part of this scene, the relationship between Steve and his lawyer is forefronted. We ask students to think about this relationship and discuss the following questions in literature circles.

- What is Steve left thinking at the end?
- What is so harmful about this ending?

- How does O'Brien's cultural background play into her response to Steve?

- What is the author hoping the reader will think at the end?

- How is this book about examining our cultural biases?

By working with particular passages before, during, or after reading the entire text, we find that students can begin to examine their own thinking from a cultural perspective, and begin to critically explore some of the assumptions they have made about themselves and others because of the cultural lens through which they view the world.

By utilizing the gradual release of responsibility (see chapter 3), teachers ensure that students actually are learning how to use culturally situated response theory. Students' learning is evident because once teachers model critical questioning and reflective thinking, students then have the opportunity to perform this behavior for themselves. For instance, while listening to a group of eighth graders discuss one of the newscast scenes from *Monster* in a literature circle, we found these middle-level students becoming more critically conscious and much more critical of the evening newscasts they watch:

Jill: [That newscast scene] reminds me of those shows on TV—you know, the judge shows on after school. The judge is always yelling at the people like they should know better or something.

Casey: Well, some of the stuff they [people] get in trouble for is stupid. They didn't know any better?

Robert: That's what this whole discussion is supposed to be. How are they going to know if they don't know?

Saundra: This reminds me of *Make Lemonade* [Wolff, 1994] when Jolly says something like "How am I supposed to know?" and she's mad because people just expect you to know when you don't.

Robert: I mean, we know, because we see it on TV and people tell us.

Casey: Or you just sort of figure it out. Like, I know I'll get in trouble for stealing...well, I did get in trouble for stealing, so I definitely figured it out!

This exchange highlights a key concept we like to address with middle-level students—the issue of knowing and when that knowing occurs. Some of the complexities middle-level students can discuss with each other and with their teachers include the following: the age at which people should become accountable for their actions, how any community or society can ensure such knowledge, the reasonableness of responsibility, and discriminatory actions based on such assumptions.

Jill: That question on the board makes me wonder about what I don't think about because I just know. That's kind of scary because then you wonder if everyone is thinking like you or when you get in trouble or in fights you wonder if it's 'cause you expected the other person to be thinking like you.

Robert: This can sure get complicated. You'll be all in your head all the time trying to figure out what you don't know, what someone else doesn't know, blah, blah, blah. It will make you crazy.

During this short exchange, students voice how complicated assumptions can be. They are beginning to understand the concept of how truth might be a matter of perspective and that multiple perspectives ensure that not everyone will think like they do.

Saundra: This scene reminds me of the news when they put the artist's pictures on the TV because I guess we aren't supposed to see the real people or something.

Jill: It does sound just like what you would expect on TV. But, this is about a kid and not some adult. They don't show too many kids on TV when they get in trouble with the law. Maybe it's against the law to see them.

Saundra: I think it's because they're too young. My cousin got in trouble and went to juvenile detention or whatever it's called, and he wasn't on TV.

Casey: I wouldn't want to be on TV for getting in trouble. I wouldn't want to be that guy in *Monster* 'cause everyone will think you did it just because you are there.

Making the connection to television shows that students are aware of how the world works outside the classroom. They are transferring what they are learning in the classroom to life outside it. By addressing the issue of age, they also are speculating about the treatment of young adults by the media and people's common perspectives based on media attention.

Saundra: And he's black, so that makes it worse. People always think the black kids do the bad stuff in the neighborhood.

Robert: Not everybody. But a lot. It's ridiculous.

Noting the issue of race in this discussion addresses two aspects of critical consciousness: (1) the discriminatory treatment of some racial groups and (2) the issue of stereotyping and how it must be avoided even when appearances would suggest otherwise.

We involve students in additional activities such as critically viewing the news, courtroom and police dramas, and afternoon court television. We discuss the limitations of government along with individual freedoms, rights, and responsibilities. We ask students to conduct their own inquiries into the penal system, juvenile detention, and the statistics that suggest more young men of color are in prisons than any other population.

We often study *Monster* in conjunction with *If You Come Softly* (Woodson, 1998) because of the incident at the end of *If You Come Softly* that also brings into focus the nature of relationships between many young men of color and the legal system.

Once students become more adept at using culturally situated response theory by reading *Monster*, we move on to other texts in which social class is addressed, as well as stories students choose from their own cultural perspectives. By working with texts that reflect a cultural identity nearer to their own, regardless of racial or ethnic background, students can become more critical about why they accept certain norms or values. This type of questioning creates opportunities for students to investigate their own thinking and its sociocultural foundations.

We use other excellent books, such as *The Buffalo Tree* (Rapp, 2002) and *Little Boy Blue* (Bunker, 1998), but they are heavy content for many middle-level learners. If teachers were to use these additional texts, they might wish to contact parents about the violent nature of the books, and then proceed by first introducing the students to prison life through a guest speaker from the juvenile court system. By building students' prior knowledge about life in juvenile detention and how that has or has not changed in the last half century, students who chose to read one of these texts in their literature circle groups would be adequately prepared to confront the issues in these texts.

With culturally situated response theory, students can explore any text through a cultural lens. We particularly ask students to explore themselves as readers when using culturally situated responses. What is it that they bring as cultural beings to the reading? What conflicts or affirmations can they identify based on their cultural identities? For instance, when reading *Monster*, did they have a hard time identifying with Steve and understanding his situation? How might this be because of the way they think about the world and adolescents who get into this kind of trouble? We also ask students to critically examine the nature of race and class, and how the cultural assumptions of the media may play a part in the tenuous relationship between citizens and the justice system. Every aspect of a society might best be viewed with an understanding of how cultural assumptions can cause breakdowns in communication and harmonious living. Each layer of a society, whether that layer is economic, educational, judicial, or social, has been created by people who have brought their assumptions to the policies and practices of that aspect of society. When individuals or a cultural group do not share those assumptions, there is bound to be confusion, miscommunication, or strife.

Diversity Issues and Young Adolescents

By using culturally situated response theory, middle-level teachers can help their students explore their resistance to certain texts because of their ideas about other cultures. Teachers also can have students examine the idea of understanding another experience or cultural situation, rather than being dissuaded when they feel as though they do not share any of the values or practices represented in the text. Middle-level readers might explore the assumptions they bring to a text that cause them to connect or disconnect from the experience being presented, whether that experience would be considered "cultural" or not. Through the use of culturally situated response theory, teachers and students can address diversity, difference, and issues of race and social class. But they also must be prepared to confront challenges such as misunderstandings and resistance as well.

One issue we typically confront when we discuss issues of race and social class with middle-level students is their misunderstanding of the concept of culture. Students still confuse race and class with culture, believing that culture can explain race and social class. This confusion allows us to emphasize that these terms are not synonymous. We do not want our students to believe that poverty or the lower class is a particular culture that people choose to embrace and, thus, our work to relieve the poor is moot. Nor do we wish students to believe that all members of any racial group hold the same ideas or values. In essence, we do not want students to essentialize the categories of race, social class, or culture by outward or physical appearances or behaviors. We want students to think more deeply than that.

Students, however, often find that the world seems to create divisions based on these categories and label these differences as cultural. We realize that some students may wish to keep these divisions in place because one group or another benefits from the artificial distinctions created from different cultural locations. We would hope that teachers might disrupt this type of thinking, however, when it occurs in their classrooms.

Another issue we address in relation to diversity is the concept of authenticity, which we discussed in chapter 3. Although we do not wish to belabor our point about middle-level students' limited ideas of what is real or authentic when it comes to different cultural, racial, ethnic, or social class situations, we do realize that they can resist discussions about how people from different cultural, racial, ethnic, or social class backgrounds are as diverse as any other cultural group. Often, students stereotype people from other cultural, racial, or class groups, believing that only their own group encompasses all types of families, people, and ideas. The use of words like *them* and *us* is part of that thinking, and we attempt to disrupt this type of thinking by using young adult literature that allows our students to see the diversity within cultural, racial, or class groups.

Another challenge we confront when discussing diversity is connected to the stereotyping we just addressed. Often, students harbor a resistance to the reality that all cultural, racial, or class groups are similar to their own. Although we want students to realize that diversity should be celebrated and differences acknowledged, we also want students to reach across those differences to embrace the universal humanness of all people. For many people, it is easier to highlight our differences because they are the anomalies we confront in life. We happily go along with our lives until dissonance stops us—and that dissonance often can be the result of cultural differences. However, if we only concentrate on difference, we are afraid that students will not attempt to become the border crossers they would need to become to be more critically and socially conscious. The result might mean that students' communities would remain the same without the transformation needed to make better relations between all those who live in their neighborhoods, cities, or regions.

Conclusion

Working with middle-level students on issues as important as race and class can be especially satisfying and rewarding. Students' interests in social justice, equity, and tolerance are sincere, and our experiences have shown that they are willing participants in the fight for making their communities and cities places where all people are treated with dignity. Although we still struggle with the complexity of these issues and how to teach them to young adolescents, we know that the challenge is worth the effort. Our students remind us that their future depends on the steps we take today that will enable all of us to work through the dilemmas we face and to be more involved in the changing world. In the next chapter, we explore what role context plays in our understandings of the world and the multiple perspectives within it.

"I thought, as we walked, that life must be like the mockingbird's song—mostly just mimicking the notes and rhythms of other folks and not thinking twice about it—until the day you make up your very own song and decide that's the one you have to sing."

From *Jericho Walls* (Collier, 2002, p. 209)

CHAPTER 8

Critical Contextualization: Using Historical Fiction to Understand Change

istorical fiction tells about life—life in the past and life in the present. Just like a mockingbird's song, very little changes from age to age; humans still struggle with similar issues. If we listen, however, we can learn from those lessons and make changes that affect how people live in the world. By using historical fiction and viewing it through a critical lens, middle-level teachers can help students learn from the past and create new songs to sing.

Whenever we look at an event or situation, we use our values, prior knowledge, and beliefs to interpret what is happening. Sometimes we are right; other times we are wrong. By examining instances when we are right and when we are wrong, we can learn about the way we view the world. And, if we talk to one another about the same event, we usually discover that each of us sees it differently. This diversity makes life interesting, and by sharing our views with each other, we grow in understanding.

When interpreting a situation, however, we also might evaluate or judge it, and this is when the concept of context becomes important. Without knowing the extenuating circumstances, we might be making judgments that are inappropriate at best and far more damaging if left unquestioned. For example, this excerpt from *Flipped* (Van Draanen, 2001; see story pp. 91–93 for a more detailed excerpt) is a good example of making and incorporating judgments; in this excerpt, Bryce's father, Chet, judges their neighbors because of the condition of their yard. He says that the neighbors are "trash" who do not care about how they represent themselves, and that there is "no excuse" for not fixing up their yard.

"No?" My grandfather takes a deep breath and seems to weigh things in his mind for a few seconds. Then he says, "Tell me this, Rick. If you had a brother or sister or child who had a severe mental or physical handicap, what would you do?"

It was like my granddad had passed gas in church. My father's eyes pinched, his head shook, and finally he said, "Chet, what does that have to do with anything?"

My grandfather looks at him for a minute, then quietly says, "Juli's father has a retarded brother..."

Excerpt from *Flipped* (Van Draanen, 2001), p. 91.

QUESTIONS FOR STUDENTS TO CONSIDER

1. Should the neighbors be given the benefit of the doubt? Why or why not?

2. Is the narrator's father hard to listen to? Why or why not?

3. How does this passage show that we need to understand a situation or person before we judge them?

4. How does knowing about a person change the context of the situation?

The importance of context and how it can influence people in any situation is an aspect of communication that students frequently miss, but should begin to understand. Recognizing the role context plays in people's interactions can help students learn how to control their feelings or behaviors when they find themselves involved in situations that are new to them.

Defining Context

Middle-level students might have an idea of how context works. However, as the previous excerpt shows, they need to know what it means in a larger sense. In our work with students, we have found that context involves more aspects of a situation, entity, or event than we realized at first. It can concern the physical location of an event or a particular geographical feature that could not be found in another part of the country or planet. In terms of geography and literature, it could mean where a story takes place. Setting is the time and place of an event, situation, or story. When students think about setting, they often forget that it can include the time of day, the historical time period, or a time in a person's or character's life. We also suggest to students that setting can be physical or mental, depending on how the plot is advanced. In many ways, context and setting are very much alike, but they are in fact different concepts.

Context is the social background of the story, what is taking place not only in the book but also during the time when the author wrote the book and what was happening in the author's life. Context also can refer to what was happening in the world at the time of the writing, as well as what is happening in the world at the time of the reading of the book. As opposed to setting, context takes into account the values and attitudes during the time of the book's publication and during the time in which a reader is engaged in the text.

Context also can include the people involved or the event at hand. It can relate to behaviors or attitudes evoked by a combination of factors, all of which are related to the situation. In this way, context is very much like discourse, which we discussed in previous chapters, in that the event, the people, the language, and the actions all influence one another.

When we examine particular events in our lives, we typically find that our emotions, behaviors, and attitudes may be affected by the context of the situation. When we discuss social context with middle-level students, we ask them to think about their embarrassment when reprimanded in front of their peers or about how the enthusiasm of the crowd at a ball game might bring them out of a bad mood. Context can be created by those within a setting, just as setting can create context or influence those within it. The following excerpts can be used to show students how people and context are connected. These excerpts also can be used to discuss context itself, or the role that context or setting plays in affecting the characters' behaviors.

In the first excerpt from *Rag and Bone Shop* (Cormier, 2001; see story pp. 88–90 for a more detailed excerpt), 12-year-old Jason has been asked to come into the police station to help with a murder investigation. He is suspected by the police of killing his younger neighbor because he was the last person to see her alive. Trent, the detective on the case, asks him about seeing anyone suspicious. Jason explains that he has not seen anyone "suspicious," but Trent then explains to him the nature of suspicion as it relates to a particular context.

> "For instance, take a druggist. Someone familiar you've done business with in the store, a pharmacy. He's not suspicious in himself. But suppose you saw him out of context from the pharmacy."
>
> Seeing the puzzlement on the boy's face, he explained. "Let's say that you saw him outside the drugstore at a time when he should be in the store. Say you saw him suddenly hurrying through the park. Then a man

Context is the social background of the story, what is taking place not only in the book but also during the time when the author wrote the book.

who was not himself suspicious would suddenly become a questionable figure because of where he was at the moment, or what he was doing...."

Excerpt from *Rag and Bone Shop* (Cormier, 2001), p. 89.

QUESTIONS FOR STUDENTS TO CONSIDER

1. How is context used in this passage?

2. Why is it important for Jason to understand the meaning of context?

3. Other than Jason and Mr. Trent's discussion of what context means, what other parts of this excerpt relate to context?

4. How would you explain context to someone else?

In the second excerpt from *No Condition Is Permanent* (Kessler, 2000; see story pp. 20–21 for a more detailed excerpt) we ask students to think about Jodie, who has traveled to West Africa with her mother, and as they enter the terminal, she is warned by her mother to "grab [the bags] as quickly as you can," which seems like the obvious thing to do at an airport. The excerpt begins as Jodie enters the baggage area. Between these two excerpts, students can begin to see that context and setting are connected; however, setting is more of a physical location, whereas context can involve people and their actions or words.

The total confusion seemed like a cross between a fire alarm in a crowded disco and a serious session of roller derby. Mom amazed me as she waded into the madness, elbows flying, ready for action.

Our first bag appeared and she fought over the handle with a very fat man wearing torn shorts. Once again she switched into her new (or old) language, and shouted, "Lef mi bo!" Whatever it meant was effective. She slung the bag back in my direction and said, "Hang on to it, Jodie."

Excerpt from *No Condition Is Permanent* (Kessler, 2000). p. 21.

QUESTIONS FOR STUDENTS TO CONSIDER

1. What is the context of this passage? How do you know?

2. How is the context unfamiliar to you? What makes it so?

3. What emotions does the character experience in this context?

4. What parts of the context influenced those emotions?

The concept of context also can be used to teach students the importance of how a particular place can create different moods, ideas, value beliefs, or behaviors in people. For example, certain ideas about medicine during early times suggested that taking a bath was dangerous because it exposed the body to the cold. Now we know that is not true.

In the following excerpt from *An Island Like You: Stories From the Barrio* (Cofer, 1995; see story pp. 1–3 for a more detailed excerpt), the setting and context create a mood, and it is this description that evokes an emotion or response for the reader. This excerpt establishes a situation in which readers must think about what values, attitudes, and beliefs they bring to a situation or setting. In this scene, the narrator is visiting her grandparents in Puerto Rico for an annual two-week vacation. She spends most of her time on the beach with her cousins, but this year her cousins are not there. She suggests that it will be a "long, hot summer." While the setting is summertime in Puerto Rico, the context could be suggested by the narrator's feelings about being in Puerto Rico without her cousins. The setting is conditioned by the context of the narrator's feelings about where she is and for what reason.

> When I stepped off that airplane in San Juan, it was like I had opened an oven door. I was immediately drenched in sweat, and felt like I was breathing water.... Of course, there was no AC [at the house]. The window was thrown wide open, and right outside, perched on a fence separating our house from the neighbors' by about six inches, there was a red rooster. When I looked at him, he started screeching at the top of his lungs.... I put a pillow over my head and decided to commit suicide by sweating to death.

Excerpt from *An Island Like You: Stories From the Barrio* (Cofer, 1995), pp. 2–3.

QUESTIONS FOR STUDENTS TO CONSIDER

1. What is it about the physical environment that produces a negative response from the narrator?

2. How would you feel if you were in that setting?

3. In what ways does this context produce negative feelings in you?

4. Why do people differ in their responses to different contexts?

In essence, context is important because it has the potential of creating situations that might not arise in another area or with other people. This is why we find it so important to discuss the concept of context with students before, during, and after they read pieces of historical fiction or work from a New Historical perspective.

Discussing Context With Middle-Level Students

Studying history can be an exciting venture. Context changes all the time as our perspectives change. People change, and the physical or social environment changes. We know that the social climate of a country or society can change when leadership changes or when the country develops into an international power. The United States was not always a super power, yet many students do not know that because they do not study the history of power, per se. Other nations have changed dramatically over time. For example, we remind students that Rome was once a great power, yet now it is not the powerful entity it once was; the kingdom of Great Zimbabwe also was a powerful force in southern Africa, but now it is no longer as powerful or called "great"; and the Aztec kingdom was powerful at one time as well, and now nothing remains. The context or social climate of regions, nations, peoples, and the world changes with the rise and fall of the politically powerful. Individuals have changed the social climate of nations, regions, and the world as well. Studying major religions shows us this. The study of medicine will also tell us about social context and what is privileged or not during particular time periods. Teachers can teach social context or climate in connection with any content area because there is such diverse literature available that addresses these topics as an aspect of a text's setting.

The context or social environment of middle schools changes as well. Students can tell stories of their own popularity, isolation, or social status. Another excerpt from *Flipped* (Van Draanen, 2001; see story pp. 101–102 for a more detailed excerpt) can be used to discuss the idea of personal positioning and social context. This passage also can be used to compare and contrast perspectives or contexts with the previous excerpt from *Flipped* (see page 170). In the excerpt, Juli is upset because she realizes that her yard, her parents' cars, and even her bicycle do not match the standards of their neighborhood. She then realizes that her family never goes on vacations like the rest of their neighbors. She begins to wonder if her family is poor even as she thinks about how much her father and mother work. She also begins to wonder about the values she has learned about hard work making people successful. She decides to ask her parents if they are poor, but cannot do it. Instead she suggests that they start a "project" to fix up their front yard.

My parents stopped eating and stared at me.
My father sighed and said, "The yard is not our responsibility, Julianna."
"It's...it's not?"
He shook his head and said, "It's Mr. Finnegan's."

"Who's Mr. Finnegan?"

"The man who owns the house."

I couldn't believe my ears. "What?"

My father cleared his throat and said, "The landlord."

"You mean *we* don't own the house?"

...My mother reached over and took my hand. "Sweetheart, I'm sorry if this is a shock. I guess we always thought you knew."

Excerpt from *Flipped* (Van Draanen, 2001), p. 102.

QUESTIONS FOR STUDENTS TO CONSIDER

1. How would you feel if you were Juli? Could you ask your parents about being poor? Why or why not?

2. What could have changed for Juli that now makes her see her life differently?

3. What would you do in this situation to make Juli feel better about her life?

For the character Juli, the context has changed. Her perspective has changed and, with it, her life. When students come to realize how context colors the lens through which they view the world—whether that lens is created by their society, family, or own thoughts—they are freer to paint the world and the way they would like it to be. We say this because we hold the perspective that there is no wrong or right way to be in the world but rather places from which to view the world and learn the lessons offered us. Through the vicarious experience literature offers, students can become more critically conscious of multiple contexts from which to view any situation, condition, or person. They can choose which perspective they will hold and become responsible for that position. For example, in *Flipped*, most of the characters make choices about how to view each other but then change those views when they became more cognizant of the context in which they all live their lives.

Examining Context Through Young Adult Literature

When we explore the concept of context, we use young adult literature so that students can bridge more easily the distance between their lives and other realities. Young adult literature allows students to live vicariously through the lives of others and to ponder the situations they do not—nor may ever—encounter. We want them, however, to have the experience of living outside their own realities. And in many cases, we also want them to reflect upon life in the past. Through the use of New Historical criticism and historical fiction, we find that students develop a depth of critical thought that they may not have achieved without this type of literature or lens through which to read it.

Using Picture Books to Question the Past

Using shorter texts to ponder history can be done through the use of picture books, many of which are sophisticated pieces displaying historical conditions and people. For example, *Nettie's Trip South* (Turner, 1995) and *Pink and Say* (Polacco, 1994) address situations concerning the treatment of African Americans and the issue of slavery, an issue that still exists for many people throughout the world. The horrors of slavery, the legitimacy of slavery, and the prejudice that produces such treatment all can be discussed in relation to the present and to the past when students read these picture books.

There are multitudes of picture books that address historical events through historical fiction. Table 18 lists some of our favorite picture books that invite young adolescents to question the past and make comparisons to the present. Through such comparisons, students can challenge current situations where oppression and power are manifested.

Using New Historicism

As we mentioned in chapter 3, New Historicism questions when texts were produced, how the social context of readers and authors influences the way we read texts, and the values that are found within texts. New Historicism asks readers to read from their current belief systems

TABLE 18

Picture Books Presenting Historical Fiction
Battle-Levert, G. (2003). *Papa's mark*. New York: Holiday House. Bunting, E. (2000). *Train to somewhere*. New York: Clarion. Heide, F. (1992). *Sami and the time of troubles*. New York: Clarion. Innocenti, R. (1985). *Rose Blanche*. San Diego, CA: Harcourt Brace. McCully, E. (1998). *The ballot box battle*. New York: Dragonfly. McLerran, A. (2001). *The ghost dance*. New York: Clarion. Oppenheim, S. (1995). *The lily cupboard*. New York: HarperTrophy. Park, F., & Park, G. (1998). *My freedom trip: A child's escape from North Korea*. Honesdale, PA: Boyds Mills Press. Sisulu, E. (1999). *The day Gogo went to vote*. New York: Megan Tingley. Uchida, Y. (1993). *The bracelet*. New York: Putnam.

and societal values, and not only to discuss how society has changed since the text was written but also to comment on historical precedent without excuse. The example we used in chapter 3 asserts that the owning of slaves is illegal in most current societies. By looking back on a text produced in the 1800s or before the Civil Rights movement in the United States, students can gain insight into the values of U.S. society.

New Historicists reject the idea that history is a unified story along one continuum. History is chaotic, and only certain texts are privileged; thus, we have only a partial view of history. The New Historicist perspective also suggests that authors reflect their own time periods, even when writing about historical events that took place prior to their time period.

When working with a novel from a New Historicist perspective, teachers can invite students to ask the following types of questions:

- How do we really know how people acted during the early history of the United States?

- Have human beings changed since this text was written, or have the stories told about them changed?

- How representative of the actual time period is this book?

- In what ways is the protagonist different from what we would expect of the people during the particular time period depicted in the text?

- In what ways does the protagonist represent how we think people would have thought and acted during the particular period depicted in the text?

- How do we feel about these people and their ideas?

- How has our society changed since the time period depicted in the text?

- How can our society continue to improve?

- What do we think the author is trying to say about the issue presented in the novel?

- How does the author's time period reflect particular ideas about the world?

By using New Historical literary theory, students can gain a greater awareness of what has been left out of the history books, or what has been represented misleadingly. Students will come to know that there is no objective story about the history of their country, but only people's ideas about what occurred in the past and their ideas about why the past is important for the future. Reading historical fiction, then, gives students access to contextualized reading and writing, and exposure to how comparisons of the past to the present are relevant for future thinking and learning.

Highlighting Historical Fiction

Lesesne (2003) suggests that "historical fiction give kids a sense of how we are all connected through time, that even though times change, the needs we have as people remain unchanged" (p. 86). Contexts, however, can change, and using historical fiction gives middle-level teachers the opportunity to ask students whether the accounts and values of the past should be judged by today's standards. Reading young adult fiction is of value to young adolescents because of the unique qualities it targets in connection to them and their concerns. Historical fiction also addresses key issues or events from the past that are also relevant to the present and to these students. (See Table 19 for a list of attributes of historical fiction.)

Historical fiction allows students to ponder human nature and the concerns of the past in the context of the past, and make comparisons to the present. Historical fiction also can be read through the lens of New Historical literary criticism and gives students the opportunity to review the past and reflect on judgments and actions made in the past that may have been distasteful or disconcerting to them as current readers. Students also may look at people who lived in the past with new ap-

TABLE 19

Attributes of Historical Fiction
Historical fiction • is set in a time period prior to when it was written. • examines a single subject or time period in depth versus the surface rendering found in many textbooks. • offers differing perspectives on the same event, which can be explained by the times in which the author lived and wrote. • encompasses fictionalized memoirs, family histories, or events based on research. • brings the event to life for the reader, so setting is important. • creates questions through plot about the time period, characters' motivations, and readers' general knowledge. • includes characters who are everyday people and not historical figures, although they may be in close contact with famous historical figures. • has a theme that is significant to the time period being depicted and to the present.

preciation for the hardships they endured and the resilience they displayed. Ultimately, studying historical fiction through a New Historical lens allows students to gain an awareness about history and human behavior and question the past.

Reading *Kezzie* and *Out of the Dust* With Middle-Level Learners

In our experience, we have found that most history textbooks highlight wars and relegate other events to the background. We want students to realize that more has happened in the world and throughout history than wars. For example, because the Great Depression in the United States affected the entire world, just as the wars of recent history have affected the world, we believe students should know more about this event. Through a number of books about the Great Depression, students can discover the unique attributes of the United States' situation during this time period, but they may not learn what happened in the rest of the world as a result of the U.S. situation. However, the young adult novel *Kezzie* (Breslin, 1993) chronicles the story of a family in Scotland as they struggle during the Great Depression. Reading this novel with middle-level students reveals a more holistic picture of the world during that time. Students can move beyond the immediate experience in the United States, and perhaps their ethnocentric ideas of history, to begin understanding the interdependence of nations.

It is important for middle-level students to understand the concept of ethnocentrism because it explains how someone can be limited by his or her value system, societal conditioning, or cultural situation. This limitation can produce biases that lead to attitudes or behaviors that are unfair to those who are not part of the same society, system, or culture.

We also teach cause and effect during this unit and attempt to have students think about this concept from a New Historical perspective. We address comparing and contrasting so students can begin to realize that some of the issues a society thought it solved in the past may still be a part of society today, only in another form. We also ask critical questions about how the books students read might be different if they were written by people at the time of the Great Depression. Would those people have the same feel for the time period, or would their writings be more detailed about the everyday matters that some of the authors who write from a later time might not think about? We ask students to connect this kind of thinking to their own lives by talking about how some of the important issues in their lives right now may not mean anything in a few years.

> Ethnocentrism explains how readers can be limited by their value systems, societal conditioning, or cultural situations.

We highlight the following two excerpts from *Kezzie* during this unit on the Great Depression. They show key ways in which the world has changed, and how individuals react to particular people or situations. Students have the opportunity to ponder the historical context of child labor and child abuse in these two scenes as well. Students discuss them in literature circles and then share their thoughts with the entire class. Individual literature circle groups discuss other excerpts as well, but these two we ask the entire class to ponder.

The first excerpt presents Kezzie as she attempts to get a job at a local factory. She has no experience, but because of the way she handles the situation, she is offered a job. Kezzie understands the setting she is in—a factory—but also the context—she is an inexperienced, young woman talking to the factory manager about a job. She knows he is the person who can decide if she gets hired or not.

Kezzie hurried into the office buildings. Out in the yard she heard them getting ready to open the gate. There was a door marked SECRETARY. For a second she faltered, then went past it to the one marked MANAGER. She knocked briskly and walked straight in.

There was a small bald-headed man sitting behind the desk. He was dictating to a lady who was writing in a note pad. They both looked up in surprise.

"Oh, I do beg your pardon," said Kezzie as politely as possible. "I thought this would be the office for the interviews. Did I make a mistake?"

The man consulted his pocket watch.

"Goodness it's ten o'clock already. I didn't realize." He stood up. "We'll continue later, Miss Dunlop. I'd better see these people right away." He glanced out the window to where the queue was assembling in the yard. "Some of them have been waiting since before dawn."

He indicated for Kezzie to sit down.

"Now what experience have you had with knitwear machines?" he asked her.

Something about his manner gave Kezzie a clue to how to react. She looked him straight in the eye.

"Absolutely none," she stated truthfully. "However, I do learn extremely quickly. I was intending to go to university but my father's death prevented that. I have my leaving certificate and a very good reference from my minister." She handed him the letter.

He examined the seal carefully before opening and reading it.

"Very impressive," he said. "It says here that you are diligent, truthful, hardworking, intelligent, punctual, and of a neat and tidy appearance." He smiled. "Do you agree with all of this."

"Yes," said Kezzie.

The manager laughed right out loud.

"How could I not employ you?" he asked. He took a card and wrote her details down. "You start on Monday. The shift is eight o'clock until five thirty, with an hour for lunch. Tea is for sale but not food, so bring sandwiches."

Kezzie stood up.

"Thank you very much," she said.

"Don't you want to know what the wage is?" the manager asked her.

She blushed and sat down again quickly.

"You will start on the coarse knitting at fifteen shillings each week, and if you show some promise you might progress to fine knitting." He consulted a sheet. "Fine knitting pays seventeen and sixpence."

Kezzie's eyes brimmed. Seventeen and sixpence! What she could do with seventeen and sixpence! She was going to show the most promise of any person on that whole factory floor.

"Thank you again," she said. She paused. Something had just occurred to her. It was worth a try. Boldness had got her this far already, and she sensed that he was sympathetic.

"Is it possible," she enquired, "for me to have an advance against my first pay?"

He stopped with his pen in mid-air and regarded the girl in front of him. He had noted the cheap suit and the make-up, and her feet sliding out of the too large shoes. He was sure that she had tricked herself in first this morning in some way. She was very thin and had a barely concealed desperation about her. But she was also striking-looking and determined and he could see the spirit shining out of her. He might probably never see her or the money again, he thought ruefully.

"I can give you five shillings," he said, and marked it on her card. "Give this to Miss Dunlop and she will give you the money and your card. Congratulations, Miss Munroe, you are our very first employee."

From *Kezzie* © Theresa Breslin 1993 (pp. 104–107). Published by Egmont Books Limited, London, and used with permission.

QUESTIONS FOR STUDENTS TO CONSIDER

1. Would Kezzie have the same chances of being hired today? Why or not?

2. How is this situation similar to and different from today's working environments?

3. Would employers give someone a money advance today? Why did the employer do it then?
4. Do the wages Kezzie is earning seem fair? Why or why not?

In this excerpt, Kezzie, unlike the subservient role she played in the first excerpt, is more forceful with the person whom she is addressing. In this scene, Kezzie is trying to ascertain whether the orphan who was placed in a slovenly, uncaring household is her younger sister, Lucy. The child has been placed in a shed in back of the house, and Kezzie is overwhelmed by the thought that a child could be treated so harshly. At this point, Kezzie also has traveled from Scotland to Canada and is overwrought by the hopelessness of never finding her sister.

"I told you," she said firmly. "I am from the home. Now take me to her at once."

The woman led the way through the yard to a lean-to at the back of the house. Here, scraggy chickens pecked in the dirt and an old cat with matted fur slunk away under the house.

The woman pushed the door of the shed open.

"She ain't been well the last few days," she whined. "I've been having to nurse her. That was soup I was making her, extra work for me on top of everything else I have to do."

Kezzie barely heard her. She had stepped past her into the darkness. By the light from the door she could see a straw mattress on which a small figure lay huddled, half-sitting against the wall. The air was foetid, it was a place one would not have kept animals in. A stench of urine and vomit made Kezzie gag. She went forward slowly and looked at the child in the bed. She was smaller and thinner than Lucy had been. Her hair was coarse and tufted and moving with lice. Her face was sallow and sunken, her skin was lacerated and covered with scabs. But worse, much worse, were the child's eyes. They stared blankly out at nothing. The woman was right. This child was indeed an idiot.

Kezzie felt anger. Anger at the woman who had treated a child so badly, and anger at the authorities which had allowed a child to be placed with people such as these. She would go straight back to Dalton, but not to the home. She would go to the police and report this. She turned toward the door. And then the fact of the matter hit her.

If this child was not her sister, where in the wide world was Lucy? She had followed the trail very carefully and had not found her. Where could she be? Not in Scotland, not in Canada. Where? There was nowhere else left for Kezzie to search. Lucy was lost to her forever.

Kezzie paused with her hand on the door. A feeling of the greatest despair came over her. The woman was watching her. Kezzie put her forehead against her hand and bowed her head in defeat.

There was a silence in the room. Nothing. Kezzie felt a breath against her cheek. She sensed something...an echo. She raised her head. The woman had not moved. She glanced in the corner of the shed. Neither had the child. Then what? Kezzie looked at the woman.

"Did the child say something?" she asked her.

"I told you," said the woman. "She be dumb..."

Kezzie held up her hand to silence her and walked towards the bed.

"Did you speak, little girl?"

The child gazed at her vacantly.

Kezzie knelt down beside the child's bed. She took one thin hand in both hers.

"Little girl," she said gently. "Did you say something?"

There was a terrible empty silence in the room. Kezzie felt as though the world had stopped turning. She moved her head slightly to try to catch the child's gaze. Was there something there? Was her imagination playing tricks? A gleam of light in her eyes. Was it a reflection of something? Kezzie felt at her throat for her little silver locket. She held it up before the child's eyes.

"See," she said.

Nothing.

Kezzie sat back on her heels. She closed her eyes. She could feel warm tears beginning to trickle through her lids.

"Oh, Lucy, where are you?" she whispered.

Then she heard, no more than a breath on the air, a sigh. One word.

"Kezzie."

From *Kezzie* © Theresa Breslin 1993 (pp. 206–209). Published by Egmont Books Limited, London, and used with permission.

QUESTIONS FOR STUDENTS TO CONSIDER

1. What would happen today if a child was treated so badly? How do we know?

2. Does Kezzie have the right to be angry? Why or why not?

3. What would you do in that situation if you were Kezzie? What do you think you could do now that she couldn't do then?

We also juxtapose *Kezzie* with the Newbery Medal–winning *Out of the Dust* (Hesse, 1997), a book that presents the hardship of the Great Depression in the United States. We read aloud this novel to adolescents because they tell us that being read to is enjoyable and it helps them enter the time period they are studying. With a read-aloud, we place the excerpts on a transparency so students can read them before discussing them in their literature circles. Although students' listening vocabulary is larger than their reading vocabulary and they can listen "faster" than they can read or talk, many students still need to see what is being read because they are visual learners.

Even though we use *Out of the Dust* as a read-aloud, we still ask students to reflect on some of the excerpts through a New Historical lens. We find key passages in the text, place them on transparencies, and then ask students to discuss in literature circles if the scene presents a situation that could happen in the present and what would be the consequences or problems with the actions involved. Teachers also can ask students to compare and contrast current and past situations, discussing which consequence or response by those involved is the better solution and why.

By analyzing and discussing particular excerpts with the entire classroom community, students can realize how differing perspectives paint the world, its changes, and its continuity. Students also become aware of how the social context has changed. The previous excerpts reflect different ideas about the world and how people treated one another for good or for bad during hard times.

Understanding Cause and Effect

The concept of cause and effect is one of the primary learning objectives when exploring history. Why did particular events occur? What is the current result of actions from the past? When students begin to wrestle with these questions, they begin to think like historians and develop their critical thinking skills. Of course, along with exploring cause and effect in short excerpts, teachers should be sure to discuss the causes of the Great Depression in a unit on that period. Also, because of a concentration on New Historicism, teachers should explore how what we know now might have changed the conditions that caused the dust bowl and the economic misfortunes of that time.

Comparing and Contrasting the Past and the Present

Because New Historical criticism asks questions about the past from a current perspective, students need to develop the ability to compare and contrast events, situations, conditions, and perspectives. The following excerpts help middle-level students easily compare the past to the present. The first excerpt from *Out of the Dust* (Hesse, 1997) presents Billie Jo's condition after she has "hopped a train" headed west from Oklahoma. The whole experience of riding trains is limited by the lack of an extensive rail system in many countries. The idea that a young girl could hop a train so easily is something students can ponder in relation to their current societies.

Gone West

I am stiff and sore.
In two endless days on this train. I have
burned in the desert,
shivered in the mountains,
I have seen the
camps of dust-bowl migrants
along the tracks.

There was one girl.
I saw her through the slat in the boxcar.
She stared up at the passing train.
She stood by the tracks watching,
and I knew her.

August 1935

Excerpt from *Out of the Dust* (Hesse, 1997), p. 199.

QUESTIONS FOR STUDENTS TO CONSIDER

1. Does this passage compare to something in your experience?

2. If the year was not posted on this passage, when do you think this could have occurred?

3. Who is the narrator of this passage? What makes you think so? How does your answer relate to the time period in which you are living?

The second excerpt from *Kezzie* (Breslin, 1993) takes place as Kezzie wakes from an accident to find that her younger sister, Lucy, is missing. Students can compare such a phenomenon to current situations, but the situation takes a twist when the matron of the children's home suggests that Lucy might have been sent to another country.

Kezzie could feel the mist clearing slowly from around her. She felt warmer. The sun must be shining and, better still, her headache was less severe. She opened her eyes. It was a very bright day, and she was not outside as she had imagined but in a room lying down in bed. He grand-dad was there, and Miss Dunlop. She wanted to laugh, they looked so serious. She smiled at them.

"I'm all right," she said. Then she remembered her dream and the thing she had been trying so hard to recall. "Is Lucy with you, Grandad?"

Kezzie became like a person demented. She discharged herself from the hospital immediately, despite the doctor's dire warnings. When she eventually realized that Lucy had not been seen for days her distress was profound. They went from house to house in the village and then started a search of Shawcross.

"A child that age, wandering off," said the sergeant at the police station, "anything could happen to her. She could fall in a burn or go away across the peats. We might never find her."

Kezzie clenched her fists and tried not to scream. It was all she could do to control herself. She felt like running up and down the streets shouting wildly.

"Or the tinkers," the sergeant went on, "taking a child's the sort of thing they would do."

"They would NEVER do something like that," said Kezzie angrily. She was just about to say something very rude when her grandfather came running in.

"One of the bus drivers at the garage saw a little girl walking on the road to Glasgow last Friday. She told him she was going to meet her sister."

"Glasgow!" cried Kezzie. "Glasgow!"

"She must have taken the wrong turn at the road end," said Grandad. He turned to the sergeant. "Can you check with the Glasgow police, if any child has turned up there?"

By evening they were speaking to the matron of the children's home.

"I don't understand how you can do something like that," Kezzie was in tears. "She's halfway to Canada with a different name and her own family don't know."

"To us she was an abandoned child," said the matron defensively. "Lots of children have been sent out over the years. Very few go now, but it gave many a good start in life. We have letters from them telling us how well their new families treat them. We were doing it for the best."

From *Kezzie* © Theresa Breslin 1993 (pp. 139–141). Published by Egmont Books Limited, London, and used with permission.

QUESTIONS FOR STUDENTS TO CONSIDER

1. With what circumstance can you compare this passage?

2. Could a similar situation happen today?

3. How is Kezzie's reaction typical in comparison to today's standards? How is it abnormal in comparison to today's standards?

4. In what ways is this situation different from kidnapping? The same as kidnapping?

5. Can the state do this with children now? In what ways does the state have rights that could compare to the situation in this passage?

Comparing and contrasting life during the Great Depression with life in the present is one way of asking middle-level students to think deeply about an issue. Asking them to compare people's reactions to their situations is another way of asking them to think critically about time and how it may or may not have affected the human condition. Finally, to ask middle-level students to think in historical contexts opens up the discussion about whether history should be judged from the present, and the arguments for and against that stance.

Conclusion

Contextualizing our thinking and seeing ourselves as historical beings allow us, as readers, greater insight into how events may occur. When we as teachers read historical fiction with middle-level students, we have the opportunity to make connections between our past and our present, our families and our communities, our countries and other nations to teach students about the changes they can make for the future. By using New Historical criticism, middle-level students can begin to recognize the connectedness of human beings that transcend borders, and how time periods, settings, and events can be evaluated and understood as necessary components of the present.

"'You've got to hold on to the things you know to be true, set your mind to a higher place, and fight like a dog to keep it there. War can be so fierce, you can forget the good. Forget what you're about in this world, what's really important. There's always going to be somebody who wants to try to make you forget it. Don't let them.'

Tree wasn't sure how you do that in seventh grade."

From *Stand Tall* (Bauer, 2002, p. 71)

CHAPTER 9

Where Do We Go From Here?
Critical Consciousness, Critical Literacy, and the Questions That Remain

Perhaps thinking about becoming critically conscious, critically literate, and concerned with social justice should not be thought about in terms of war, yet there are people within our communities who are fighting for equal opportunity, dignity, and justice. Their fight can be as crucial as any war because wars often are about power, ideologies, and people's lives. When thinking about social justice, it may be difficult to believe that young adolescents are interested in such matters, but this is not the case. Just before this book was published, Holly walked into a sixth-grade classroom just as one Latino student was reading to his class his response to a current event. His last sentence asserted that "one day we will have our justice."

Knowing what justice is and how it relates to their lives as middle-level students involves the ability to think critically and to develop critical consciousness. Young adolescents care about issues of justice, and they are developmentally ready to wrestle with the ambiguities and complexity that accompany such attention. We know that when middle-level teachers address the issues we have highlighted in this text, they infuse new life—and change—into their classrooms—change that can infuse new life into a school, a community, or a nation. In this final chapter, we address some of the issues that still challenge us as educators. We also present the direction we and other teachers concerned about critical consciousness and social justice can take toward a better world for all people.

The Issues That Remain

Just as we know we will continue to read and reexamine our approaches to teaching for critical consciousness and social justice, we also know that there will be issues to confront along the way. We will have to address the limitations within ourselves, our school systems, and our societies. Regardless of those limitations, however, our biggest challenge may involve holding on to hope and the belief that each of us can and does make a difference. We can make a difference in our teaching, our communications with others, and the direction that young adult literature is headed. Some of the issues with which we currently are wrestling include our teaching methods, censorship, and the type of literature to use with students when addressing critique and pleasure.

Critical Teaching Methods

One of the critical issues teachers face is developing and implementing critical teaching methods. We have shared some of the strategies we have used to involve students in literature and literary theory, and in their growth as critical consumers of texts and theories. We believe, however, that teachers need a bigger repertoire of teaching methods that will address critical consciousness, critical literacy, and social justice.

For example, service learning should become part of our teaching and our students' learning. Inviting students to join their communities on a level that involves not only their physical presence but also their emotional and cognitive involvement can lead them to a greater awareness of how their communities are addressing issues of poverty, literacy, and discriminatory practices. Through such an awareness—and action that can begin to alleviate some of the challenges to liberty and justice in their immediate vicinities—middle-level students can transform their lives and their worlds. Service learning, when approached with a sense of equity and appreciation for all people, can become one of the most powerful ways in which students can learn about concepts we have addressed in this book.

Service learning projects can be developed and implemented through thematic units of study that address the concepts and issues that encourage critical thinking. Literature units in which literature plays a key role in students' learning, interdisciplinary units that involve more than one content area, and integrative units that transcend particular content areas can create holistic experiences for students, disrupting the barriers that schooling often erects for ease of delivery. Such distinctions—and discussions about the artificial nature of them—can be addressed with students so they, too, remember that knowledge and people are connected and frequently interdependent.

Inquiry is another method of teaching that engages students and addresses both critique and pleasure. Inviting middle-level students to ask their own questions and discover or create their own answers allows for the type of learning that is pleasurable to them. Inquiry combines personal interest with dialogue that can lead to more meaningful engagement with others. Students are asked to reflect on their learning and to present their new ideas to others. With this cycle of independent and whole-class reflection, students grow as critical thinkers and more socially conscious members of their communities.

We know that middle-level students are passionate about injustice and have a desire to understand their world. We are excited by the curricular changes that service learning, thematic teaching, and inquiry can produce. Finding ways to implement these teaching methods in classrooms and to move beyond a standard curricular framework in which one size frequently fits all is the challenge we must continue to address.

Censorship

Another challenge teachers face is the reality of censorship. As the world becomes smaller, there are times when our societies seem to be more fragmented. The tension between school learning and family values appears greater than ever, and the objectives of the two often are blurred or confused. Censorship of particular pieces of literature resides in the center of this tension with little resolution in sight. Learning how to talk across the different—yet often overlapping—"jobs" of teachers and parents is also at the center of the censorship issue.

Censorship is a complex issue, yet it often comes down to value systems and what is acceptable for students to know, think, or be like. The diversity of values and beliefs in the world needs to be addressed on community, if not national, levels. Too often assumptions about what is right or normal limit the freedoms of others, and schools in a democracy need to address such issues. The purpose of schooling, however, is seldom questioned, thus leaving how and what students should learn subject to the various interests, values, and beliefs specific groups espouse as appropriate.

For us, the purpose of schooling is about raising citizens who will honor the U.S. Constitution and the dignity of all people. Schools are about creating equity for individuals as well as groups of people, and are places where favoritism is not appropriate or beneficial. Schools in a democracy are about democracy, tolerance, and an acceptance of multiple voices and multiple perspectives. When we censor texts based on differences of value systems, we close the door to students' learning about others in the world. Addressing censorship, then, has to do with a public dialogue that focuses on the purpose of schooling. Such a dialogue will not directly alleviate the problem of censorship, but it will allow for attention to the very public issue of education, which should not be overshadowed by private interest. Censorship based on discriminatory beliefs cannot be tolerated in a free and democratic society.

Teachers who wish to transform their classrooms, the lives of their students, and the communities in which they live will find ways to discuss this issue when given the opportunity. The struggle is local more often than not, and thus censorship is typically a battle that is fought by one teacher, one school, or one community. With more public discussions about the purpose of schooling, perhaps such struggles will no longer be so isolated.

Writing the Critical: Access to Appropriate Materials

Who writes for whom is a question that remains both viable and pertinent. In regard to the critical awareness of middle-level students, having more materials available to them allows for greater learning in areas outside of novels and picture books. Access to materials that address issues of poverty, discriminatory practices, and ways in which these issues can be challenged needs to become part of the landscape of middle schools across the world. Middle-level students have the intelligence, the interest, and the passion to engage in studies that will transform them.

However, finding the materials that address the issues in a real way can be problematic. This could be the result of economic considerations or authorial interest. More likely the reason such materials do not exist in abundance is because of a general lack of interest at the adult level. The issues and concepts we have addressed in this text are complex; they cannot be taught in one or two quick lessons, nor can they be easily explained. While we believe units of study can be developed to address the concepts and issues we suggest, materials that can be introduced in a middle-level classroom can be difficult to find. It is our hope that as teachers find the courage to engage in such studies with their students, more authors and publishers will make the materials available and more adults outside the classroom will be willing to discuss the issues with students.

Continued Care: Creating Inclusive Classroom Environments

There are times when we all can become discouraged with the work of social justice and the need for developing critical consciousness. We know there are times when our best efforts have been rewarded with the misunderstanding and discomfort of our students—not because we planned such results, but because working with human beings always includes unknown variables. We continue to hope and continue to broach discussion of the sensitive issues of identity and representation, racism and sexism, and multiple perspectives with increasing care. Creating classroom environments in which such issues can be discussed requires our full attention to the students with whom we work so we are ever more inclusive, rather than alienating.

As we analyzed the transcripts of discussions included in this text, we realized that we have an obligation to disrupt some of the problematic statements students generate. Simultaneously, such disruption must be broached gently, taking care to avoid silencing students. The obligation to disrupt and to care is based on our ideas about the purpose of schooling: to raise a democratic citizenry. Attempting such a balance is similar to walking a tightrope, but we know that when teachers extend their care toward students, more often than not, students' forgiveness of a teacher's oversight is readily granted. It is this balance of disruption and care that is very similar to critique and pleasure. If a paradox exists, it reflects the reality of a relationship based on respect and hope.

New Directions, Continued Promise

As teachers face continued challenges, they also face new directions and a promising future. Our focus on fiction throughout this text has prompted us to examine other ways of approaching the concepts we have discussed and other aspects of our world that cannot be ignored. Social justice, representation, identity, and discriminatory practices need to be explored in relation to other formats and to other elements in the world.

Other Genres, Other Formats

Although we concentrated on young adult fiction and picture books in this book, we know that critical consciousness can be developed by using all types of literature. We concentrated on young adult fiction and picture books because of our own interests and because of the many quality pieces of fiction that are available to young adolescents and their teachers. As we continue to read and reflect on the issues of identity, representation, power, oppression, and perspective, we know that the genres we did not directly address, such as fantasy and mystery, also present situations and characters that would allow middle-level readers to enjoy reading and discussing social justice and the concepts addressed in this book. Books such as *Perloo the Bold* (Avi, 1998) for younger students and *Heaven Eyes* (Almond, 2000) for those interested in magical realism present conditions that allow for discussions of social justice, equity, and possibility for our own communities. We also realize that science fiction that is more "earthbound," such as *Shade's Children* (Nix, 1997), *Armageddon Summer* (Yolen & Coville, 1998), and *Feed* (Anderson, 2002), also will intrigue middle-level students while pushing them to become more critically conscious about the conditions of the world. Mysteries such as *Eagle Strike* (Horowitz, 2004) from the Alex Rider Adventure series and *Riding the Flume* (Pfitsch, 2004), which is also historical fiction, bring intrigue and excitement to students as they predict and contemplate the critical elements presented such as oppression, power, and issues of justice.

We also would like formats such as informational texts and poetry to become more prominent in our teaching and sharing of texts that can lead toward critical consciousness and social justice. Informational texts such as *Voices From the Fields: Children of Migrant Farmworkers Tell Their Stories* (Atkin, 1993) and *Remembering Manzanar: Life in a Japanese Relocation Camp* (Cooper, 2002) can help bring to life some of the situations that students either do not think about or do not encounter in their textbook reading. Poetry books such as *The Pain Tree* (Watson, 2000) and *You Hear Me? Poems and Writing by Teenage Boys* (Franco, 2001) also help bring to life some of the struggles adolescents experience in the world, while books such as *The Dream Keeper and Other Poems* (Hughes, 1932/1996) allow students to transcend the limitations frequently set before them.

We also realize that students can study identity, assumptions, binary opposites, representation, and similar issues by examining advertisements, commercials, and other media in more critical ways. We started with fiction and picture books because we see these formats and the particular genres we selected as a good way to introduce the topics we have found especially salient for young adolescents to study. By extending our visions to all types of texts, we can provide students the opportunity to grow and become more critically literate.

Other Entities, Other Elements

This book addresses very human issues, yet when thinking about social justice, representation, and discriminatory practices, we also know that there are other elements connected to humanity that must be considered. For example, the environment is a cause for concern, as is the animal kingdom. Students can be encouraged to think about how language is used to dissuade them from exploring real issues such as environmental protection and animal rights.

As the media present more about environmental issues and animal stories, reading about and discussing such issues is timely, and these activities are sure to engage most students because the issues evoke powerful emotions and allow students to voice their thinking about current issues. For example, exploring the issue of stewardship in relation to the earth is as complex and critical as any of the other issues we have discussed in this book. We say this because these issues directly involve the concepts of identity and the issue of assumptions, perhaps on an even deeper level than we can imagine. Students are keenly interested in the issues involving their environments and the complexity of animal rights. Learning to examine these interests is one more way students engage in critique and pleasure.

Students Writing the Critical: Applying Knowledge

We already have discussed the issue of writing the critical, but not from the perspective of middle-level students and their stories. Middle-level students everywhere should be allowed to voice their own understandings of the world without censure. This does not mean, however, that their ideas are not open to conjecture or revision. When students write, they also have the opportunity to engage their peers in real ways. When they share with others in their classrooms, student writers address an audience that may or may not understand what they are attempting to share. By writing, reading, and discussing their own writings with others, middle-level students gain a sense of their own voices; their own power to persuade, inform, or entertain; and their own convictions. They learn to use language in more precise ways while also discovering firsthand how language is used to represent, oppress, or empower them or others. By asking students to write from a critical standpoint, teachers complete a powerful cycle of learning. Their students read, discuss, and then create their own critical understandings of the world.

The poetry books we mentioned previously are excellent examples of students writing about aspects of their lives, many in critical ways. These are perfect examples of our contention that critique and pleasure often intermingle. By creating opportunities for students to tell their own stories about representation, identity, assumptions, power, and oppression, teachers can engage students in actions that can transform the world.

Conclusion

In *Memoirs of a Bookbat* (Lasky, 1994), the character Harper states,

> I realized then a very weird but simple truth: although books were as much
> a part of my life as anything had ever been, as much a part of me as the air

I breathe or the blood that runs through my veins, nothing I had ever read in a book in itself caused me to be really, truly unhappy. (p. 72)

Just as they are for Harper, books are a part of our lives and part of our teaching, so using them as a way to teach issues that concern us as educators and concern middle-level students as citizens becoming aware of social issues seems not only feasible but also exciting. By creating opportunities for students to become more critically conscious, however, we know that there will be times when reading a book will cause students discomfort. It is not the pain that the character Harper addresses because in *Memoirs of a Bookbat*, books are Harper's escape, guide, and salvation from the world of people who cannot tolerate freedom, nor remember innocence. The pain students can experience involves their empathy and their budding understandings about the condition of the world. Thus, to bring about awareness means we also must bring about hope, with the understanding that hope should be linked to action.

The use of literature to bring about change gives us the hope that such action can bridge the gap between the present and a more just and understanding community. We know middle-level students are up to the challenge, we know that teachers can inspire such a journey, and we know that our communities are prepared for the change that occurs when people commit to such a cause.

Social Justice Unit

This unit combines many of the ideas addressed in this text. We have used much of this unit with sixth graders over a two-month period, focusing heavily on read-alouds, picture books, literature circle discussions, student journals, and minilessons that emphasize the concepts or topics under study. A major element of this unit is the inquiry project that students can either do individually or as groups. (The groups are selected by membership in literature circles that discuss the novels students select in week three.) An extension of this unit is the service learning project we present in weeks seven and eight. During most weeks, teachers can overlap the literary theory highlighted, because all of these theories can be used together or interwoven. Teachers should not spend large amounts of time on the theories, but rather the questions and topics highlighted by the theories.

Assessments for writing assignments and projects would depend on individual teachers' purposes. The sixth graders with whom we worked used their inquiry project posters for parent night and wrote about their inquiry discoveries for a six-week assessment their district used to gauge their research and computer skills. The writing assignments can be used in portfolios.

Week One
Purpose: Students will learn the concept of social justice and its connections to language, identity, and assumptions.

Books Used for Read-Alouds
Conrad, P. (1996). *The rooster's gift*. New York: HarperCollins.
Gregorowski, C. (2000). *Fly, eagle, fly!* New York: Margaret K. McElderry.
Jiménez, F. (2001). *La mariposa*. New York: Houghton Mifflin.
Raschka, C. (1998). *Yo! Yes!* New York: Orchard Books.
Stanek, M. (1989). *I speak English for my mom*. New York: Albert Whitman & Co.
Waddell, M. (1991). *Farmer Duck*. Cambridge, MA: Candlewick.

Topics Addressed

Identity

Assumptions

Descriptive Language

Literary Theory: Reader Response and Rhetorical Criticism

Activities

1. Literature Circles: Students meet in literature circles after each read-aloud and discuss the book read. Teacher prompts invite students to address language usage, the issue of identity, and the role of assumptions on alternate days.

2. Journals: Students write in journals before and after literature circle discussions. Prior to meeting in literature circles, individual students respond to the text. After literature circles, students write what they have learned about the book and the concept of identity, assumptions, or language (the concept addressed that day). Journals can be spiral-bound notebooks or notepaper placed in a binder or folder (with enough sheets of paper to provide adequate space for responding to the readings each day and to be used as a gathering place for notes during their inquiry research project in weeks five and six).

3. Whole-Group Discussions: Students and teacher discuss their ideas on the topic addressed (assumptions, language, or identity), as teacher does a minilesson on the concept.

Week Two

Purpose: Students write personal narratives about social justice in their lives.

Books Used for Read-Alouds

Daly, N. (2003). *Once upon a time*. New York: Farrar Straus Giroux.

Lorbiecki, M. (2000). *Sister Anne's hands*. New York: Puffin.

Madrigal, A. (2001). *Erandi's braids*. New York: Penguin Putnam.

Morrison, T., & Morrison, S. (2002). *The big box*. New York: Hyperion/ Jump at the Sun Books.

Rahaman, V. (1997). *Read for me, Mama!* Honesdale, PA: Boyds Mills Press.

Woodson, J. (2001). *The other side*. New York: Penguin Putnam.

Topics Addressed

Representation

Power

Literary Theory: Reader Response and Feminist Criticism

Activities

1. Literature Circles

2. Journals

3. Personal Narratives: These essays address aspects of individual students' lives in which they have either abused power or have felt unfairly represented. This topic is taught along with the writing process during the week, and it takes about two weeks to complete. Students work on these essays for a part of each day. Drawing in Rhetorical Criticism through the selection of language used in the essay helps students better understand the theory. With middle-level learners, essays can be from two to five handwritten pages. Students work on editing and revising their essays with their literature circle group members.

Week Three

Purpose: Students read young adult literature to expand ideas of social justice.

Books Used for Read-Alouds

Marsden, J., & Tan, S. (1998). *The rabbits*. Port Melbourne, Australia: Lothian Books.

McGovern, A. (1997). *The lady in the box*. New York: Turtle Books.

Shange, N. (1997). *White wash*. New York: Walker & Co.

Waddell, M. (1991). *Farmer Duck*. Cambridge, MA: Candlewick.

Wiles, D. (2001). *Freedom summer*. New York: Simon & Schuster.

Woodson, J. (2002). *Visiting day*. New York: Scholastic.

Topics Addressed

Oppression

Binary Opposites

Bullying

Literary Theory: Culturally Situated Response and Rhetorical Criticism

Activities

1. Literature Circles

2. Journals

3. Novels: Students select books in literature circle groups after teacher does short discussions of the book through Book Talks. The students read the novels over a two-week period, again using class time to read for a few minutes and then meeting in literature circles. (Students can choose to meet after an agreed upon number of chapters; otherwise, they meet in literature circles after completing the book.) Students also complete their personal essays during this week.

Week Four

Purpose: Students will address issues of language usage and its connection to power.

Books Used for Read-Alouds

Altman, L. (1995). *Amelia's road*. New York: Lee & Low.
Bradby, M. (1995). *More than anything else*. New York: Orchard Books.
Pinkney, A. (2003). *Fishing day*. New York: Jump at the Sun.
Rappaport, D. (2000). *Freedom river*. New York: Sagebrush.
Williams, V. (1982). *A chair for my mother*. New York: Greenwillow.
Yolen, J. (1992). *Encounter*. New York: Harcourt.

Topics Addressed

Language as Description and Mediator of Power

Literary Theory: Culturally Situated Response and Feminist Criticism

Activities

1. Literature Circles

2. Whole-Group Discussions

3. Journals

4. Comparison/Contrast Essays: These short essays (two to three pages) involve students comparing and contrasting two of the texts they have heard read aloud (students should be able to borrow the books from the teacher to review particular plot lines and so forth), or students can compare and contrast their lives with one of the characters' lives from the texts. These essays take about one week to complete.

Week Five

Purpose: Students explore historical evidence of social justice through inquiry.

Books Used for Read-Alouds

Battle-Levert, G. (2003). *Papa's mark*. New York: Holiday House.

Bishop, G. (1999). *The house that Jack built*. Auckland, New Zealand: Scholastic.

Coleman, E. (1996). *White socks only*. Morton Grove, IL: Albert Whitman & Co.

Littlesugar, A. (2001). *Freedom school, yes!* New York: Philomel.

Ransom, C. (2003). *Liberty street*. New York: Walker & Co.

Turner, A. (1998). *Drummer boy: Marching to the Civil War*. New York: HarperCollins.

Topics Addressed

Context

Ethnocentrism

Multiple Perspectives

Literary Theory: Culturally Situated Response and New Historicism

Activities

1. Library and Internet Research: Students generate and select questions to research about issues of social justice or injustice, or people involved in movements that promoted social justice. Examples include the following: the U.S. Civil Rights movement, the women's movement in the United States, abolitionists, Gandhi, Malcolm X, suffrage movement, apartheid, slavery, and the Holocaust.

2. Journals: This week, students divide their journals into two sections. The front section is the continuation of responses to student reading. The back section is used as a learning log for notes gathered about students' inquiry projects.

3. Literature Circles: Literature circles are used to discuss the issues found in the novels they finished over the weekend and to support students' inquiry projects.

Week Six

Purpose: Students develop a better understanding of a particular aspect of social justice through completing and presenting inquiry projects.

Books Used for Read-Alouds

Bunting, E. (1999). *Smoky night*. New York: Voyager.

Lacapa, K., & Lacapa, M. (1994). *Less than half, more than whole*. Flagstaff, AZ: Northland.

Lionni, L. (1967). *Frederick*. New York: Knopf.

Lorbiecki, M. (1996). *Just one flick of a finger*. New York: Dial.

Shange, N. (2004). *Ellington was not a street*. New York: Simon & Schuster.

Topics Addressed

Sign Systems and Transmediation

Connotations and Denotations

Literary Theory: Culturally Situated Response and Reader Response

Activities

1. Inquiry Project Presentations (if students are ready): At the beginning of the week, students brainstorm, under the guidance of the teacher, how they could present their inquiry questions and discoveries on posters. A checklist of essential elements is created by the teacher and the students and either typed up by the teacher or placed on a bulletin board. This checklist also becomes the scoring guide for poster presentations.

2. Journals

3. Literature Circles

4. Whole-Group Discussions: Discussions center around inquiry presentations.

Weeks Seven and Eight

Purpose: Students plan and present a service learning project as an extension of one of the inquiry projects. Prepare and make presentations to the local Parent–Teacher Association (PTA) with suggestions of how the PTA could help sponsor the project.

Books Used for Read-Alouds

Atkins, J. (1999). *A name on the quilt*. New York: Atheneum.

Madonna. (2003). *Mr. Peabody's apples*. New York: Callaway.

Romain, T. (2002). *Jemma's journey*. Honesdale, PA: Boyds Mills Press.

Smothers, E. (2003). *The hard-times jar*. New York: Frances Foster.

Vaughan, M. (2003). *Up the learning tree*. New York: Lee & Low.

Topics Addressed

Service Learning

Making Presentations to an Outside Audience

Language Registers (using language for different purposes and for different audiences)

Decision Making Through a Problem-Solving Process and Criteria

Literary Theory: Rhetorical Criticism and Reader Response

Activities

1. Literature Circles: Students will read all five of the above books in literature circles over three days.

2. Whole-Class Discussion: Discussion centers on books and the merits of each.

3. Service Learning Project: Each of the above books presents ideas that could be turned into a project that students could undertake as part of a service learning extension. For instance, students can create a scrapbook of memories for the community or individuals at nursing homes, make a quilt that addresses social justice to be hung in the school library or foyer, create posters that draw attention to language that can hurt others, or collect money for the underprivileged and use it for a holiday fundraiser or to buy books for the underprivileged or library. Students come up with an idea for a service learning project and present it to the PTA.

Over 100 Books That Encourage Critical Consciousness

Marginalization

Green, B. (1973). *Summer of my German soldier*. New York: Laurel Leaf.

Hamilton, V. (1993). *Plain city*. New York: Scholastic.

Jones, R. (1976). *The acorn people*. New York: Laurel Leaf.

Koje, K. (2003). *Buddha boy*. New York: Farrar Straus Giroux.

Krumgold, J. (1987). *Onion John*. New York: Scholastic.

Lisle, J.T. (2000). *The art of keeping cool*. New York: Scholastic.

Mazer, A. (1993). *The oxboy*. New York: Knopf.

McGraw, E. (1996). *The moorchild*. New York: Scholastic.

Meyer, C. (1996). *Gideon's people*. Orlando, FL: Gulliver/Harcourt Brace.

Philbrick, R. (1993). *The mighty*. New York: Scholastic.

Rapp, A. (1997). *The buffalo tree*. New York: HarperCollins.

Sachar, L. (1998). *Holes*. New York: Scholastic.

Wittlinger, E. (2000). *Gracie's girl*. New York: Simon & Schuster.

Yep, L. (1991). *The star fisher*. New York: Scholastic.

Power and Oppression Issues Outside the United States

Bell, W. (2001). *Stones*. Toronto, ON, Canada: Doubleday Canada. (Canada)

Clinton, C. (2002). *A stone in my hand*. Cambridge, MA: Candlewick. (Gaza City)

Ellis, D. (2001). *The breadwinner*. Toronto, ON, Canada: Groundwood. (Afghanistan)

Ellis, D. (2002). *Parvanna's journey*. Toronto, ON, Canada: Groundwood. (Afghanistan)

Fletcher, S. (1998). *Shadow spinner*. New York: Scholastic. (Persia)

Hautzig, E. (1968). *The endless steppe: Growing up in Siberia*. New York: HarperTrophy. (Russian Siberia)

Ho, M. (1990). *Rice without rain*. New York: Lothrop, Lee & Shepard. (Thailand)

Jiang, J.L. (1997). *Red scarf girl: A memoir of the cultural revolution*. New York: Scholastic. (China)

Kurtz, J. (1998). *The storyteller's beads*. Orlando, FL: Gulliver/Harcourt Brace. (Ethiopia)

Levin, B. (1990). *Brother Moose*. New York: Greenwillow. (Canada)

Levitin, S. (2000). *Dream freedom*. San Diego, CA: Harcourt. (Sudan)

Vos, I. (2000). *The key is lost by Ida* (T. Edelstein, Trans.). New York: Scholastic. (Holland)

Whelan, G. (2000). *Homeless bird*. New York: Scholastic. (India)

Race/Culture/Ethnicity

African Americans (Slavery/Segregation/Jim Crow)

Beatty, P. (1992). *Who comes with cannons?* New York: Scholastic.

Hamilton, V. (1974). *M.C. Higgins the great*. New York: Simon & Schuster.

Myers, W.D. (1994). *The glory field*. New York: Scholastic.

O'Dell, S. (1989). *My name is not Angelica*. New York: Yearling.

Paterson, K. (1996). *Jip, his story*. New York: Scholastic.

Pearsall, S. (2002). *Trouble don't last*. New York: Knopf.

Rinaldi, A. (2002). *Numbering all the bones*. New York: Scholastic.

Taylor, M.D. (1981). *Let the circle be unbroken*. New York: Puffin.

Taylor, M.D. (1990). *The road to Memphis*. New York: Puffin.

Tillage, L.W. (1997). *Leon's story*. New York: Scholastic.

Wesley, V.W. (1993). *Where do I go from here?* New York: Scholastic.

Woodson, J. (1995). *From the notebooks of Melanin Sun*. New York: Scholastic.

Woodson, J. (2002). *Hush*. New York: Putnam.

Class

Avi. (2002). *Crispin: The cross of lead*. New York: Hyperion Books for Children.

DeFelice, C. (1999). *Nowhere to call home*. New York: HarperTrophy.

Estes, E. (1973). *The hundred dresses*. New York: Scholastic.

Hunt, I. (1970). *No promises in the wind*. New York: Berkley Books.

Recorvits, H. (1999). *Goodbye, Walter Malinski*. New York: Frances Foster Books.

Simmons, M. (2003). *Pool boy*. New York: Simon & Schuster.

Gender/Sexual Orientation

Bauer, J. (1992). *Squashed*. New York: Laurel Leaf.

Cather, W. (1992). *O pioneers!* New York: Vintage.

Cushman, K. (1995). *The midwife's apprentice*. New York: HarperTrophy.

Greene, B. (1974). *Philip Hall likes me. I reckon maybe*. New York: Puffin.

Hartinger, B. (2003). *Geography club*. New York: HarperTempest.

Holm, J.L. (1999). *Our only May Amelia*. New York: HarperTrophy.

Kerr, M.E. (1994). *Deliver us from Evie*. New York: HarperTrophy.

Lasky, K. (1994). *Beyond the burning time*. New York: Scholastic.

Hispanic Americans

Cisneros, S. (2002). *Caramelo*. New York: Knopf.

Hesse, K. (1993). *Letters from Rifka*. New York: Puffin Books.

Isaacs, A. (2000). *Torn thread*. New York: Scholastic.

Jiménez, F. (1997). *The circuit: Stories from the life of a migrant child*. New York: Scholastic.

Jiménez, F. (2001). *Breaking through*. Boston: Houghton Mifflin.

Laird, C. (1989). *Shadow of the wall*. New York: Greenwillow.

Laird, C. (1993). *But can the phoenix sing?* New York: Greenwillow.

Lobel, A. (1998). *No pretty pictures: A child of war*. New York: Avon.

Martinez, V. (1996). *Parrot in the oven*. New York: Scholastic.

Immigrants to the United States

Buss, F.L. (1991). *Journey of the sparrows*. New York: Yearling/Random House.

Levitin, S. (1970). *Journey to America*. New York: Scholastic.

Sachs, M. (1982). *Call me Ruth*. New York: Scholastic.

Japanese Internment

Houston, J.W., & Houston, J.D. (1973). *Farewell to Manzanar*. New York: Bantam Dell.

Reeder, C. (1998). *Foster's war*. New York: Scholastic.

Uchida, Y. (1991). *The invisible thread*. New York: HarperTrophy.

Jewish Holocaust

Matas, C. (1996). *After the war*. New York: Aladdin Paperbacks.

Matas, C. (1998). *Greater than angels*. New York: Aladdin Paperbacks.

Perl, L., & Lazan, M.B. (1996). *Four perfect pebbles: A Holocaust story*. New York: Greenwillow.

Reiss, J. (1972). *The upstairs room*. New York: Scholastic.

Reiss, J. (1976). *The journey back*. New York: Scholastic.

Williams, L.E. (1996). *Behind the bedroom wall*. Minneapolis, MN: Milkweed Editions.

Yolen, J. (1988). *The devil's arithmetic*. New York: Scholastic.

Native Americans

Banks, S.H. (1993). *Remember my name*. New York: Scholastic.

Bruchac, J. (2002). *The winter people*. New York: Dial.

Erdrich, L. (1999). *The birchbark house*. New York: Scholastic.

Hamm, D.J. (1997). *Daughter of Suqua*. Morton Grove, IL: Albert Whitman & Co.

Highwater, J. (1977). *Anpao, an American Indian odyssey*. New York: Scholastic.

LaFarge, O. (1957). *Laughing Boy*. New York: Signet.

McKissack, P.C. (1997). *Run away home*. New York: Scholastic.

O'Dell, S. (1970). *Sing down the moon*. New York: Laurel Leaf.

Stewart, E.J. (1994). *On the long trail home*. New York: Scholastic.

Science Fiction/Fantasy Communities

Bradbury, R. (1953). *Fahrenheit 451*. New York: Del Rey/Random House.

Haddix, M.P. (1998). *Among the sidden*. New York: Aladdin Paperbacks.

Lowry, L. (2000). *Gathering blue*. Boston: Houghton Mifflin.

Lowry, L. (2004). *The messenger*. Boston: Houghton Mifflin.

Nix, G. (1997). *Shade's children*. New York: HarperCollins.

Orwell, G. (1946). *Animal farm*. New York: Signet.

Sleator, W. (1974). *House of stairs*. New York: Dutton.

References

Allington, R. (2002). *Big brother and the national reading curriculum: How ideology trumped evidence.* Portsmouth, NH: Heinemann.

Alvermann, D.E. (2002). Effective literacy instruction for adolescents. *Journal of Literacy Research, 34*(2), 189–208.

Alvermann, D.E., & Hagood, M.C. (2000). Fandom and critical media literacy. *Journal of Adolescent & Adult Literacy, 43,* 36–46.

Barrs, M., & Pidgeon, S. (Eds.). (1994). *Reading the difference: Gender and reading in elementary classrooms.* York, ME: Stenhouse.

Beach, R. (1993). *A teacher's introduction to reader response theories.* Urbana, IL: National Council of Teachers of English.

Brown, A.L. (1997). Transforming schools into communities of thinking and learning about serious matters. *American Psychologist, 52*(4), 399–413.

Buehl, D. (2001). *Classroom strategies for interactive learning* (2nd ed.). Newark, DE: International Reading Association.

Burke, K. (1969). *Rhetorical criticism: A grammar of motives.* Berkeley: University of California Press.

Coles, G. (2003). *Reading the naked truth: Literacy, legislation, and lies.* Portsmouth, NH: Heinemann.

Comber, B., & Nixon, H. (1999). Literacy education as a site for social justice: What do our practices do? In C. Edelsky (Ed.), *Making justice our project: Teachers working toward critical whole language practice* (pp. 316–352). Urbana, IL: National Council of Teachers of English.

Croteau, J.M., Talbot, D.M., Lance, T.S., & Evans, N.J. (2002). A qualitative study of the interplay between privilege and oppression. *Journal of Multicultural Counseling and Development, 30*(4), 239–258.

Daniels, H. (2001). *Literature circles: Voice and choice in book clubs and reading groups.* York, ME: Stenhouse.

Dewey, J. (1929). *Democracy and education: An introduction to a philosophy of education.* New York: Macmillan.

Edelsky, C. (Ed.). (1999). *Making justice our project: Teachers working toward critical whole language practice.* Urbana, IL: National Council of Teachers of English.

Espelage, D. (Summer, 2004). Bullying: An old problem gets new attention. *The Classroom Teacher,* 4–8.

Evans, K. (1996). *Just when you thought it was complicated enough: Literature discussions meet critical theory.* Unpublished doctoral dissertation, University of Arizona, Tucson.

Fairclough, N. (1989). *Power and language*. New York: Longman.

Fetterley, J. (1978). *The resisting reader: A feminist approach to American fiction*. Bloomington: Indiana University Press.

Freedman, L., & Johnson, H. (2004). *Inquiry, literacy, and learning in the middle grades*. Norwood, MA: Christopher Gordon.

Freire, P. (2000). *Pedagogy of the oppressed*. New York: Continuum International. (Original work published 1973)

Freire, P. (2002). *Education for critical consciousness*. New York: Continuum. (Original work published 1973)

Gee, J.P. (1996). *Social linguistics and literacies: Ideology in discourse*. Bristol, PA: Taylor & Francis.

Gee, J.P. (1999). *Social linguistics and literacies: Ideology in discourse* (2nd ed.). Bristol, PA: Taylor & Francis.

Giroux, H. (1990). Rethinking the boundaries of educational discourse: Modernism, Postmodernism, and Feminism. *College Literature, 17*(2/3), 41–50.

Goffman, E. (1974). *The presentation of self in everyday life*. New York: Anchor.

Gomez, M.L. (1993). Prospective teachers' perspectives on teaching diverse children: A review with implications for teacher education and practice. *Journal of Negro Education, 62*(4), 459–474.

Harvey, S., & Goudvis, A. (2000). *Strategies that work: Teaching comprehension to enhance understanding*. York, ME: Stenhouse.

Howard, G.R. (1999). *We can't teach what we don't know: White teachers, multiracial schools*. New York: Teachers College Press.

Hynds, S. (1997). *On the brink: Negotiating literature and life with adolescents*. Newark, DE: International Reading Association.

Johnson, H. (1997). *Reading the personal and the political: Exploring female representation in realistic fiction with adolescent girls*. Unpublished doctoral dissertation, University of Arizona, Tucson.

Johnson, H. (2000). "To Stand Up and Say Something": "Girls Only" literature circles at the middle level. *The New Advocate, 13*(4), 375–389.

Johnson, H., & Chen, X. (2004). [Reading requirements in secondary schools: A comparison of reading selections across the United States]. Unpublished raw data.

Johnson, H., & Miller, R. (2004). *Using picture books to teach social justice: A case study at the middle level*. Unpublished manuscript.

Kidder, L. (1997). Colonial remnants: Assumptions of privilege. In M. Fine, L. Weis, L.C. Powell, & L. Mun Wong (Eds.), *Off white: Readings on race, power, and society* (pp. 158–166). New York: Routledge.

Kohl, H.R. (1995). *"I won't learn from you": And other thoughts on creative maladjustment*. New York: The New Press.

Kohl, H.R. (1996). *Should we burn Babar? Essays on children's literature and the power of stories*. New York: The New Press.

Kuhn, D. (1999). A developmental model of critical thinking. *Educational Researcher, 28*(2), 16–25, 46.

Lesesne, T.S. (2003). *Making the match: The right book for the right reader at the right time: Grades 4–12*. Portland, ME: Stenhouse.

Luke, A. (2000). Critical literacy in Australia: A matter of context and standpoint. *Journal of Adolescent & Adult Literacy, 43*(5), 448–461.

Luke, C. (1997). Media literacy and cultural studies. In S. Muspratt, A. Luke, & P. Freebody (Eds.), *Constructing critical literacies: Teaching and learning textual practice* (pp. 19–49). Cresskill, NJ: Hampton Press.

Macedo, D., & Freire, P. (1987). *Literacy: Reading the word and the world.* Westport, CT: Bergin & Garvey.

Marano, H. (Ed.). *Psychology Today, 28*(5). New York: Sussex.

McIntosh, P. (1998). White privilege: Unpacking the invisible knapsack. In M. McGoldrick (Ed.), *Re-visioning family therapy: Race, class, and gender in clinical practice* (pp. 147–152). New York: Guilford.

Meier, D. (1996). *The power of their ideas: Lessons for America from a small school in Harlem.* Boston: Beacon Press.

Mitchell, D. (2003). *Children's literature: An invitation to the world.* Boston: Allyn & Bacon.

Moll, L., Vélez-Ibáñez, C., & Greenberg, J. (1988). *Project Implementation Plan. Community knowledge and classroom practice: Combining resources for literacy instruction* (Tech. Rep. No. L-10). Tucson: University of Arizona, College of Education and Bureau of Applied Research in Anthropology.

Moon, B. (1999). *Literary terms: A practical glossary.* Urbana, IL: National Council of Teachers of English.

Morgan, W. (1997). *Critical literacy in the classroom: The art of the possible.* New York: Routledge.

Neeld, E.C. (1986). *Writing* (2nd ed.). Glenview, IL: Scott Foresman.

Paul, R. (1990). *Critical thinking.* Doctoral dissertation, Center for Critical Thinking and Moral Critique, Sonoma State University, Rohnert Park, CA.

Pearson, P.D., & Gallagher, M.C. (1983). The instruction of reading comprehension. *Contemporary Educational Psychology, 8*(3), 317–344.

Peterson, R., & Eeds, M. (1990). *Grand conversations.* New York: Scholastic.

Powell, L.C. (1997). The achievement (k)not: Whiteness and "black underachievement." In M. Fine, L. Weis, L.C. Powell, & L. Mun Wong (Eds.), *Off white: Readings on race, power, and society* (pp. 3–11). New York: Routledge.

Rabinowitz, P.J., & Smith, M.W. (1997). *Authorizing readers: Resistance and respect in the teaching of literature.* New York: Teachers College Press; Urbana, IL: National Council of Teachers of English.

Rathes, L., Jonas, A., Rothstein, A., & Wassermann, S. (1967). *Teaching for thinking: Theory and application.* Columbus, OH: Charles Merrill.

Richardson, J.S. (2000). *Read it aloud! Using literature in the secondary content classroom.* Newark, DE: International Reading Association.

Rogers, R. (2002). "That's what you're here for, you're suppose to tell us": Teaching and learning critical literacy. *Journal of Adolescent & Adult Literacy, 45*(8), 772–787.

Rosenblatt, L.M. (1978). *The reader, the text, the poem: The transactional theory of the literary work.* Carbondale: Southern Illinois University Press.

Rosenblatt, L.M. (1995). *Literature as exploration.* New York: Modern Language Association. (Original work published 1938)

Shannon, P. (1992). *Becoming political: Readings and writings in the politics of literacy education.* Portsmouth, NH: Heinemann.

Short, K., Harste, J., & Burke, C. (1996). *Creating classrooms for authors and inquirers.* Portsmouth, NH: Heinemann.

Simon, R.I. (1992). *Teaching against the grain: Texts for a pedagogy of possibility*. Westport, CT: Bergin & Garvey.

Simpson, A. (1996). Fictions and facts: An investigation of the reading practices of girls and boys. *English Education, 28*(4), 268–279.

Sims, R. (1982). *Shadow and substance: Afro-American experience in contemporary children's fiction*. Urbana, IL: National Council of Teachers of English.

Smith, F. (1988). *Joining the literacy club*. Portsmouth, NH: Heinemann.

Tannen, D. (2001). *You just don't understand: Women and men in conversation*. Kolkata, Canada: Quill.

Wardle, F., & Cruz-Jansen, M.I. (2004). *Meeting the needs of multiethnic and multiracial children in schools*. Boston: Allyn & Bacon.

Wilhelm, J.D. (with Baker, T.N. & Dube, J.). (2001). *Strategic reading: Guiding students to lifelong literacy 6–12*. Portsmouth, NH: Heinemann.

Young, I.M. (1990). *Justice and the politics of difference*. Princeton, NJ: Princeton University Press.

Literature Cited

Abelove, J. (1998). *Go and come back*. New York: Penguin

Allende, I. (2002). *City of the beasts*. New York: HarperCollins.

Almond, D. (2000). *Heaven eyes*. New York: Delacorte Press.

Anderson, L. (1999). *Speak*. New York: Penguin.

Anderson, M.T. (2002). *Feed*. Cambridge, MA: Candlewick.

Armstrong, J. (2002). *Shattered: The stories of children and war*. New York: Knopf.

Atkin, S.B. (1993). *Voices from the fields: Children of migrant farmworkers tell their stories*. Boston: Little, Brown.

Avi. (1991). *Nothing but the truth*. New York: Avon.

Avi. (1998). *Perloo the bold*. New York: Scholastic.

Bauer, J. (2002). *Stand tall*. New York: Putnam.

Bawden, N. (1993). *The real Plato Jones*. New York: Puffin Books.

Beale, F. (1998). *I am not Esther*. New York: Hyperion.

Bechard, M. (2002). *Hanging on to Max*. Bolton, ON, Canada: Roaring Book Press/H.B. Fenn & Co.

Bennett, J. (1994). *Dakota dream*. New York: Scholastic.

Bertrand, D.G. (1999). *Trino's choice*. Houston, TX: Arte Publico.

Bertrand, D.G. (2001). *Trino's time*. Houston, TX: Arte Publico.

Birdseye, T. (1992). *Just call me stupid*. New York: Puffin.

Bloor, E. (2001). *Tangerine*. New York: Scholastic.

Breslin, T. (1993). *Kezzie*. London: Egmont Books Limited.

Bunker, E. (1998). *Little boy blue*. New York: Griffin Trade Paperback.

Bunting, E. (1994). *A day's work*. New York: Clarion.

Cannon, A. (1992). *Shadow brothers*. New York: Turtleback Books.

Carlson, R. (2003). *The speed of light*. New York: HarperTempest.

Cisneros, S. (1992). Eleven. In *Woman Hollering Creek and other stories* (pp. 6–9). New York: Vintage.

Clapp, P. (1991). *Constance: A story of early Plymouth*. New York: Puffin.

Clark, J. (2002). *Wolf on the fold*. Asheville, NC: Front Street.

Clavell, J. (1963). *The children's story*. New York: Dell Books.

Cofer, J. (1995). *An island like you: Stories from the barrio*. New York: Puffin.

Collier, K. (2002). *Jericho walls*. New York: Henry Holt & Co.

Cooney, C. (1998). *Among friends*. New York: Bantam Doubleday Dell.

Cooper, M. (2002). *Remembering Manzanar: Life in a Japanese relocation camp*. New York: Clarion.

Cormier, R. (1986). *The chocolate war*. New York: Laurel Leaf.

Cormier, R. (2001). *Rag and bone shop*. New York: Laurel Leaf.

Creech, S. (1994). *Walk two moons*. New York: Scholastic.

Creech, S. (2000). *The wanderer*. New York: HarperCollins.

Creech, S. (2004). *Heartbeat*. New York: HarperCollins.

Crow Dog, M. (with Erdoes, R.). (1990). *Lakota woman*. New York: Grove/Atlantic.

Crutcher, C. (2001). *Whale talk*. New York: Random House.

Cushman, K. (1994). *Catherine, called Birdy*. New York: HarperTrophy.

DuPrau, J. (2004). *The people of Sparks*. New York: Random House.

Farmer, N. (1996). *A girl named Disaster*. New York: Penguin.

Fiegel, S. (1996). *Where we once belonged*. New York: Kaya Press.

Filipovic, Z. (1995). *Zlata's diary: A child's life in Sarajevo*. New York: Penguin.

Fleischman, P. (1997). *Seedfolks*. New York: Joanna Cotler Books.

Franco, B. (2001). *You hear me? Poems and writing by teenage boys*. Cambridge, MA: Candlewick.

Freedman, R. (1998). *Kids at work: Lewis Hine and the crusade against child labor*. New York: Clarion.

Freedom Writers (with Filipovic, Z.). (1999). *The Freedom Writers' diary: How a teacher and 150 teens used writing to change themselves and the world around them*. New York: Main Street Books.

Gallo, D. (Ed.). (2001). *On the fringe*. New York: Dial.

Giff, P. (2002). *The pictures of Hollis Woods*. New York: Wendy Lamb Books.

Glenn, M. (1999). *Foreign exchange: A mystery in poems*. New York: HarperCollins.

Hesse, K. (1996). *The music of dolphins*. New York: Scholastic Press.

Hesse, K. (1997). *Out of the dust*. New York: Scholastic.

Hesse, K. (2001). *Witness*. New York: Scholastic.

Hinton, S.E. (1967). *The outsiders*. New York: Puffin.

Horowitz, A. (2004). *Eagle strike*. New York: Philomel.

Hughes, L. (1996). *The dream keeper and other poems*. New York: Knopf.

Hughes, M. (2000). *The keeper of the Isis light*. New York: Aladdin. (Original work published 1932)

Hyman, T. (1983). *Little Red Riding Hood*. New York: Holiday House.

Irwin, H. (1988). *Kim/Kimi*. New York: Puffin.

Isaacs, A. (2000). *Torn thread*. Troy, MI: Blue Sky Press.

Johnson, A. (1995). *Humming whispers*. New York: Orchard Books.

Johnston, T. (2003). *Any small goodness: A novel of the barrio*. New York: Scholastic.

Jordan, S. (2000). *The raging quiet*. London: Simon & Schuster.

Kessler, C. (2000). *No condition is permanent*. New York: Philomel.

Koller, J.F. (1992). *The primrose way*. Orlando, FL: Gulliver Books.

Konigsburg, E.L. (2000). *Silent to the bone*. New York: Aladdin.

Krisher, T. (1994). *Spite fences*. New York: Laurel Leaf.

Lacapa, K., & Lacapa, M. (1994). *Less than half, more than whole*. Flagstaff, AZ: Northland.

Lasky, K. (1994). *Memoirs of a bookbat*. New York: Harcourt.

Lee, H. (1960). *To kill a mockingbird*. New York: HarperCollins.

Levine, G. (1998). *Ella enchanted*. New York: HarperTrophy.

Lord, B.B. (1986). *In the year of the boar and Jackie Robinson*. New York: HarperTrophy.

Lowry, L. (1989). *Number the stars*. New York: Yearling.

Lowry, L. (1993). *The giver*. New York: Laurel Leaf.

Lynn, J. (2002). *Glory*. New York: Puffin.

Mahy, M. (1982). *The haunting*. New York: Random House.

Major, K. (2003). *Hold fast*. New York: Delacorte.

Marsden, C. (2002). *The gold-threaded dress*. Cambridge, MA: Candlewick.

Martin, A. (2001). *Belle Teal*. New York: Hyperion Books for Children.

Martin, N. (2002). *A perfect snow*. New York: Bloomsbury.

Martin, R. (1998). *The rough-face girl*. New York: Puffin.

Mazer, N. (1991). *Silver*. New York: Turtleback Books.

McKinley, R. (1993). *Beauty: A retelling of the story of Beauty and the Beast*. New York: HarperCollins.

Morrison, T., & Morrison, S. (2002). *The big box*. New York: Hyperion/Jump at the Sun Books.

Myers, W.D. (1996). *Slam!* New York: Scholastic.

Myers, W.D. (1999). *Monster*. New York: Amistad Press.

Napoli, D. (1995). *The magic circle*. New York: Puffin.

Napoli, D. (1996). *Zel*. New York: Puffin.

Nix, G. (1997). *Shade's children*. New York: HarperTrophy.

Oates, C. (2002). *Big Mouth & Ugly Girl*. New York: HarperTempest.

Osa, N. (2003). *Cuba 15*. New York: Delacorte.

Park, L.S. (2001). *A single shard*. New York: Clarion.

Pfitsch, P. (2004). *Riding the flume*. New York: Aladdin.

Philbrick, R. (2002). *The last book in the universe*. New York: Scholastic.

Polacco, P. (1994). *Pink and say*. New York: Philomel.

Popov, N. (1996). *Why?* New York: North-South Books.

Rapp, A. (2002). *The buffalo tree*. New York: HarperTempest.

Rees, C. (2000). *Witch child*. Cambridge, MA: Candlewick.

Rennison, L. (2001). *On the bright side, I'm now the girlfriend of a sex god*. New York: HarperCollins.

Rowling, J.K. (2003). *Harry Potter and the order of the phoenix*. New York: Scholastic.

Ryan, P. (2000). *Esperanza rising*. New York: Scholastic Press.

Saldana, R. (2002). *The jumping tree*. New York: Laurel Leaf.

Salisbury, G. (2002). *Island boyz*. New York: Laurel Leaf.

Savin, M. (1992). *The moonbridge*. New York: Scholastic.

Scieszka, J. (1995). *The true story of the three little pigs by A. Wolf*. New York: Dutton.

Shakespeare, W. (1990). *William Shakespeare: The complete works*. New York: Gramercy.

Shange, N. (1997). *White wash*. New York: Walker & Co.

Shelley, M. (1818). *Frankenstein*. New York: Bantam.

Soto, G. (2000). *Baseball in April and other stories*. New York: Harcourt.

Spinelli, J. (1990). *Maniac Magee*. Boston: Little, Brown.

Spinelli, J. (2002). *Stargirl*. New York: Knopf.

Sullivan, P. (2003). *Maata's journal*. New York: Atheneum Books.

Taylor, M. (1976). *Roll of thunder, hear my cry*. New York: Puffin.

Tillage, L. (1997). *Leon's story*. New York: Farrar Straus Giroux.

Tolan, S. (1991). *The plague year*. New York: Fawcett.

Turner, A. (1995). *Nettie's trip south*. New York: Aladdin.

Twain, M. (1962). *The adventures of Huckleberry Finn*. New York: Penguin.

Van Draanen, W. (2001). *Flipped*. New York: Knopf.

Waddell, M. (1991). *Farmer duck*. Cambridge, MA: Candlewick.

Walker, A. (1982). *The color purple*. New York: Harcourt Brace.

Watson, E. (2000). *The pain tree*. Boston: Houghton Mifflin.

Watts, L. (2002). *Stone-cutter*. Boston: Houghton Mifflin.

Whelan, G. (2000). *Homeless bird*. New York: HarperCollins.

Wiles, D. (2001). *Freedom summer*. New York: Simon & Schuster.

Williams, V. (1982). *A chair for my mother*. New York: Greenwillow.

Wolff, V.E. (1993). *Make lemonade*. New York: Henry Holt.

Woodson, J. (1994). *I hadn't meant to tell you this*. New York: Bantam Doubleday Dell.

Woodson, J. (1998). *If you come softly*. New York: Penguin.

Yolen, J., & Coville, B. (1998). *Armageddon summer*. New York: Scholastic.

Young, E. (1989). *Lon Po Po*. New York: Philomel Books.

Zindel, P. (1968). *The pigman*. New York: HarperCollins.

Index